Valentine Baker's Heroic Stand at Tashkessen 1877

In memory of my grandfather, Orland Dale King (1938–2016)

Valentine Baker's Heroic Stand at Tashkessen 1877

A Tarnished British Soldier's Glorious Victory

Frank Jastrzembski

Pen & Sword
MILITARY

First published in Great Britain in 2017 by
Pen & Sword Military
an imprint of
Pen & Sword Books Ltd
47 Church Street
Barnsley
South Yorkshire
S70 2AS

ISBN 978 1 47386 680 5

A CIP catalogue record for this book is
available from the British Library.

Typeset in Ehrhardt by
Mac Style Ltd, Bridlington, East Yorkshire

Printed and bound in Malta
By Gutenberg Press Ltd.

Pen & Sword Books Ltd incorporates the Imprints of
Pen & Sword Archaeology, Atlas, Aviation, Battleground, Discovery,
Family History, History, Maritime, Military, Naval, Politics,
Railways, Select, Transport, True Crime, Fiction,
Frontline Books, Leo Cooper, Praetorian Press,
Seaforth Publishing, Wharncliffe and White Owl.

For a complete list of Pen & Sword titles please contact
PEN & SWORD BOOKS LIMITED
47 Church Street, Barnsley, South Yorkshire, S70 2AS, England
E-mail: enquiries@pen-and-sword.co.uk
Website: www.pen-and-sword.co.uk

Contents

Acknowledgements

I am first and foremost in eternal gratitude to Valentine Baker, who without his hardships and exile, this book would have never occurred. I am also indebted to the Ottoman, Russian, Romanian, and Bulgarian soldiers of the Russo–Turkish War whose names are forgotten to history, but will live on in immortality.

Without the individuals listed below, this book would have only been an afterthought, lost forever in the barren wasteland of ideas that never came to fruition.

First to my wife Asha, for never giving up on me, and for the countless hours of support when negativity threatened to get the best of me. Ever since thrusting herself into my life, she has helped me to mature and to eradicate a large portion of my self-doubt. She inspired me to further my studies by completing graduate school, and encouraged me to write. She will continue to inspire me to do great things. I will love you always.

To all of my family members and friends for their endless support. To my grandparents for the persistent support they provide for pursuing my dreams. Thanks to my father for passing down his appetite for history and for providing me with a plethora of history books beginning at a young age. To my mother for appreciating all of my work, regardless of how significant or insignificant it may be.

Dan Zawacki, for tweaking and fine tuning my countless drafts, and his excellent advice over the last couple of years. Thanks for giving me the confidence to write. Pen and Sword Books for giving me the opportunity to produce this book, and to my excellent commissioning editor Linne Matthews, who put faith in me to tell Baker's story. The excellent illustrations provided by Zsuzsi Hajdu.

The authors Bruce Catton, Byron Farwell, and Joseph Lehmann, all three who are no longer with us, but who have influenced me by their literary styles.

The Victorian Military Society for keeping the memory of the soldiers of the Victorian era alive through their quarterly publication, *Soldiers of the Queen*.

To all those institutions and individuals in the United States, Great Britain, and Bulgaria for their assistance along the way contributing to the completion of this book, including, but not limited to: the Panorama Pleven, the National Park Museum Shipka-Buzludzha, the US Army War College Library and Archives, and the Combined Arms Research Library (CARL). To my friend, Yakup Ünişen, for locating information related to Baker's role in Armenia during the 1880s, and to Alexander Schweig of the University of Arizona, for translating this material from Turkish into English.

I would also like to give a special thanks to all of the faculty members of my respective universities who over the years have shaped me as a scholar, listed in no specific order. My hope is that I created something that they deem worthy of the labour they put into my education:

John Carroll University: Dr George Vourlojianis, Dr James Krukones, Dr Anne Kugler, Dr David Robson, and Dr Maria Marsilli.

Cleveland State University: Dr Stephen Cory, Dr Thomas J. Humphrey, Dr José O. Solá, and Dr J. Mark Souther.

Book jacket illustrations

The 'Inglese Pasha', also known as Baker Pasha.
Illustration by Zsuzsanna Hajdu (www.facebook.com/zsuzsihajduarts).

All other illustrations on the jacket were reproduced from Edmund Ollier, *Cassell's Illustrated History of the Russo-Turkish War*, 2 vols, Cassell, Petter & Galpin, London, 1879.

Introduction

It is all very well now to sing paeons over the grave where General Valentine Baker has been buried. He recks not of any war-trumpet that may be busy with his name or fame. The poet may sing of his sorrowful and tempestuous life, and the novelist may make of him a hero to adorn many a tale and romance; but he is past all heeding now – he has crossed over the river to rest, it may be, with another soldier under the shades of the trees.

An excerpt by John N. Edwards from 'Poor Valentine Baker', in the *Kansas City Times*, 6 January 1888.

History has not been sympathetic to Colonel Valentine Baker, remembering him for his checkered past, rather than his remarkable persona. The small number of scholars and military history enthusiasts that would recognize Baker's name would immediately attach it to one of the most notorious scandals of nineteenth-century Victorian Britain. His name next surfaces as a soldier-of-fortune serving in Egypt during the 1880s, where he had the unfortunate fate of leading an Egyptian column to a crushing defeat in the Sudan at the Battle of El Teb on 5 February 1884. The role he played during the Russo-Turkish War of 1877–78, situated between these two discreditable events, is rarely ever mentioned in much detail.

Finalizing his twelve-month prison sentence after the scandal that led to his dismissal from the army in 1875, Baker packed his luggage, loaded his wife and two daughters aboard a steamer, and left Britain for Constantinople. His old friend from the 10th Hussars, the Prince of Wales (Edward VII), offered him a chance for redemption. He furnished Baker with an appointment as a major general in the Ottoman Army to organize and train the Ottoman gendarmerie, which led to his subsequent service in the war that erupted in April 1877 between the Russians and Ottomans. Shrouded in ignominy is the exhilarating tale of Baker's pivotal role in this conflict. This book is the telling of the long-forgotten saga of Valentine Baker's role in this war, and his perpetual search for redemption in the wake of his dismissal.

The Battle of Tashkessen remains undoubtedly one of the most brilliant rearguard actions fought during the nineteenth century. The exiled Baker, in command of roughly 3,000 Ottoman soldiers, was dispatched to the village of Tashkessen (Sarantsi, Bulgaria) to stall three advancing columns of 25,000 Russian soldiers from descending on the rear of the Ottoman position at the Kamarli line in December 1877. Through his superb leadership and the brilliant disposition of his battalions, Baker was able to stall the three Russian columns for four crucial days. The Spartan stand of Baker and his little command of brave soldiers have been all but forgotten today.

Despite this modern obscurity, Baker's performance at Tashkessen was applauded by his colleagues as a prototype of effective leadership, an aggressive defence, and the successful display of the 'spirit of tactics'. They urged that Baker's tactical arrangements should be analyzed by all students of war. The final chapter of this book is dedicated to evaluating if the Battle of Tashkessen is worthy of the acclaim as 'the most wonderful rearguard action of our times, if not of all times', as recorded by Colonel Sir John Frederick Maurice in his presentation to British officers of the Military Society of Ireland in 1892.

There have been only two other books written on the life of Valentine Baker, and both are well researched and well organized. The first book, written by a distant relative through marriage to Valentine Baker, Anne Baker (Salmond), was published in 1996 under the title *A Question of Honour: The Life of Lieutenant General Valentine Baker Pasha*. In *Crisis of the Ottoman Empire: Prelude to Collapse 1839–1878*, Dr James Reid praised that 'this biography has great value for the present study for the reason that it has converted Valentine Baker from merely a soldier who wrote a military memoir to a human being with foibles and strengths.' Anne Baker relied heavily on the few unpublished letters in her family's personal possession to give a broad overview of his life. Baker explained how very few secondary sources on Valentine Baker 'describe the character of the colonel, his greatness, his kindness, and thoughtfulness, his love of horses,' which she successfully resolved in her book.

The second book was written by the professional librarian and author Dorothy Anderson, and was published in 1999 under the title *Baker Pasha: Misconduct and Mischance*. The New Zealand native claimed that she began her research forty years beforehand in the 1970s, while working on another book she published related to the foreign relief workers serving in the Russo-Turkish War. Anderson intended her book to focus solely on Baker's service in the Sudan during the 1880s, but found that it was 'essential to provide a rounded account of Baker', by examining the events that brought him to this region. She expressed that Baker 'deserves better than to be remembered for only that one incident [his dismissal],' as this book also sets out to do.

Both Baker and Anderson briefly discuss Baker's role during the Russo-Turkish War. This is where the most fascinating events of Baker's life can be exhumed. The lack of attention devoted to this period in these books is not due to either author's carelessness, or a disregard for his role in the war, but rather that unveiling this period of his life in detail was not the main objective in either of their own studies. The goal of this book is to fill this large void in the historiography of Baker's life related to the Russo-Turkish War, as seen through his eyes and supplementary accounts from eyewitnesses during the conflict.

A brief psychohistorical inquiry into Baker's shameful dismissal that led to his imprisonment has been included in this book. The author does not claim to be an expert in psychohistory; but there are intense emotions, reactions and visible signs of irregular behaviour Baker demonstrated following his trial in 1875 that will be dissected for the first time. A case of an officer being knocked off of his illustrious pedestal under a slew of accusations is not a unique occurrence during the Victorian period; one notable example of an officer who dealt with comparable accusations, Major General Hector Archibald MacDonald, committed suicide under the strain of the allegations attributed to his homosexual behaviour. Baker carried the psychological scars of the accusations, imprisonment, and humiliation until his death in 1887.

A subtle objective of this book is to reintroduce the overlooked Russo-Turkish War of 1877–78 to English readers. Dr Stephen M. Woodburn, in the translator's introduction of *Woe to the Victors: The Russo-Turkish War, the Congress of Berlin, and the Future of Slavdom*, illuminated the obscurity of the Russo-Turkish War to modern readers when he wrote:

> The Russo-Turkish War of 1877–78 is an obscure corner of the past for many in the present, completely unknown to most Americans, largely forgotten not only by Europeans, whose forebears watched the events with great concern, but even by Russians, for whom the tsarist past is doubly removed.

Dr Edward J. Erickson, in his outstanding book published in 2003, *Defeat in Detail: The Ottoman Army in the Balkans, 1912–1913*, dedicated a few short paragraphs to the Russo-Turkish War and reminded his readers that 'Unfortunately, there is no recent major study of this war available in the English language, and the episodic coverage of the campaigns tends to focus on the great siege battles of Plevna, Shipka Pass, Kars, and Erzurum.' Nine years later, Quintin Barry pierced this English language barrier by publishing an all-encompassing modern English study of the campaigns of the war. This book has given special attention to the overlooked, but equally important, operations along the Lom River in the autumn of 1877, and the operations that took place around Sofia leading up to the final Ottoman defeat.

This book is by no means a comprehensive study of the war, as it dwells on the portions of the conflict in which Valentine Baker played a direct role. The role of the Caucasia Theater in the war was omitted for this reason, not that it played an insignificant role in the outcome of the war. One chapter has been specifically dedicated to defining the major Western reforms (mostly superficial), ideologies (principally the flaws), the condition of the officer corps, their adherence to obsolete strategies and tactics, and the uniforms and armaments of the Ottoman and Russian armies leading up to 1877. This chapter also does not attempt to cover the reforms and elements of each of these armies in entirety; it instead covers the elements most important to providing a general understanding of these 'ancient enemies'. Such all-inclusive dedication would have led to an exhaustive study on each army, which was not the intention of this book.

This war played two very important roles on a global scale. First, it shaped the political dynamics of the Balkans in the latter part of the nineteenth century, and some claim can be interconnected to the outbreak of the First World War. Second, it introduced technological advances in warfare that would become painfully apparent on a much larger scale less than forty years later in 1914. In his comprehensive novel-length bibliography on Balkan military history, Dr John E. Jessup added that army officers and war correspondents from throughout the world came to spectate the war, and that 'No war up to that time, with the possible exception of the American Civil War, had so much contemporary material formulated about it.' So significant to the participants, soldiers, and international leaders during the latter part of the nineteenth century, why is this war virtually forgotten today?

Modern American and British historians generally convey a lack of interest in the conflict that tore the Balkans apart 140 years ago. The American Civil War has captured the popular imagination of most modern studies related to nineteenth-century warfare in the United States, leaving other noteworthy wars and even some smaller American wars neglected. The Russo–Turkish War produced an international crisis in Great Britain, and still there seems to be little modern attention dedicated to the actual conflict outside of the overarching theme of the 'Eastern Question'. This book will attempt to promote the additional publication of modern English studies dedicated to the Russo–Turkish War.

Another explanation for the war being snubbed by historians was that the participants wanted the memory of the conflict to pass into oblivion. Dr Woodburn explained that the political meddling of Great Britain, Germany, and Austria-Hungary following the Treaty of San Stefano in 1878 spoiled the achievements of the Russian military victory and abolished their dreams of accessing the Mediterranean. The Ottomans sought to forget the war altogether, as it signified the end of the 400-year-old absolute Ottoman rule in the Balkans, and provided a bitter reminder that the fortunes of their once proud empire were in decline. The war today is most celebrated only by the Bulgarians, who rightfully view 3 March 1878 as Bulgaria's Liberation Day – the day the Treaty of San Stefano was signed, ending the war.

The pronunciation of villages, battles, and leaders of the Russo–Turkish War can be imposing and gruelling to articulate to English readers, and may deter some fainthearted scholars from undertaking the study of the war altogether. The names of many of the villages and cities has changed or have been altered since 1877–78 (i.e., Plovdiv: Philippopolis; Edirne: Adrianople; and Pleven: Plevna), even further complicating the study of the war. Some contemporary accounts included two, three, or more transliterations of the same landmarks, battles, or key personalities. The author has identified at least seventeen different spellings for the village Tashkessen used in contemporary and modern accounts of the war: Tashkessin, Taskesend, Tash-Kessan, Tackeran, Tashkosen, Tachkessen, Tashkesen, Taskesen, Tashkessen, Tashkessan, Tasheksan, Taskosen, Tashkent, Taskisen, Tashkennan, Sarikhantsi, and Sarantsi (modern-day name of the village). For this reason, this book will use the version of spelling most readily recognized or adopted in accounts when it comes to physical locations, landmarks, names, or battles, but when able, modern Turkish punctuation has been used for the proper names of Ottoman leaders. Any spelling discrepancies between the period maps and in the book have been identified in the captions.

A large number of modern sources were intertwined with contemporary sources to assemble the content of this book. This was done to provide a well-rounded and in-depth view of Baker the man, the Battle of Tashkessen, and the war. Valentine Baker chronicled and published his experiences during the war in two volumes in 1879, which was a true asset to writing this book. The author is indebted to Anne Baker and Dorothy Anderson for providing excerpts of original letters and newspaper clippings in their books related to Baker's life, used in some instances within this book. The absence of a large number of Russian or Turkish primary or secondary sources – which do existence in an unsoiled condition as alluded to by Dr Ömer Turan – is attributed to the author's own deficient fluency in both languages. Hopefully, a resurgence of interest in this conflict will eliminate the language barriers that exist in studying this war, instead uniting Russian, Bulgarian, British, and Turkish scholars.

Chapter 1

Epitome of the Mid-Victorian Gentleman

A wandering spirit is in my marrow which forbids rest.
Samuel White Baker in a letter
to his sister, 26 January 1861.

It did not take long for the robust son of a merchant father to grow disheartened as a clerk in his dull London office. Samuel White Baker longed for more than this monotonous lifestyle could offer. He described his restlessness in a letter to his sister dated 26 January 1861:

A wandering spirit is in my marrow which forbids rest. The time may come when I shall delight in cities but at present I abhor them. Unhappy the bird in its cage! None but those who value real freedom can appreciate its misery.

The free-spirited Samuel was destined to become more distinguished than his three brothers – John, Valentine, and James. He is remembered for serving as a pasha and governor general in Egyptian service. His exploits as a well-travelled African explorer and hunter was stuff of legend in Victorian Britain. Self-determination, ambition, fortitude, and a 'wandering spirit' were traits inherited by the other three Baker brothers cloaked in their older brother Samuel's monumental shadow.

The Baker family had a legacy of producing seafarers, in search of exotic voyages around the globe to satisfy their roving spirits. The grandfather of the Baker brothers, Captain Valentine Baker, left the Royal Navy following the War of American Independence to pursue a career as a privateer in the late eighteenth century. He fought a David and Goliath fashioned naval battle in command of the eighteen-gun privateer vessel, christened the *Caesar* on 27 June 1782. In this action, he defended a convoy of vulnerable British merchant vessels from Bristol being pursued by a well-armed French thirty-two gun frigate. Despite his inferior armament, smaller sized ship, and numerical disparity, Captain Baker dauntlessly engaged the French frigate and outfoxed the sluggish vessel.

The contest adjourned with the mangled French frigate striking its white flag to surrender. The *Caesar* was badly damaged, with all of the boarding boats smashed, the riggings crippled, and the hull pierced and leaking. The captain of the French ship took advantage of the *Caesar*'s pitiful condition, hoisted his tricolour flag, and cowardly made his escape. Another British vessel seized the French frigate shortly after it had evaded capture. The French captain was said to have become so distraught over discovering he had been defeated by such an inferior adversary that he excused himself to the privacy of his quarters and committed suicide by slitting his own throat.

Captain Baker was presented with an ornate silver vase and a fine oil painting depicting the contest in a show of appreciation from the Bristol merchants. These short spoken but ennobling words were etched on the silver vase:

Presented to Captain Valentine Baker by the merchants and insurers of Bristol for gallantly defending the ship *Caesar* against a French sloop of war greatly superior in force to his own ship, and battling her off, on June 27, 1782.

His share in additional privateer profits in the aftermath of the battle allowed Captain Baker to purchase property on the islands of Jamaica and Mauritius. He cultivated plantations on both islands, operated by a large crew of slaves. His investment in the sugar and shipping industry led to financial prosperity.

Captain Baker chose to cast out to sea the youngest of his seven sons in 1807 to mellow his adolescent spirit. Samuel was immersed in the sufferings and depravities of life by the age of fourteen. By adulthood, he developed a notorious reputation for his hard drinking and intrepidity, but was esteemed as a sensibly minded man. Upon the death of his father, Samuel inherited the rich family estates in Jamaica and Mauritius. He matured into an energetic and successful merchant, navigating the Pacific and Atlantic with his own fleet of merchant vessels, and later served as director of the Great Western Railway and the chairman of the Gloucestershire Bank.

Upon one of his return voyages to Britain, Samuel settled down in Enfield and married Mary Ann Dobson. Mrs Baker gave birth to five boys (Thomas, Samuel, John, Valentine, and James) and three daughters (Mary, Ann, and Ellen). Their firstborn, Thomas, died at the age of twelve in 1832. The fourth son of the couple was born on 1 April 1827, and was christened after his intrepid grandfather, Captain Valentine Baker. 'Val', as he was known in the family, was as plucky as his grandfather. Perhaps Samuel Sr shared with Val bedtime stories of his grandfather's exploits the boy would later rival.

Samuel Sr intended his offspring to mature into 'doers and makers', as efficiently phrased by author Brian Thompson. He made sure they were all well educated before they would be thrust into 'the great stage of the world'. Valentine received his education in the one-room schoolhouse of King's School in Gloucester established by King Henry VIII in 1545, and afterwards studied under a private tutor. He may well have been privately educated by his older brother Samuel's tutor, Reverend H.P. Dunster. The holy scholar tutored him in Latin and Greek, and permitted the reading of specific sagas of scientific exploration to appease his appetite, such as Giovanni Belzoni's *Travels in Egypt and Nubia*, and Richard Madden's *Travels in the East*.

Samuel and John appeared to be destined for futures administering the merchant domain of the Baker family, while the two younger boys were to pursue careers in the army. Samuel Sr purchased officer's commissions as cornets for Val in the 10th Royal Hussars and James in the Royal Horse Guards (James first entered the Indian Navy in 1845 until he left the service to honour his commission). Queen Victoria required a plethora of young men to serve as army officers in order to protect her colonial interests in Asia, Africa, and the Middle East over her 63-year reign. Officer commissions in the army provided a chance for distinction, adventure, and helped to cast adolescent youths into well-polished gentlemen. There was no nobler deed than to put one's line on the line for Great Britain.

Samuel Sr sent his two oldest sons abroad to manage his properties in Mauritius, located off Madagascar. While attending to their father's business, the brothers visited the island of Ceylon, 2,500 miles away, drawn by fascinating accounts of elephant hunts. The climate of the region was comfortable and the land fertile, and the collapse of the coffee market in 1847 allowed land on the island to be purchased for a fraction of its worth. Samuel and John travelled back to London with the intention of gathering supplies and manpower for forming an English colony in the region of Newera Ellia.

Upon their homecoming to Britain, Samuel and John chartered a vessel christened the *Earl of Hardwick* for their ambitious plans of settlement after convincing their father of the fiscal opportunity of the enterprise. They loaded the vessel with their families, including their younger brother Valentine – who intended to remain in the settlement until required to report to the 10th Hussars – a bailiff and twelve other emigrants, livestock, and plenty of provisions. The vessel took roughly six weeks to reach its destination. Despite early struggles, they successfully cultivated potatoes, beans, peas, carrots, and cabbage on the settlement. Samuel would remain on the colony for nearly seven years, while John would remain there for another forty years until his death in 1883.

In August 1848, Valentine briefly joined the green-jacketed Ceylon Rifle Regiment as an ensign at the age of twenty-one while in Ceylon. His short-lived service with the regiment allowed him to become acquainted with military discipline, drill, and organization. It also provided him with the opportunity to become familiar with commanding Muslim soldiers, the regiment being composed of native Malays. British officers in the regiment believed that allowing the Malays to practise religious customs freely would assist with maintaining discipline. Baker would learn the importance of respecting ethnic and religious customs in both military and political circumstances, which he would demonstrate time and again throughout his life.

Samuel and Valentine shared a close bond and sought out the hazards and thrill of the 'extraordinary sport' of elephant hunting while in the jungles of Ceylon. The elephant, when threatened by man, could easily turn rogue and evolve into a dangerous foe. In one week, the brothers tracked and slew thirty-two elephants. Beyond the threats from being skewered or trampled by rogue elephants, other wild beasts hidden in the jungle could pose an even greater danger. Samuel recorded one incident when the brothers were ambushed on a typical hunt that nearly turned deadly:

I remember an instance of carelessness, which might have had a disastrous result, many years ago, when I was hunting in Ceylon. My brother, the late General Valentine Baker, was riding with me through the jungles in the district called 'The Park'. I had been caught by a rogue elephant a few days before, and my right thigh was so damaged that I could only walk a few yards with difficulty. Suddenly the man who walked before my horse ran back, and shouted 'Wallahah, Wallahah' ('Bears, Bears'), and we caught sight of some large black objects rushing through the jungle, close to our horses' heads. Valentine Baker jumped nimbly off, and I heard a shot almost immediately … I now heard my brother shouting my name at only a few yards' distance; running towards him, as I feared some accident, I found a large bear half lying and half sitting upon the ground.

In April 1851, Valentine Baker travelled to India to honour the conditions of his commission purchased by his father in the 10th Hussars. Baker must have been mesmerized when he joined this prestigious regiment, stationed in the British colony since 1846. Service in the regiment appeased his lifelong love for horses, while also providing him with a chance to serve in a regiment with a 130-year-old legacy. The 10th had a commendable record dating back to 1715, fighting in a litany of legendary battles: Culloden in 1745, Minden in 1759, the Peninsula War from 1807–14, and Waterloo in 1815.

After a year of monotonous garrison duty with his regiment, the restless Baker transferred to the 12th (The Prince of Wales's) Regiment of Dragoons (Lancers) with a chance to join the largest British army to take the field in South Africa in over fifty years. Two squadrons of the regiment were transported to South Africa to take part in Major General George Cathcart's invasion of the Sotho kingdom of Chief Moshoeshoe. Instead of immediate action, the 12th Lancers were exposed to routine marching and countermarching for miles under the blistering African sun. The 12th Lancers developed an 'exceptional stamina' from their longevity in the saddle while battling threats of sunstroke. Baker soon discovered the tight-fitting wool jackets of the cavalrymen were brilliant for parades at home to attract the young ladies, but were a poor choice for active campaigning under the African sun, and that in melee combat, 'the lance is comparatively useless.'

On 20 December 1852, 700 Sotho horsemen under Moshoeshoe's second son, Molapo, ambushed a British detachment under the command of Lieutenant Colonel George Napier composed of 119 men of the Cape Mounted Riflemen and 114 men of the 12th Lancers at Berea Mountain. The men of the 12th, under the command of the brave and efficient Major William Heathcote Tottenham, formed the rearguard upon ambush in order to allow the Cape Mounted Riflemen to flee with 4,500 captured enemy cattle. The men of the 12th discovered their lances were virtually useless in the close-quarters fighting over the rugged terrain against Sotho horsemen armed with battleaxes and assegais. Tottenham's detachment, which included Cornet Baker, were driven down along a dried-up watercourse and cut off. Tottenham and his command lost twenty-seven men in the melee, but managed to cut their way out of the perilous situation.

The pluck and spirited leadership of Major Tottenham won the admiration of all those present at the battle. The 37-year-old Tottenham joined the 12th in 1833 as a cornet, alike to Baker, and within ten years received the promotion to major. One officer observed the major during the fight at Berea and wrote that 'Tottenham behaved like a hero; the last to turn, he remained almost the last in the retreat, and by cool courage and good riding managed to save a sergeant – Tottenham, by shooting a Basuto [Sotho] while just about to stab him.' Tottenham would become a protégé and friend to Baker.

The 25-year-old Cornet Baker received praise for his gallantry in his first major action. His service in the conflict earned him the South Africa Medal, and in July 1853 he received promotion to lieutenant. The conflict ended when peace was concluded between Moshoeshoe and Cathcart after numerous setbacks to the British invasion force. The 12th Lancers were sent back to Mysore in Southern India, where they remained until 1855. Baker chose to remain in the 12th instead of requesting a transfer back to the 10th Hussars.

In 1853, war broke out between the Ottoman and the Russian empires for the tenth time in a 280-year-period. This time, Great Britain, France, and Sardinia bolstered the Ottomans with military and financial support, chiefly for their own economic welfare and to curb the growing influence of the Russian Empire in the Balkans and Asia. Britain and France sent large contingents of soldiers to the Crimean Peninsula located in the northern portion of the Black Sea to conduct a land campaign against the stronghold of Sevastopol.

The 12th Lancers were one of the British cavalry regiments subsequently ordered to Crimea. The regiment first moved to Cairo from India, then on to Constantinople, and finally landed on the Crimean Peninsula on 19 April 1855. They were attached to the Light Brigade, shattered at the Battle of Balaclava during their legendary charge on 25 October 1854. What remained of the brigade continued to be devastated by the outbreak of infectious diseases such as typhus, typhoid, cholera, and dysentery, and due to the inadequate system of transporting supplies to the men on the front.

Lieutenant Baker distinguished himself in the war despite missing the major battles of Alma, Balaclava, and Inkerman. He was present at the Battle of the Chernaya on 16 August 1855, where a combined British, French, Sardinian, and Ottoman force repulsed a furious Russian assault. He was detached from the main body of the 12th Lancers to serve as the headquarters escort for the Commander-in-Chief of the British forces, the ancient Lord Raglan, and then his successor upon his death from dysentery, the uninspiring General James Simpson. Baker took part in the Allied siege of Sevastopol along with his brother James, having transferred to the 8th (The King's Royal Irish) Hussars in 1854.

With the conclusion of the Crimean War in February 1856, the 12th Lancers and the 8th Hussars left Crimea for Constantinople to await their departure to their former stations. Both regiments were stationed at the Scutari Barracks, located within the confines of the Ottoman capital. Lieutenant Colonel Frederick C.A. Stephenson of the Scots Guards described the 'lovely view' from the barracks that 'often makes me think of Switzerland.' Inside the actual barracks, the atmosphere was quite the opposite. Stephenson remembered that 'the filth and stench of the rooms is beyond description, and it swarms with fleas.'

Valentine and James opted to rent an Ottoman cottage outside of the capital to escape the toxic environment of the barracks, and were soon joined by the recently promoted Lieutenant Colonel Tottenham and their brother Samuel, who had arrived on a visit to Constantinople. The brotherly reunion came to an abrupt end when the 12th Hussars were ordered back to India and the 8th Hussars to Great Britain. Desiring to return to Britain for the first time since departing ten years beforehand, Baker requested to exchange regiments with Captain William Murray in May 1857, and thereafter returned to the 10th Hussars with the same rank. James Baker would leave the 8th Hussars soon after the Crimean War, entering politics and residing for the remainder of his life in British Columbia.

Baker very well may have taken away some appreciation of the decrepit Russian 'shock tactics' used during the Crimean War. The Russian military doctrine stressed the use of large numbers of soldiers in column formation to swiftly plunge into the enemy line of battle with the cold steel of their bayonets, engaging them in hand-to-hand combat before they would be able to get off more than one of two volleys. 'The bullet's a fool, the bayonets a fine lad,' acclaimed Russian General Alexander Suvorov in his notorious maxim praising the bayonet over the musket. The technological advances in war, first with the rifled musket during the Crimean War, and then the breech-loading rifle in the latter part of the 1860s, made these shock tactics horribly obsolete, giving the British soldier the advantage with a greater range, greater accuracy, and a greater rate of fire. The Russian high command disregarded the technological advances and suffered setbacks throughout the Crimean War.

Baker returned to Britain upon his request for transfer after the war and received warranted laurels. In August 1856, he received the promotion to captain and the Crimea Medal with the Sevastopol clasp, along with the Turkish Crimean War Medal. Baker received the well-deserved promotion to major three years later, in June 1859. He spent most of the 1860s peacefully stationed in Great Britain with the regiment.

He became widely known as one of the most renowned cavalry theorists during this period. In 1858, he published a 100-page pamphlet titled *The British Cavalry*, devoted to identifying areas of needed reform within the cavalry arm. These concepts were collected from Baker's own experiences in India, South Africa, and Crimea. He called for improving transportation, outfits, armaments, and tactics of the cavalry. He 'sorrowfully' dedicated his book to the memory of his old friend and protégé Lieutenant Colonel Tottenham, who succumbed to a fever on his return journey to India from Crimea on 6 July 1857.

The 32-year-old Baker assumed command of the 10th Hussars after his promotion to lieutenant colonel on 31 March 1860. The former commander of the regiment, Colonel John Wilkie, retired after twenty-two years of uninterrupted service, paving the way for Baker's promotion less than ten years after being commissioned a cornet. In 1865, he was promoted to full colonel. Two years before his promotion to colonel, the son of Queen Victoria, the 24-year-old Prince of Wales (later King Edward VII), was appointed to the superficial role of colonel-in-chief of Baker's Hussars, and the regiment was rechristened the Prince of Wales's Own in his honour. The young prince became immersed in his ceremonial duties with the regiment, where he was able to play the part of a soldier.

Baker and the young prince took to each other from the start. Baker was invited to join the Prince's inner circle of friends and colleagues known as the 'Marlborough House Set', made up of wealthy and esteemed playboys notorious for indulging in such pursuits as the theatre, hours of card playing, gambling on horse races, extravagant parties, and loose women. This free-spirited group pursued their 'own wayward course', becoming notorious for their unconventional behavior. The young prince, as author Virginia Cowles explained, was 'desperately anxious to be one of the boys'. Queen Victoria bitterly disapproved of these acquaintances and the negative media attention they brought upon her son, plagued with scandals, divorces, and sexually promiscuous behaviour.

As a member of the Marlborough Club, Baker first met Captain Frederick Burnaby, an officer of the Royal Horse Guards (The Blues), who had earned the admiration of and admission into the exclusive club for his larger-than-life personality. Burnaby defied his 'modest' background to earn admission into the bourgeoisie Marlborough Club. The 6-foot 4-inch daredevil would become known for his hot air balloon rides across the English Channel and his adventures as a war correspondent in Spain during the Third Carlist War. He later published an account of his solo travels in Central Asia titled *A Ride to Khiva*, in 1874, which became an instant success in Britain. Private George Radford, another muscular trooper from the Royal Horse Guards, accompanied Burnaby on many of his adventures, the duo forming a bond alike to Doyle's Sherlock Holmes and John Watson.

The 10th Hussars forged a reputation as one of the most impressive regiments in the British Army, under Baker's tutelage earning the playful moniker of 'Baker's Light Bobs'. Baker devoted the majority of his time and energy to enhancing the efficiency and organization of his command, and endeavoured to shape it into the most polished regiments in the British Army, even if it meant spending extra time rehearsing manoeuvres with his cavalrymen. One observer noted that he felt it unnecessary for Baker to keep his men out after a tiring parade to demonstrate its machine-like drill, but declared that 'Valentine Baker was a man of great energy and enthusiasm and did not get tired himself or see why others should.' He demonstrated their flawless drill and crisp manoeuvres on a number of official military reviews, attended by persons such as Queen Victoria and a number of foreign military observers. He left a lasting impression on the spectators, who were mesmerized with the gracious bearing and genius of the hussar colonel.

Baker requested official leave to act as an observer to study cavalry tactics and the organization of other cavalry regiments from around Europe. He familiarized himself with the tactics and organization of these foreign regiments enough to translate the knowledge for use in the British cavalry arm. He visited the Austrian Army in 1863, returning to implement a system of non-pivot drill within his own regiment. He was an observer during both the Austro-Prussian War of 1866 and the Franco-Prussian War of 1870-71, where Prussian armies soundly defeated both the Austrian and French armies. During the Franco-Prussian War, he was captured by French soldiers and falsely accused of being a spy, but later released when his true identity was discovered.

The Austro-Prussian War and the Franco-Prussian War demonstrated that the Austrian and French military doctrines ill-advisedly depended on outdated shock tactics, which led to their defeat by Prussian armies armed with modern breech-loading firearms. Emperor Franz Joseph of the Austro-Hungarian Empire did not put much faith in firepower after the defeat he suffered against the French at Solferino in 1859 during the Franco–Austrian War, boldly declaring, 'only *motion* will bring victory'. He misguidedly did everything in his power to imitate the French shock tactics used against him, instead of arming his men with modern firearms and adapting to the shifting methods of waging war, leading to the Austrian defeat during the war of

1866. Baker took note of these outdated tactics used by both the Austrians and the French while acting as an official observer. A little over a decade later, he employed an aggressive defence and appreciated the significance of breech-loading firepower to counter Russians tactics, who instinctively stuck by cumbersome close-column assaults comparable to the Austrians.

On 13 December 1865, Baker decided to settle down and embrace the 'great stumbling block, marriage', as designated by Sir Garnet Wolseley. His bride, Fanny Wormald, was the only daughter of Frank Wormald, Esq, of Potterton Hall, Yorkshire. The ceremony took place in the village of Barwick-in-Elmet, West Yorkshire, and the Prince of Wales provided Baker with a splendid white Arabian stallion as a wedding gift. In Fanny, Baker found a hidden gem; she validated her fortitude and devotion to her husband time and again until her death. Their first daughter, Hermione, was born in 1867, followed by their second daughter, Sybil, the next year.

The tranquility of his life was disrupted in 1872, when the 10th Hussars received orders transferring it back to India, after being stationed in Britain for more than ten years. On 23 March 1873, Baker submitted his formal resignation as colonel of the regiment. He had spent ten years as commander of the 10th Hussars, and had accomplished wonders in its reorganization and development. He became rooted in Great Britain, close to his family, friends, and colleagues, and chose to remain as an alternative to transplanting to India with the regiment. The decision to hand over command of his beloved regiment nonetheless tore at his heart.

In April 1873, less than a month after submitting his resignation, Baker took leave of absence on half pay to travel on a 'Central-Asian Expedition'. His destination was Northwest Persia, a congested region of Russian scheming against British-controlled India. Baker clarified the swiftness in desiring to set out on his journey when he wrote:

I knew that some little time must remain at my disposal before a fresh military appointment would claim my services. I determined to devote this interval to useful purpose to endeavour to penetrate the mystery which hung over those Eastern deserts, and to bring back, if possible, political, geographical, and strategical information that might be valuable.

Great Britain had grown fearful of the Russian threat to India from 1870, providing an ideal time for Baker's proposed exploration into this hotbed of intrigue. Although the Russians had been soundly defeated in the Crimean War over a decade earlier, they still posed a viable threat to India as Baker determined the 'British Lion [Great Britain] was getting morosely bellicose'. Russian military excursions into Central Asia were becoming fearfully close to the boundaries of the Northwest Frontier of British India. The British perceived that Russia furnished a direct menace to 'Indian supremacy' and that it must be checked 'at all costs and at all hazards'.

Baker departed Britain accompanied by Captain William John Gill of the Royal Engineers and Captain William C. Clayton of the 9th Queen's Royal Lancers. The party travelled by railroad to Vienna, then by boat down the Danube River to the Black Sea, to reach their destination of Constantinople. Captain Clayton had to depart rather early from the party since he had contracted cholera, and would tragically die in 1877 during a polo accident while stationed in India. Baker and Gill were strangely given permission to travel on to Persia by the Russian Grand Duke Michael upon arriving to Tiflis, located in modern day Georgia. From Tiflis they travelled roughly 400 miles by carriage to Baku, and trekked another 500 miles to Tehran.

Along his journey of exploration in Northwest Persia, Baker became frankly aware of the differences of the Russian and the British methods of administering their 'conquered dependencies in the Eastern world colonies'. He perceived that, 'Nothing can be more distinctive than the two.' In one instance, he was accompanied to a mosque by a Russian superintendent, who Baker forcibly halted from entering with his muddy boots, which would have led to a sacrilegious act against the occupants' religious customs. Baker expanded on the dissimilarities demonstrated between the Russians and British:

> We show the utmost delicacy for the religious feelings of the races we subject, and even punish any violation of their prejudices. The Russians, on the contrary, though professing religious toleration, really act as proselytizing conquerors. Which course will be the most successful in the long run, time alone can prove.

The expedition was far from a pleasurable sightseeing holiday. Baker was exposed to a number of deadly encounters, such as threats from hostile bandits and thieves, exposure to the harsh elements of the Persian landscape, and threats from infectious diseases. When confronted by a group of twenty bandits, 'trusting to the effect of a sudden initiative,' Baker charged the fiends head-on with his pistol pointed in their direction, causing them to panic and flee. He suffered bouts of dysentery and malaria on the journey and at one point swallowed large quantities of quinine to remain balanced upright in his saddle as his grey stallion, named Imaum, led the way.

When Baker concluded his expedition and finally returned to Great Britain he was a mere skeleton. He gave a hearty handshake to Gill when they arrived at Charing Cross Station in congratulation of their success and survival. His expedition had paid off; the two gathered vast amounts of information related to the Russians, the inhabitants, and the geography. Baker learned an important lesson from his travels in North Persia that he would attempt to mimic in his later encounters: 'Never halt or retreat in face of an Eastern enemy, it is always fatal.'

Baker became regarded as an expert in respect of Russian expansion and all matters related to the East upon his return to London. He gave presentations and lectures on his travels, illuminating the dangers of Russia's advances into Central Asia. In 1875, he published *Clouds in the East*, which recollected his travels in Persia. His tales of the landscape, people, and deadly encounters were followed by his assessment of a pre-emptive foreign policy that Great Britain needed to adopt to counter the Russians.

In the midst of the acclaim he received for his Northwest Persia expedition, Baker was appointed the Assistant Quartermaster General at Aldershot. This post was far from the exhilaration he had experienced on his Persian travels. He had always been regarded as an expert of organization, and would be put to work assisting with maintaining and overseeing the supply of the British Army. Baker may have found some relief in the quiet assignment to give himself some time to recuperate from the arduous expedition. Aside from the quiet post, he was scheduled to organize a grand review for the Sultan of Zanzibar, scheduled to take place on 28 August 1875.

On 17 June 1875, the 48-year-old Baker boarded the 3.00 pm train at Liphook Station, destined for London. He made arrangements to dine that night upon his arrival with the Commander-in-Chief of the British Army and the cousin of Queen Victoria, the Duke of Cambridge. Upon entering the railway carriage, he noticed that a lone passenger was his only company. In the compartment sat a young lady, the beautiful Rebecca 'Kate' Dickinson, the 21-year-old sister of a physician, traveling alone to London to meet her brother for the first part of a planned holiday in Switzerland. Colonel Valentine Baker, an illustrious army officer with a fruitful future ahead of him, had no reason to suspect that his life would be dramatically transformed upon entering the compartment with this lovely female companion.

Chapter 2

Exodus

An ordinary man would have succumbed to the blow; but he was not an ordinary man.

Major General Frank S. Russell referring to Valentine Baker
in *Blackwood's Magazine*, 1909.

Whatever truthfully transpired on that train ride bound for London on 17 June 1875 will forever remain a mystery. The consequences of the event would change how Valentine Baker was perceived by the public for the remainder of his life. The public's sentiment was fuelled by newspaper accounts that vilified Baker as a sexual deviant influenced by an immoral act of passion. His supporters consisted of family members, close friends, and army colleagues who believed that his female companion misinterpreted his intentions and panicked, leading to one of the greatest scandals of the nineteenth century. A portion of the truth may be disinterred in both of these perspectives.

Rebecca Dickinson climbed aboard the train that summer's day as a naïve, but articulate, adolescent girl. She discreetly positioned herself in the corner of the car with her face turned towards the open window, allowing the cool summer breeze to flow freely into the compartment. Upon halting to load passengers at Liphook Station, Baker lowered his head and climbed into the car, sitting on the leather cushioned seat opposite the beautiful girl. He had an air of coolness and self-confidence about him that made Rebecca somewhat uneasy, maybe even bashful. Casual small talk commenced between the two passengers, first initiated by Baker. He politely asked her if the breeze of the open window was a nuisance, but she answered that she was quite satisfied with it.

Baker scooted towards the middle of the seat situated in a more relaxed position, interested in the small talk he had engaged his company thus far.

They gossiped on a variety of topics to pass the time and pointed out the natural beauty of the landscape through which they passed. They spoke of Aldershot, and Baker noted his delight for the pictures hanging on the walls of the Royal Academy. Baker inquired as to where she was destined, and she informed him of her planned vacation to the emerald hills of Switzerland.

When Rebecca mentioned the destination of her intended vacation, Baker's raised eyebrows and stroke of his mustache revealed his concern. He paused and asked in an uneasy tone, 'Are you going alone?' She replied, 'No, my brother and sister accompany me.' It was unusual for a lady of rigid morals in the Victorian era to travel unchaperoned. She had departed the company of her mother and sister at Midhurst, and would be joined by her brother awaiting her arrival in London before heading out to Switzerland.

The uneasiness escaped Baker with her clarification, and the carefree conversation resumed. The topics turned to the social atmosphere of London as the train rattled through the countryside and clouds of smoke rose from the chimney. Baker suggested that she should stay in the city long enough to visit the theatre, which he relished. Rebecca informed him that she had recently attended the grand performance of Shakespeare's *Hamlet*. Now this was a refined woman.

Baker turned the conversation to a controversial topic and probed her thoughts on mesmerism. It involved gaining control of an individual through hypnosis, a psychic phenomenon gaining popularity in Victorian Britain. He asked if she had seen the stage performances of John Nevil Maskelyne and George Alfred Cooke. Baker grew more and more absorbed in the young girl as she met each of his questions with a polished answer and expressed her viewpoints.

What developed between this moment and the end of the train ride is ambiguous. The only testimony of what materialized in these next few moments in the compartment came from Rebecca during Baker's subsequent trial. According to *her* testimony, Baker casually pulled the car's window closed that she had requested to be left open.

Rather bluntly, he asked, 'Will you give me your name?' Rebecca, feeling that Baker was attempting to make a sexual advance upon her either due to his tone or gesture replied, 'I shan't.' Somewhat taken aback, Baker fumed, 'Why not?' She feared that he regarded her as a woman of loose virtue with which he planned to wet his sexual appetite. 'Because I don't choose; I don't see any reason why I should,' she indicated in an abrasive manner.

This animated reply changed Baker's approach of seduction. He then proceeded to swap sides of the car's seat and sat uncomfortably close to Rebecca, violating her sense of space, and began to caress her hand. Rebecca testified that she forcibly shoved him off her, causing him to act out more aggressively. He proceeded to wrap his hands around her waist, followed by laying a subtle kiss on her cheek. He petitioned her, 'You must kiss me, darling.'

Rebecca reached for the emergency bell in the centre of the compartment, and pulled tightly. To her horror, it was disconnected and unserviceable. Baker kissed her again on the lips and she next 'felt his hand underneath my dress, on my stocking, above my boot', which sent her into a frenzied panic. She screamed, broke free from his clutch, and flung open the window with both hands. She forced her head and shoulders out of the car's window, causing her oversized hat to rip off her head in a gush of wind.

She pushed down on the door handle, opening it, and tumbled outside on to the car's footboard. There she held on for dear life as the train rumbled 40 miles an hour through the countryside. She tightly held on to the door handle to steady herself from falling to her death, and with the other hand she grasped the extended arm of her assailant reaching to help her back in. Baker had reached out to retrieve her by the waist, causing her outfit to become dishevelled, as he pleaded, 'Get in dear!' Passengers on the other cars dangled their heads outside their windows to identify the cause for the commotion.

The awkward scene continued for 5 miles as Rebecca Dickinson hesitated to get back into the car with her assailant, while also fearful of toppling to her death. Pedestrians on the platform at Walton Station had seen the young girl hanging from the car as it raced past, and telegraphed ahead to the station at Esher to stop the train. As the train came to a screeching halt, a crowd congregated around the awkward scene. A railway guard, by the name of Henry Bailey, pushed his way through the crowd towards the faint girl, with her hair clearly in a jumbled mess and her blouse torn and dangling, exposing some bare skin.

She lifted her trembling hand with what strength remained and pointed Baker out to the uniformed guard, declaring, 'That man would not leave me alone.' She later testified that Baker whispered to her, 'Don't say anything; you don't know what trouble you'll get me into; say you were frightened.' Baker was locked into another car under the vigilant guard of two fellow passengers, by the names of Pike and Burnett. The flustered girl was escorted by Reverend Aubrey Browne to his own car, and he would accompany her for the remainder of the journey to Waterloo Station.

Baker sat silently under his captor's supervision, trying to rehash the events that led to the hysteria of his young companion. Surely he would see to it that everything would be straightened out when he arrived at Waterloo Station. Upon the train's arrival, Rebecca Dickinson and Valentine Baker were escorted by Sergeant William Atter to the superintendent's office. Baker attempted to apologize to Rebecca and remarked, 'I am very sorry if anything I did frightened you.' Atter took down their names and addresses, and afterwards Rebecca Dickinson was escorted by the Reverend Browne to her physician brother's home on Chesterfield Street.

The following day, a warrant was issued for Baker's arrest. Deputy Chief Constable of Surrey Constabulary, Charles Walter Barkes, appeared before Baker at Guildford Railway Station and served the warrant. When Baker was confronted by the uniformed constable he remarked with disbelief, 'Who laid the information?' Constable Barkes simply replied, 'The young lady herself.' Baker probed the constable if the young lady was still in London, and Barkes informed him that she was in town, residing with her brother, Dr William Howship Dickinson. Baker mentioned to Barkes that he should be able to privately settle Rebecca Dickinson's claim with her brother, as this was a grossly exaggerated misunderstanding.

Is it possible that the well-respected Valentine Baker, a married man with two delightful young daughters at home, allowed his sexual appetite to supersede rational thought? Even though he rubbed shoulders with members of the 'Marlborough House Set', whose unconventional behaviour was well established among its members, this kind of behaviour was not characteristic of the illustrious cavalry colonel. Certainly something took place in that car that sent Rebecca Dickinson into a wild hysteria. If her accusations were precise, Baker endangered his reputation, his army career, and the relationship with his wife and children to quench this sexual yearning. Colleagues and friends recalled Baker's mild demeanor, polished character, and courteous and hospitable conduct, and those closest to him could hardly believe that he would act out in such a fashion.

A reputable duo of legal gurus made up Baker's defence. Serjeant William Ballantine previously served as the prosecutor in the case of Franz Müller, a German tailor hanged for murdering a 69-year-old city banker in 1864. This was the first recorded murder on a British train, which led to the establishment of the emergency cord that had failed Rebecca Dickinson. Henry Hawkins was recognized as the man who defended Simon François Bernard, tried for his involvement in the 1858 plot to assassinate Napoleon III. He helped Bernard to be acquitted of all charges.

Baker appeared before a panel of eight magistrates in the County Court of Guildford to face the charges of common assault, indecent assault, and attempted rape. Samuel and a number of loyal army officers from the garrison at Aldershot accompanied him for moral support. The defendant's bail was set at £4,000 and 'a large number of gentlemen spontaneously offered themselves as bail for the defendant,' a local newspaper reported. This display of generosity demonstrated the strong support he had from his friends and colleagues. The bail was divided in half and posted by his brother Samuel, and the Eleventh Viscount Valentia, a former lieutenant of the 10th Hussars.

The case opened on 30 July 1875 at Summer Assizes at Croydon. The judge presiding over the trial was the 60-year-old William Brett, known for his sound judgment and harsh sentences. Ballantine requested for the case to be adjourned until a later date, and that a special jury be gathered for the case. This request was put forth by Ballantine so the jury would be 'composed as it would be of the same rank of society' and 'will look with a more impartial view of the case'. The defence feared the existing jury would hold a biased view against the accused, who was regularly associated with the aristocracy. The request for a fresh jury was denied by Judge Brett, and Baker's trial was set for 2 August 1875.

The events of the scandal made the newspapers headlines as the lowliest workers up to noblest gentlemen maliciously gossiped. 'The case was the talk of all of England,' recorded one American newspaper. Tensions ran high, and the highly publicized trial fuelled the discontent of the commoners. The outcry 'one law for the rich and another for the poor' rang throughout the streets of London. This backlash was in response to the slew of preceding controversies and scandals that the Prince of Wales and his 'Marlborough House Set' were charged with but had eluded.

The American author Mark Twain even mocked Colonel Baker, speaking of the 'atrocious story'. Twain pronounced:

If a lady, unattended, walk abroad in the streets of London, even at noonday, she will pretty likely be accosted and insulted – and not by drunken sailors, but by men who carry the look and wear the dress of gentlemen. It is maintained that these people are not gentlemen, but are a lower sort, disguised as gentlemen. The case of Colonel Valentine Baker obstructed that argument, for a man cannot become an officer in the British army expect he hold the rank of gentleman.

On 2 August 1875, Baker and his lawyers forced their way past the surge of onlookers gathered in front of the doorway of the courtroom. *The Times* chronicled the chaos that surrounded the building and the courtroom:

From as early as eight o'clock in the morning, the account runs, people had begun to assemble round the doors of the Court, and long before the time for opening them a dense crowd had congregated before the court-house, and not only obstructed the entrance, but completely blocked up the roadway before and for some distance on each side of the courthouse. No case had ever been within living memory which appears to have caused such excitement.

Judge Brett, in his elegant robe and ivory wig, was forced to temporarily suspend the trial in order to allow the streets to be cleared and to silence the disrupting racket.

Baker stepped forwards and pleaded not guilty in a 'firm voice' in the suffocating and noiseless courtroom. Testimony was heard by the jury from fellow train passengers, eyewitnesses outside of the train, and Rebecca Dickinson herself. Two employees of the London and South Western

Railway Company, the bricklayer William Burrowes, and the platelayer George Godsmark gave their testimonies of witnessing the victim dangling from the train as it passed them while at work. Reverend James Baldwin Brown, who rode in the third car back from where the incident took place, recorded he saw her 'gesticulating violently' and thought that her car was engulfed in flames. Henry Bailey, the railway guard who initially confronted Baker, and Sergeant William Atter, who interviewed Baker at Waterloo Station, also gave critical testimonies.

The testimonies of Sergeant Atter, the two gentlemen who guarded him, and the accuser were the most damning to Baker's case. Sergeant Atter testified that he overheard Baker remark, 'I am sorry I did it; I don't know what possessed me to do it, I being a married man.' The two gentlemen in the car into which he was placed testified that his trousers appeared unbuttoned and dishevelled. Rebecca Dickinson, accompanied by her mother and sister, coolly made her way to the bench and gave her own testimony in vivid detail.

A number of prominent individuals testified on Baker's behalf. Sir Richard Airey, Adjunct General of the British Army, testified in favour of Baker's reputation as an officer. Sir Thomas Steele, in command at Aldershot and later of the land forces in Ireland, also gave strong evidence in favour of Baker's character. The mere presence of these distinguished soldiers, politicians, and aristocrats in the courtroom spoke louder than words: Colonel Thomas George Alexander Oakes of the 12th Lancers; Major General Charles Cameron Shute, formerly of the 6th (Inniskilling) Dragoons; George Charles Bingham, the 3rd Earl of Lucan, famous for issuing the orders that led to the charge of the Light Brigade during the Crimean War; the Honourable Grantley Berkeley; Viscount Halifax; and the Marquis of Tavistock.

Colonel Baker's testimony was the only one missing. If the behaviour that brought him to trial appeared completely out of character, how he responded during the trial did not. Baker had a handwritten statement read by his counsel:

I am placed here in the most delicate position. If any act of mine on the occasion referred to could have given any annoyance to Miss Dickinson, I beg to express my most unqualified regret. At the same time, I solemnly declare, upon my honour, that the case was not as it has been represented today by her under the influence of exaggeration, fear and unnecessary alarm. To the evidence of the police constable Atter, I give the most unqualified denial. I may that I don't intend in the least to say that she willfully misinterpreted the case, but I say that she has represented it incorrectly, no doubt under the influence of exaggerated fear and unnecessary alarm.

Baker refused to allow the accuser to be cross-examined by his defence team. 'I was debarred by his express command from putting a single question,' Henry Hawkins later conveyed with frustration. Baker felt that by allowing his lawyers to examine Rebecca Dickinson under intense scrutiny, it would compromise the young lady's honour. The defence had the fruitless task of downplaying the accuser's description of events in an attempt to exonerate their client. They fought to convince the jury that she had misinterpreted Baker's intentions, and the events of that day were overblown.

Without placing the accuser on the stand under the scrutiny of the defence team, Baker's chance of evading conviction was virtually hopeless. He refused to dislodge from his stance despite the pleas of his lawyers, and ultimately condemned himself. He could only hope that the jury would appreciate the testimony conveyed of his character, and show sympathy in their conviction. Henry Hawkins expounded:

I say to his honour, that as a gentleman and a British officer, he preferred to take to himself the ruin of his own character, the forfeiture of his commission in the army, the loss of his social status, and *all* that make life worth having, to casting even a doubt on the lady's veracity in the witness box.

Despite nearly all of Britain appearing to be waging a witch hunt against Valentine Baker, those most loyal to him stood close by as his repute was left in shambles. The members of his family and dearest friends still felt the whole incident had been sensationalized by the papers and dramatized by the accuser. Fanny Baker must have initially felt betrayed by her husband's suspected advances upon this attractive young lady. She put her misgivings aside and loyally supported her husband through the vicious slandering.

The jury took less than an hour to reach a verdict. Valentine Baker was found not guilty of the more severe charge of 'assault with the intention to ravish', i.e., rape, but was found guilty of indecent assault and common assault. Both of these charges came with a prison sentence. Judge Brett ordered him to serve twelve months in the common prison of Horsemonger Lane Gaol, pay a fine of £500, and pay all the costs of the prosecution. These verses dictated by Judge Brett must have replayed like a broken record in Baker's head as he was led away to an unornamented milk train to avoid being waylaid on his way to serve his prison sentence:

I hope that, some future day, you may be allowed, by some brilliant service, of which you are so well capable, to wipe out the injury you have done to yourself, and the dishonour you have done to your country.

Henry Hawkins, though exasperated by being debarred from questioning Rebecca Dickinson, was mesmerized by his client's demeanor during the trial. He added:

The manliness of his defence showed him naturally to be a man of honour, who, having been guilty of serious misconduct, did all he could to amend the wrong that he had done; and so he won my sympathy in his sad misfortune and misery.

It appears that those not buying the criminal charges felt that Baker was at least guilty of carelessness. One individual was sympathetic towards the defendant when he proclaimed, 'Poor fellow, he destroyed his career by a momentary indiscretion.' His brother, Samuel, may have given a hint to the truth when he penned to a friend on 25 June 1875:

With regard to Val's affair, I know more from him than I have the right to divulge. He has confided the *whole* to three friends, including myself, but you know in such a case a man is at the mercy of a lady, and his tongue must on point of honour be absolutely sealed.

Samuel continued in another letter to the same friend:

> Although he has been guilty of *much indiscretion* the punishment is
> terribly severe in proportion to the offence. In such cases a gentleman's
> tongue is sealed, but no man of common sense can suppose that he
> acted without some attraction that he accepted as encouragement.

Baker's culpability on that train ride will be left to the judgment of the
reader.

Baker was a ruined man and shamed in all social circles. He was banned
from all the prestigious social organizations of which he had been a member.
Even though a staunch supporter of Baker, the Prince of Wales travelled to
India in 1875, and was forced to distance himself publicly from his close
relationship with Baker. Queen Victoria continually kept a worrisome eye on
the Prince of Wales, who tended to associate himself with less than satisfactory
acquaintances. Now one of these acquaintances was accused of rape.

Queen Victoria found out about the 'dreadful business' of Baker's trial
while casually glancing through the *Daily News*. She was disturbed that a
gentleman officer of her army could commit such a heinous act. In a private
letter to her daughter, Princess Victoria, she furiously penned:

> I wanted to mention to you that awful trial of Colonel V. Baker! Was there
> ever such a thing and such a position for a poor young girl [Rebecca
> Dickinson]? And what a disgrace to the Army. No punishment is severe
> enough. Sir William Jenner knows the brother, who is a distinguished
> doctor and she is a very nice girl – though some officers and people tried
> to excuse him by abusing the poor, unprotected girl but the country are
> furious with him, and he will be disgraced for life. The articles in *The
> Times*, *D. News* (especially), and *D. Telegraph* were excellent. What is to
> happen if officers, high in position, behave as none of the lowest would
> have dared to do, unless a severe example is made. I owe I feel most
> indignant. Should you care to see the two last-named articles I will
> send them for you and Fritz [Frederick III] to see. Colonel Baker has
> a very bad moral character and Sr S. Baker his brother also does not
> stand very high in that respect.

Baker offered his resignation from the army, but it was vetoed by Queen Victoria. The Duke of Cambridge was another prominent personality that stood staunchly by Baker. He received a reprimanding letter from Lord Ponsonby, forwarded from Queen Victoria, concerning an appeal he had made to allow Baker to honourably resign. Her scalding tone could resonate through the words of the letter he received on 30 August:

> The Queen desires me to assure Your Royal Highness that she never for a moment thought that Your Royal Highness defended the conduct of the prisoner, but that she desired to explain to Your Royal Highness how necessary Her Majesty thought it, that this man should be removed from the army with a mark of disgrace, and not be permitted to retire.

A 'severe example' was to be made of Baker to exemplify what happens to officers who commit such decadent crimes. Instead of being allowed to honourably resign, he was humiliated by being cashiered from the army. To be cashiered meant the amount paid for the original purchase of the officer's commission in the regiment was forfeited. Major General Frank S. Russell estimated the original amount paid by Baker's father for his officer's commission was nearly £5,000, which would equate to nearly half a million pounds today. Beyond financially stripping the officer, being cashiered carried the mark of disgrace.

Now everything that defined his life – honour, reputation, and the army – vanished. All that made 'life worth having' for Valentine Baker ceased to exist. His actions left a horrible blotch on not only his reputation, but the repute of his family and even the legacy of the 10th Hussars. Baker was condemned to carry the mark of disgrace for the remainder of his life. Twelve months in Horsemonger Lane Gaol would be spent contemplating everything lost and how he might set everything right.

Horsemonger Lane Gaol was located in the county of Surrey and established seventy-seven years before, in the year of 1798. The prison was built to accommodate 400 prisoners separated into separate wings occupied by less dangerous debtors and those with more severe criminal charges. Public executions for Surrey took place outside this prison, and in 1849, the hanging of the Mannings on the prison roof was witnessed by 40,000 onlookers, including Charles Dickens, sickened by amusement surrounding public executions. The poet Leigh Hunt was confined here for two years, in response for defaming George IV in the *Examiner* by labelling him as 'a despiser' and one who 'closed half a century without one single claim on the gratitude of his country'. The fellow poets Thomas Moore and Lord Byron paid a visit and dined with Hunt while in the prison in June 1813.

Activist William Hepworth Dixon, in his book *The London Prisons*, published in 1850, noted that the condition of the prison was quite different from when Moore and Byron had visited their friend. Dixon explained:

> Time and rules are changed since then: 'the luxurious comforts – the trellised flower-garden without the books, busts, pictures, and pianoforte within' – which Moore describes on the occasion when Byron dined with him in prison, would be looked for in vain now.

He reported the prison provided little control, and failed to segregate a majority of its prisoners. He described the decrepit prospect of a common prisoner who 'finds himself in a low, long room, dungeon-like, chilly, not very clean, and altogether as uncomfortable as it can conveniently be made.' He further illuminated the pitiable conditions:

> This room is crowded with thirty or forty persons, of all ages and shades of ignorance and guilt – left to themselves, with no officer in sight. Here there is no attempt to enforce discipline. Neither silence nor separation is maintained in the largest prison in the metropolitan county of Surrey!

Baker's prison sentence in Horsemonger Lane Gaol was criticized by journalists for not being harsh enough and that he was treated as a 'gentleman felon'. Mark Twain was critical of Baker's prison sentence when he exploded, 'Baker was "imprisoned" – in a parlor; and he could not have been more visited, or more overwhelmed with attentions, if he had committed six murders ...' *The Bee-Hive* criticized that:

If Colonel Baker had been a rider in a third class carriage, and if he had been a poor man, there is no reason to believe that any leniency of any kind would have been extended to him by the judge.

In *The Bible Echo*, it was written that Baker's prison sentence was a blatant display of injustice. 'To call Mr Baker's incarceration *punishment* is completely absurd. The lesson of this trial is to confirm the words of the Bible, that equity is not found in the earth,' the weekly religious newspaper grumbled.

Baker was certainly allowed accommodations that other inmates in the prison were not. He was permitted to buy his own food, wear his own clothing, and to furnish his rooms 'with what is reasonable, necessary, and not extravagant', according to *The Morning Post*. One account recorded that his enclosed chamber or 'apartment' consisted of two rooms in a portion of the debtor's section, provding him access to freely exercise in the attached courtyard. He was allotted a small portion of wine at his own expense (not exceeding one pint per day) or instead malt liquor (one quart). He was permitted to see visitors in his 'apartment' between the hours of 9.00 am and 6.00 pm.

Even if Baker's prison sentence was not nearly as harsh as many would have liked, the emotional and psychological effects of it and the shame attached to it were detrimental to his overall health. Baker was forced to rehash the events of that fearful train ride that led to his disgrace and humiliation when faced with the idleness and monotony of prison life. He had the recurring reminder of the many people he had disappointed, and the disgrace he had brought down upon his family. He was castigated by the public, and many would have gladly seen him broken by back-breaking prison labour. Fanny Baker pleaded to *The Times* that within the first three months of his sentence, she was fearful of the fluctuating condition of his health:

I am thankful to state that the symptoms which recently caused so much alarm, both to myself and his friends and family, have yielded to medical treatment. I cannot, however, hide from myself the terrible fact that such continued and trying confinement after his active and useful life, had rendered him finally out of health, and his condition caused me the most constant and distressing anxiety.

The psychological repercussions of being accused of a shameful incident and ensuing wrongful imprisonment can have sobering consequences on the individual indicted. Psychological repression of humiliation, according to psychologists Walter J. Torres and Raymond M. Bergner, can cause individuals to plunge 'into major depressions, suicidal states, and severe anxiety states, including ones characteristic of post-traumatic stress disorder'. The late Dr John P. Wilson of Cleveland State University studied the psychological impact of individuals faced with wrongful imprisonment. He explained that for those wrongfully imprisoned, it can leave permanent scars of the mental psyche, such as bouts of severe depression, anxiety disorders, post-traumatic stress disorder, and can lead to instances of self-destructive behaviour for the remainder of their lives. Dr Wilson indicated that:

> One of the real existential dilemmas every day for a person is they know that when they go to their grave, this experience is going to be right here, in the forefront of their mind, even though they try to push it away and get on with their normal life afterwards.

Even if not sympathetic to the assessment that Baker's imprisonment was unwarranted, he unquestionably demonstrated some of the visible characteristics as defined by Dr Wilson. Shock and disbelief during the individual's arrest, followed by a period of belief that it can be corrected, is the first major emotional indication that you are dealing with a wrongly accused victim. Baker was stunned when he was served with a warrant by Deputy Chief Constable Barkes, and rationalized to the constable that he could correct the mistake. Next, a sense of injustice takes over for the falsely accused, which was revealed through Baker's written statement during his trial. The permanent loss of freedom, external lack of belief in their innocence, and loss of purpose in life wears down on the individual while in confinement, leading to a psychological and physical decline, verified by Fanny Baker's own letter published in *The Times*.

Dr James J. Reid briefly made mention of Baker's psychological dispositions during the Russo-Turkish War in his excellent book *Crisis of the Ottoman Empire: Prelude to Collapse, 1839-1878*. Dr Reid claimed that

Baker exhibited characteristics of self-destructive behaviour that could be amounted to what he judged as a 'death wish', similar to the after effects recognized by Wilson, Torres, and Bergner with the repression of humiliation and wrongful imprisonment. Dr Reid concluded that:

> A death wish did not mean that the afflicted one consciously wished to die or to commit suicide, though cases of this type existed. In many instances, the individual harbored an unconscious desire at least to defy fate by exposing himself to extremely dangerous situations.

A subtle death wish could have easily been buried in the recesses of Baker's mind, and may have guided him to unconsciously act with reckless bravery and total disregard for any form of danger on multiple battlefields following his dismissal.

The effects of shame and humiliation certainly scarred Baker's mental psyche for the remainder of his life. The journalist Edward Vizetelly observed that even later in his life, Baker 'had never been able to forget the past. You could see that written on his face plain enough.' One newspaper commented on 'How heavy a burden of past misdoing hangs perpetually round the neck of Valentine Baker' years after the trial. The same kind of public humiliation drove another Victorian soldier, Major General Hector 'Fighting Mac' MacDonald, to commit suicide after accusations of being a homosexual threatened to derail his illustrious military career.

A literary example of a character stalked by a shameful past alike to Baker can be found in Joseph Conrad's 1900 novel, *Lord Jim*. The protagonist, only known as Jim, abandons a sinking ship, the *Patna*, in a moment of cowardice by jumping overboard, leaving all of its passengers to perish. For his cowardly action, he is publicly condemned and suffers from the 'acute consciousness of lost honour'. Throughout the novel, Jim tries to come to terms with his past, but this incident 'followed him casually but inevitably' anywhere he went or tried to hide. Upon his death, Jim 'passes away under a cloud, inscrutable at heart, forgotten, unforgiven, and excessively romantic.'

The accusations made against Valentine Baker by Rebecca Dickinson also trailed him 'casually but inevitably'. No matter where he travelled, through the mountains of Bulgaria, or to the deserts of Sudan, the cloud of disgrace lingered overhead. His trial was so widely circulated that the reprehensible deeds of Colonel Baker became a topic of conversation not only in households of mid-nineteenth-century Britain, but throughout the world. He remained unforgiven, and the shame persisted to eclipse his heroic deeds.

Once an individual is overtaken by shame and humiliation, he or she has to find a way to rebound through various coping methods. Humiliated individuals hunt for an opportunity for a 'second chance' to find redemption, not only for themselves, but also in the eyes of others. Dr Murray Bilmes listed three ways individuals deal with shame. They try to hide or conceal it, they try to gain forgiveness for their misdeeds, or they pursue praiseworthy achievements to overshadow their shame. These 'heroic' achievements used to overshadow shame, according to Dr Bilmes, can 'lead to image enhancement, restored pride and ultimately, as the Japanese expression puts it, the saving of face.'

The 1902 novel *The Four Feathers*, written by Alfred E.W. Mason, is another literary example of a character coping with a dishonourable past. Harry Faversham, a young British officer from a distinguished military family, is disgraced when he resigns from the Royal North Surrey Regiment before his regiment is to be deployed to Egypt in 1882. His actions are viewed as an act of cowardice, and in response, his fellow officers, named Castleton, Willoughby, and Trench, sent three white feathers to him through the mail to signify their censure of his act. The most devastating was the fourth feather, given to him by beloved fiancée Ethne. Unlike Conrad's Jim, who fought to conceal his shame, the character of this book is on a quest to confront it.

Faversham is distraught and decides he cannot live with the shame, obsessed with returning each feather to redeem his honour. He travelled to Sudan disguised as a Greek musician and gained redemption by braving danger and personally delivering the feathers to his accusers. Castleton was killed at Tamai, emancipating Faversham of delivering his feather. He managed to return a feather to Willoughby, while also recovering the lost letters of General Charles George 'Chinese' Gordon in Berber. He allowed himself to be captured and thrown into the hellish prison at Omdurman, where he found Trench and returned the third feather, and later rescued him. With his reputation restored, he returned to England and married Ethne.

Baker emulated Harry Faversham and chose to confront his shame and humiliation, actively seeking redemption through his achievements to overshadow his shame. Unlike Faversham, who clearly identified how he would regain his honour by personally delivering each feather to his comrades, Baker's attempt at redemption was ambiguous. Instead, he committed himself to aiding British political and military interests whenever and wherever he could be of service. Sir Garnet Wolseley once wrote, 'What nobler heritage can poor, sinful man leave his children than the fact that he willingly died that England might be renowned and great, and her people safe and prosperous?' He acknowledged that through his brave and worthy achievements in the interests of the British Empire, there always existed a chance that he could exonerate his shame and be reinstated honourably into the British Army. He set out on what would be a lifelong mission to unearth this heroic achievement.

In August 1876, Baker was released from Horsemonger Lane Gaol, one year after the trial. With a burning desire to exonerate himself to his countryman and to Queen Victoria, he began to search for an opportunity of redemption as soon as he left his stuffy incarceration. Major General Frank S. Russell, a friend of Baker, stated that he 'felt much for him' as he was 'a disgraced and ruined man'. However, Russell felt that Baker possessed the fortitude to overcome these setbacks validated by his subsequent actions after his release. Russell afterwards proclaimed:

> Any ordinary man would have succumbed to the blow; but he was not an ordinary man. No sooner did he come out of prison than he lost not a moment in endeavouring to regain his position, and not one word of complaint did I ever hear him utter.

No longer permitted to don Her Majesty's scarlet, and blacklisted in his homeland, Baker was offered a unique opportunity. His old friend the Prince of Wales helped to acquire for him a position serving British interests in an unofficial capacity in the Ottoman Empire. Due to his expertise in all matters related to the East and his aptitude for organization, he was appointed to the rank of *Mirliva*, or major general, and tasked with organizing the Ottoman civil gendarmerie (quasi police force). The unit was composed of fifteen other retired or unemployed British officers who joined him in Constantinople. Journalist and fiction writer David Christie Murray conveyed:

> Many of them were men who had done good service in their day and held unblemished records, but there is no disguising the fact that a large contingent of the discredited riffraff of the British Army was collected in the city at that time.

Baker, accompanied by his wife and daughters, set out for Constantinople in September 1876. When he arrived, he entered a city in turmoil, beset by revolutionary movements in the Balkans and strained relations with the Russian Empire that dwindled to the point of hostility. In the summer of 1875, peasants of Bosnia and Herzegovina revolted following failed crop yields, destroying Ottoman property and burning towns and villages in response to Ottoman tax collectors demanding their customary extortion. Agitated Bulgarian peasants followed next and revolted in April 1876. The de facto Slavic principalities of Serbia and Montenegro declared war on the Ottomans on 30 June 1876 to lend support to their Slavic brothers, and the Serbians invaded Ottoman-held Bosnia, while the Montenegrins invaded Ottoman-held Herzegovina. The revolutionaries likewise found an ally in their Slavic brothers to the north.

Pan-Slavism had blossomed in the Russian Empire in the nineteenth century among the bourgeoisie, with the ultimate goal to unite all Slavs under one banner. Ambitious Russian politicians used this sentiment to advance their own interests into the Balkans, with the ultimate aim to wrestle control of these territories and undercut Ottoman control to the Black Sea and the Mediterranean Sea. Fuelled by the Pan-Slavic movement, Russian volunteers arrived in droves to support the Serbians and Montenegrins without the Russian Empire formerly declaring war on the Ottoman Empire. A section in the Pan-Slavist journal *Russkkii Mir*, published in April 1877, personified what Russian Pan-Slavists saw as a unified front against the Ottomans:

> All the Slavs of the Balkan Peninsula have served the cause of Slavdom: Bosnians and Herzegovinians, having begun a heroic uprising, not yet

victorious, and having withstood all the horrors of destructive war and all the soothing seduction of diplomacy; the Bulgarians, by their martyrdom; the Montenegrins by their victories; the Serbs by their, perhaps imprudent, but courageous, resoluteness to raise the standard of Slavic independence at the risk of their own existence. It must not be forgotten that precisely these Serbs with their glorious Russian chief also aroused the spirit of the Russian people.

Russian mercenary General Mikhail Chernyayev, made famous by his exploits in Central Asia, led the brown-jacketed and red-legged Serbian forces into Bosnia. Chernyayev served as the editor of the *Russkkii Mir* for a time, and his pro-Slavic sentiments ran thick in his veins. In May 1876, Chernyayev arrived in Belgrade along with 700 Russian officers and volunteers. Count Leo Tolstoy's novel *Anna Karenina* portrayed these Russian volunteers as no more than 'drunkards, misfits', and who 'had nothing to live for'. By the end of the war, nearly 4,000 Russian 'volunteers' would come to Serbia's support, and two-thirds would die in the war, a precursor of the Russian strategy of *maskirovka* used in Crimea in 2014.

Süleyman Pasha led an Ottoman army in a counteroffensive to derail the Serbian invasion. The 38-year-old Süleyman Pasha had been born into an impoverished family in 1840, but was the archetype of a rags-to-riches story. Valentine Baker noted that he showed 'very great capacity' as a scholar, having been initially educated for the priesthood, but instead joined the army. He had previously served in secretarial and administrative positions in Montenegro, Crete, and Yemen, and served as professor and later the director of the Military Academy in Constantinople. Baker noted that he had characteristics of a megalomaniac and was 'gifted with great shrewdness and cunning', and in consequence, 'soon gained rapid military advancement.'

The initial military successes of Chernyayev's invasion of Bosnia were short-lived. The Montenegrins, easily identified by their fierce garb of long white coats and jewelled knives protruding from their belts, proved to be dismal allies. They instead restricted their fighting to Herzegovina, refusing to coordinate attacks with their Serbian allies in Bosnia. Despite Süleyman Pasha's lack of battlefield experience, he routed Chernyayev's ill-organized and badly led peasant army at the Battle of Djunis on 29 October

1876, leading one correspondent of the Otago *Evening Star* to declare, 'This Sabbath day has been the worst twenty-four hours Servia [Serbia] has seen since the little principality declared war against Turkey.' It was estimated that 10 per cent of the male population of Serbia was killed within five months of the short war.

Meanwhile, the harsh repression and atrocities committed against Christian Bulgarian civilians by the Ottomans led to an outcry throughout the world. Most of these massacres were committed by the unmanageable Ottoman *Bashi-bozuks*. Stories circulated of rape, butchery, and the decapitation of women and children in popular Western newspapers branded as the 'Bulgarian agitation'. Western readers were appalled. Though greatly exaggerated in some instances, civilian casualties were estimated as a high as 30,000.

The American correspondent for the *London Daily News*, Januarius A. MacGahan, left the most vivid accounts of the atrocities committed following the April Uprising in Bulgaria. He attained prominence as the leading advocate for helping to initiate anti-Ottoman opinion to Western readers. On his tombstone, located in New Lexington, Ohio, his epitaph appropriately reads: 'MacGahan, Liberator of Bulgaria.' He describes the ghastly scene he came upon following the massacre of at least 1,000 civilians from the village of Batak:

> We looked again at the heap of skulls and skeletons before us, and we observed that they were all small and that the articles of clothing intermingled with them and lying about were all women's apparel. These, then, were all women and girls. From my saddle I counted about a hundred skulls, not including those that were hidden beneath the others in the ghastly heap nor those that were scattered far and wide through the fields. The skulls were nearly all separated from the rest of the bones – the skeletons were nearly all headless. These women had all been beheaded.

Opposition to supporting the Ottomans in Great Britain was led by William Gladstone. He was referred to as 'God's Only Mistake' by Prime Minister Benjamin Disraeli. Gladstone published a popular pamphlet that emphasized the grotesque acts of inhumanity in Bulgaria. The pamphlet sold 40,000 copies in one week, and 200,000 by the end of September. It almost single-handedly turned the majority of Britons against the Ottomans, who were outraged at the thought their country would support a power that allowed their soldiers to commit these horrendous acts.

The widespread circulation of MacGahan's reports and Gladstone's pamphlet placed Great Britain in a grave political dilemma. Benjamin Disraeli, backed by Queen Victoria, intended to serve as the backbone for the Ottomans against probable Russian belligerence. Disraeli and his supporters feared that Russian occupation of Constantinople would upset the balance of power in the region, and would be catastrophic to their economic and strategic interests in the Suez Canal, the Persian Gulf, and India. This public backlash divided the cabinet and left Disraeli powerless to promise military support to the Ottomans if the Russians chose to pursue an invasion into Ottoman territory.

Fixing Baker in an influential position in the Ottoman government as the war clouds loomed, allowed for him to report on the political and military situation inside the Ottoman Empire back to the British. In one letter to the Prince of Wales, he warned, 'But a war between Turkey and Russia menaces English interests so closely, that we are sure to be, in some way, involved.' He drafted various offensive plans of how to counter a Russian invasion if war was declared on the Ottomans. Frank S. Russell, who travelled to Constantinople at the time as a junior officer, recalled Baker's preparation of these plans: 'I found Colonel Baker, as usual, working very hard – he was never idle, – surrounded by maps and memorandums, drawing out plans of operations for the Turks.'

While visiting the Ottoman capital, Russell, accompanied by Reginald Brett, 2nd Viscount Esher, asked if he would care to meet the ill-starred Baker, who was staying at a hotel not far from their quarters. Brett seemed bothered at Russell's proposal and politely declined. When Russell prodded why he appeared sombre at the thought of meeting Baker, Brett shot back, 'Cannot you guess? My father sentenced him.' Reginald was the son of Judge William Brett, the man who had administered Baker's trial.

A few days later, Reginald Brett and Baker bumped into one another at a dinner party. Brett feared for the worse. Baker conversed 'with great tact' with the cautious son of the iron-willed judge. Baker broke the ice when he revealed his lack of concern that Brett's father had convicted him, and that he held no grudge against either party. Baker once again validated his honourable character, and Russell recalled that the two became 'fast friends'.

War correspondent and artist Frederic Villiers of the *Graphic* was another visitor to Constantinople that described his encounter with the notorious exile. He was not very impressed with the officer who sat across from him at the dinner table while dining at the Club Commercial et Maritime. Villiers evoked, 'At dinner one night at the club I sat opposite a pleasant-faced but taciturn man. He always seemed depressed and dejected. I shortly discovered that he was Colonel Valentine Baker, the famous British cavalry officer.' The two would meet again on two other occasions; by that time, Villiers' appraisal would be much different.

The Constantinople Conference convened on 23 December 1876, assembling diplomats from the major European nations (Germany, Austria-Hungary, Russia, France, Italy, and Great Britain) to petition the Ottoman Empire to enact political reforms for the discontent peoples of the Balkans. Ultimately, the Ottoman Sultan Abdülhamid II rejected several solutions put forth by the Western nations, leading to the conference being dissolved on 20 January 1877. This was the last chance for the impending clash in the Balkans to end peacefully, and the rooted dogma of the Ottomans gave the Russians a legitimate cause to declare a holy war to liberate their Slavic brothers. Russia mobilized for war, while Great Britain's divided public sentiment hindered intervention to support the Ottomans in any capacity.

The Ottoman Sultan Abdülhamid II, having ascended to the throne following the deposition of his brother Murad on 31 August 1876, failed to appreciate the severity of his actions. The 34-year-old sullen-faced sultan suffered from extreme paranoia and kept himself virtually isolated from the outside world in fear of assassination or an attempted coup. In every room of his vast estate, he had thousands of revolvers strategically placed in order to protect himself, and had his slaves personally test all of his food and take the first puff of his hand-rolled cigarettes to evade poisoning. In one tragic instance, he accidentally shot and killed a servant in his garden who he presumed was a would-be assassin. He refused to meet regularly with his ministers, leading author Noel Barber to conclude, 'No wonder that he took little heed of the gathering storm clouds.'

Russia sent its own implausible memorandum to the Ottomans following the disintegration of the Constantinople Conference. Their demands included: Bulgaria would become a vassal state under European supervision with administrative guarantees to the other Christian providences; additional Ottoman territory would go to Serbia and Montenegro; autonomy would be granted to Bosnia-Herzegovina; and Europe would regulate relations in the Balkans. This was followed by the most insulting demand: the annexation of a selected handful of Ottoman territories by Russia. With the evident Ottoman rejection, war was declared by the Russian Empire on 24 April 1877.

The Grand Vizier of the Ottoman Empire, Ibrahim Edhem Pasha, showed interest employing Baker to serve on the Balkan front as a staff military adviser to the Ottoman Commander-in-Chief, Abdülkerim Nadir Pasha. This came to nothing, as the War Minister, Redif Pasha, was fearful of employing European mercenaries dating back to his experiences during the Crimean War. Even though Baker was not involved in the conflict for monetary gain, Redif cancelled the order. Baker soon after fell ill with typhoid fever and was bedridden, taking three months to fully recuperate.

While Baker remained incapacitated, Russian soldiers first crossed through Romania, liberating the Romanians who embraced the Russian colours and declared independence from the Ottomans on 9 May 1877. Thousands of Romanian soldiers would bolster the invading Russian force in the coming months. From the Romanian border, the Russians faced the task of fording the Danube River, which formed a natural obstacle between the boundaries of Bulgaria and Romania. A ring of Ottoman fortresses known as the Quadrilateral (situated at Rushchuk, Silistria, Shumla and Varna), located to the south of the Danube, provided an intimidating obstacle, having bogged down the Russian invasion of 1828–29 for nearly twelve months.

The foremost Russian objective of the war was to conduct a blitzkrieg strike towards Constantinople, brining thousands of Russian soldiers to the gates of the Ottoman capital within weeks, bypassing the well-fortified Quadrilateral fortresses altogether. Once they crossed the Danube in force, two Russian corps would be posted to protect the left flank of the main advance column while most of the men marched through the Balkan Mountains, occupied Adrianople as a base of operation, and then renewed the advance on Constantinople. Two major pathways were sufficient for passage through the Balkan Mountains: Shipka Pass to the east, opposite to Adrianople, and the Araba Konak Pass, further to the west, near Sofia. The Russians presumed they would be able to end the war before the harsh Balkan winter would obstruct their operations in the Ottoman interior. The element of speed and surprise was essential to the plan.

Senior Ottoman leadership did not anticipate the Russian flawlessness with conducting an offensive over the Danube River and into Ottoman territory. Roughly 160,000 Ottoman soldiers were foolishly strung out along a 300-mile front along the banks of the Danube, beginning at Widin and ending in Silistria. The Ottomans incorrectly anticipated a crossing would take place somewhere near the fortress of Nikopol. At Sistova, about 30 miles to the east of Nikopol, Russian infantrymen in wooden pontoon boats rapidly drove them forwards with their oars to gain a foothold south of the Danube. Edward Smith King, an American correspondent travelling with the Russians, observed that the 'audacious tactics, or "lack of tactics", as the Austrian military attaché insisted upon saying, had succeeded, and at the cost of comparatively few lives.'

By 1 July 1877, four Russia corps were south of the Danube. The IX Corps (Lieutenant General Baron Krüdener) outflanked the fortress of Nikopol, which fell on 16 July 1877, and left 7,000 Ottoman soldiers in the garrison as prisoners of war. The XII Corps (Lieutenant General Vannofsky) and the XIII Corps (Lieutenant General Hahn) headed in the direction of the fortress of Rushchuk in order to block an Ottoman counteroffensive on the Russian left flank from that direction. The VIII Corps (Lieutenant General Radetzky) moved south towards Tarnovo, about 50 miles from Sistova, and halted in order to wait for the arrival of the IV Corps (Lieutenant General Zotov) and the XI Corps (Lieutenant General Prince Shakofskoi). A detachment under the command of Major General Joseph Gourko broke from the VIII Corps and hurried to occupy the major pathway through the Balkan Mountains in the east, Shipka Pass.

As thousands of Russian soldiers marched under the scorching Bulgarian sun and down the dusty roads southwards, the Ottomans turned to Baker for help. Frank S. Russell recorded that 'It was only after the fortune of war seemed to be turning against them that they actually gave him employment.' Upon his recovery in August, Baker received a telegram requesting that he and a small group of his English officers of the gendarmerie report to Varna. Baker sprang from his bedside with eagerness, later reporting, 'I had long been pining under the forced inactivity of life in Constantinople, and no time was lost in preparations for departure.'

A diverse collection of adventure seekers and men down on their luck would be picked to accompany Baker to Varna. His staff included Colonel Charles Noel Allix, formerly of the Grenadier Guards, Captain Robert Marcus Briscoe, formerly of the 15th (The King's) Hussars, Major George Conrad Sartorius, and Major Jenner. Australian surgeon Charles Snodgrass Ryan described Briscoe 'as a fire-eating, devil-may-care Irishman', who 'was the life and soul of the club'. Major Sartorius, attached to Baker's party in an 'unofficial capacity', was an officer of the British Indian Army bred from a distinguished military family – both of his brothers, Euston Henry Sartorius and Reginald William Sartorius, earned Victoria Crosses. Major Jenner acted as an interpreter for Baker as he was fluent in Turkish (Baker did not speak Turkish), while Baker's British servant, known as Reilly, attended to his personal articles and his horses.

Baker and his staff left Constantinople for the Black Sea port of Varna on 14 August 1877 by one of the largest steamers of the Austrian Lloyd Steamship Company, the 2,046-ton *Polluce*. Baker remembered with a heavy heart those who saw them off from Constantinople, evoking that 'Many of our friends turned out to bid us *adieu* by a general waving of a pocket-hand-kerchief.' Fanny and his two daughters were among those teary-eyed civilians bidding them farewell. He was uncertain of what role he would be destined to play in the developing conflict as he gazed off into the horizon. Having exchanged a red Ottoman fez for his pillbox cap, he was confident that he would find his redemption somewhere in Bulgaria.

Chapter 3

Ancient Enemies

A war between the one-eyed and the blind.

Attributed to Prussian Emperor
Frederick the Great, referring to
one of the numerous Russo–Turkish wars.

The Russo-Turkish War of 1877 was 'without a doubt, one of the most important wars of the nineteenth century', claimed Ottoman military history experts Dr Mesut Uyar and Dr Edward J. Erickson. The war is one of the least studied conflicts of the nineteenth century, despite this appraisal. During the nineteenth century, Western Europe did not view the Russians on equal terms socially or culturally, bogged down in the middle of their own military, political, and social reforms. The Ottomans were engulfed in an aged method of administration, with author Quintin Barry stating that 'mediaeval barbarity was still a feature of everyday life'. What makes the eleventh Russo-Turkish War worthy of evaluation by English readers?

Barry described the struggle as a war between 'two ancient enemies'. Russo-Ottoman wars consumed the two countries for more than 300 years up to 1877, fought in numerous conflicts dating back to the sixteenth century. The economic significance of the topography surrounding the Black Sea, coupled with each country's own religious and ethnic ideologies, generated a deep-rooted animosity between these two adversaries. Even during the Russo-Turkish War of 1877–78, a large portion of Russian soldiers believed they were waging a holy war against their sacrilegious neighbours. Hundreds of thousands of men from both sides perished in 300 years of warfare, dying in harsh winter marches, maimed while besieging fortresses or on the battlefield, and succumbing to epidemics such as typhoid fever, cholera, and dysentery.

Half a million Ottoman and Russian soldiers battled for control of the Balkans and Caucasia in the bloody contest that lasted from April 1877 to March 1878. Within roughly ten months, the Russian and the Ottoman armies suffered a combined 285,000 casualties. This total number of casualties suffered in the war surpassed the total casualties suffered in the two conspicuous conflicts of the mid-to-late nineteenth century: the Austro-Prussian War of 1866 (150,000 casualties) and the Franco-Prussian War of 1870–71 (250,000 casualties). Both of these wars garner greater attention from scholars, despite the greater loss of life in the Russo-Turkish War.

The military casualty figures of the Russo-Turkish War fail to consider the millions of Muslim civilian refugees forced into exile in the face of the Russian offensive. Cossack units operated in the vanguard of the Russian advance, intimidating and murdering Muslim inhabitants living in the surrounding villages. Bulgarian rebels were supplied with armaments by the Russians to wage their own brutal guerilla warfare against the Ottoman soldiers and civilians. Millions left their homes after living in these regions for centuries, and hundreds of thousands perished due to deadly disease, starvation, or murder. The conqueror of Robert E. Lee's Army of Northern Virginia, Lieutenant General Ulysses S. Grant, arrived in Constantinople near the war's end in the early months of 1878, and observed the chaos of this flight when he recorded:

> In a small portion of the city is stowed away in the Mosques and public buildings, probably more than a hundred thousand refugees, men women and children who have fled to the capital before a conquering army. They are fed entirely by charity and mostly by foreigners. What is to become of them is sad to think of. Besides these, many tens of thousands have been shipped to places in Asia Minor and turned loose upon the inhabitants.

The Ottoman refusal to grant autonomy to the rebellious provinces in the Balkans not only led to an outbreak of war between the Russians and Ottomans, but had a long-lasting global impact for years to come. Austria-Hungary, Germany, and Great Britain feared the growing strength of Russia in the Balkans, and the anarchy that would ensue if the Ottoman administration of the region crumbled. The rebellions created political disarray in the region and shifted the balance of power, leading Dr Ömer Turan to conclude that the war 'had dramatic consequences for the political, military, administrative, demographic and social structures of countries in the vast area extending from Russia to the Middle East, from Cyprus to the Balkans, and Caucasia.' The anticipated Russian occupation of Constantinople in 1878 nearly brought Great Britain to the brink of war, and an Anglo-Russian war could have prompted a pre-eminent world war by thirty-six years. The transfer of authority of Bosnia and Herzegovina to Austria-Hungary following the war further incited disgruntled revolutionaries, leading to the assassination of Archduke Franz Ferdinand in Sarajevo in June 1914.

Foreign military attachés, war correspondents, and artists travelled from countries such as the United States, France, Germany, Japan, Great Britain, and Denmark to observe, study, and chronicle the events of the war. Dr Genov Roumen of the New Bulgarian University reported that at least sixty-seven of these camp followers accompanied the Russians, and roughly the same number accompanied the Ottomans. Lieutenant General William T. Sherman of the United States Army selected a bright engineer officer by the name of Lieutenant Francis Vinton Greene (future general) to observe the effects of modern breech-loading weapons and fortifications during the war. Retired Major General George B. McClellan, former commander of the Army of the Potomac during the American Civil War, composed a paper on two significant battles of the war titled the 'Capture of Kars, and the Fall of Plevna'. McClellan projected that 'a new era was now about to commence for the Russians', and many of these camp followers earned first row seats to witness this death and destruction.

McClellan cautioned his readers to brace for the modern age of warfare that would tear the Balkans apart in 1877–78, imitated on a grander scale in 1914. Dr Maureen P. O'Connor indicated that the Russo-Turkish War provided 'a glimpse of the carnage of future wars', as one of the last major European wars to take place before the eruption of bloodshed in the First World War. The days of elegant columns manoeuvring on open battlefields, heroic hell-for-leather cavalry charges, and the dependence of the massed bayonet charge, were replaced by electric telegraph lines, steel railways, breech-loading firearms, and entrenchments in this new methodical system of waging war. The battles surrounding Plevna, Gorni Dubnik, Shipka Pass, and even Tashkessen demonstrated that well-entrenched soldiers armed with rapid-firing and long-range rifles would be nearly impossible to dislodge from strong defensive positions. Heroism, glory, and the laurels of war died in the mountain passes and trenches of Bulgaria.

The Blind Turk

The once mighty Ottoman Empire began to show subtle signs of political and military decay by the end of the sixteenth century. For hundreds of years it had threatened Western Europe with conquest, extending its domain as far as the gates of Vienna in 1683. Instead of expanding, it was fighting for survival in the nineteenth century. A number of factors contributed to the decline.

The vastness of the empire, the growth of nationalism, coupled with economic, administrative, religious, and military elements, left the once mighty Islamic empire a mere shell of its former self. In 1877, the multi-ethnic Ottoman Empire stretched from Anatolia with its base in Constantinople, to the Caucasus, Arabia, and North Africa, and extended into Europe, encompassing the Balkans. The sheer enormity of the Ottoman Empire's frontiers hindered its ability to garrison its territory and quell the emerging nationalist revolts. Economic stability waned for the Ottomans in the eighteenth and nineteenth centuries due to one-sided treaties with Western trade partners, such as the Anglo-Ottoman commercial treaty of 1838. Dr Kemal Karpat revealed that these one-sided trade relations led to the vast Ottoman domains turning 'into colonial markets for British goods', crippling their economy.

This decay seeped down into the foundation of the army well before the nineteenth century. The Ottoman slave soldiers known as the *yeniçeri*, or Janissaries, were recognized as one of the most formidable military formations in the world in the fifteenth to seventeenth centuries. A levy issued in the Christian provinces of the Balkans obtained young Janissary recruits, followed by private education and training in the art of war. The Janissaries depreciated from an elite and exclusive military formation over the years following the seventeenth century, into corrupt and greedy businessmen intertwined in the Ottoman economy. By the end of the eighteenth century, many of its members refused to fight and instead sent untrained levies to serve as their replacements in Ottoman wars.

The progressive Ottoman Sultan Selim III initiated sweeping reforms to replace the Janissaries near the turn of the eighteenth century. A number of military defeats suffered at the hands of the Austrians and Russians during the Russo-Turkish War of 1787–92 inspired Selim's enthusiasm for Westernization. Selim aimed to mirror the organization, training, and armament of a European army and to implement it within his own army. He organized a new force in 1797, which he entitled the *Nizam-i-Cedid* (the new order), officered and trained by German and Austrian mercenaries. The corps exploded in size from 2,500 men in 1797, to 25,000 men within ten years.

The Janissaries viewed the creation of the innovative *Nizam-i-Cedid* as a threat to their own authority as the supreme military arm of the Ottoman Empire. In response to Selim's Western reforms, the Janissaries had him deposed and murdered, replacing him with the less reform-minded Sultan Mustafa IV. Janissaries hunted down and killed the soldiers and officers of the *Nizam-i-Cedid*, while survivors fled to the farthest corners of the empire to go into hiding.

Mustafa's reign came to an abrupt end when ousted and replaced by Sultan Mahmud II two years later in 1808. Mahmud II wished to enact similar reforms that Selim had attempted before his assassination. He contrived political support against the Janissaries more than twenty years before he struck. In 1823, the Ottomans became absorbed in the Greek Revolt. The disorderly and ill-trained Ottoman levies called up to fight proved to be pitiable material, and the revolt demonstrated that military reform had to be implemented in order for the Ottoman Empire to survive the nineteenth century.

In order to move forwards with reform, Mahmud had to eradicate the strangulating hold on all facets of the army by the Janissaries. On 15 June 1826, he ordered the Janissaries ambushed in their barracks, which led to the massacre of 6,000 of their number, thousands more sent into exile, and hundreds later executed. Mahmud officially abolished the Janissaries and cleansed them from the army once and for all. Their destruction allowed him to have a free hand to continue forwards with the modernization of the army. The *Asakir-i Mansure-i Muhammediye* (Victorious Mohammedan Soldiers) was subsequently formed to replace the Janissaries.

Mahmud began the task of searching for a new cadre of officers to serve as replacements for the exterminated Janissary officer corps. He turned to those he felt born to command, the Ottoman ruling elite. He also relied on the officers who had evaded execution two decades earlier from the former *Nizam-i-Cedid*. Mahmud chose to promote his own loyal court and palace officials to high military ranks with little or no military preparation. The majority of the replacements recruited by Mahmud proved unequal to the task, and did not translate into able military commanders.

Though Mahmud intended towards refining the army along Western lines, he found it difficult to educate enough new officers. Mahmud attempted to instruct his new officers by setting up special training companies, while also sending Ottoman officers to study in London, Vienna, and Paris in the 1820s. A formal military academy was founded in 1834 in Constantinople, but it lacked qualified professors and resources to educate the young cadets. Mahmud also was undersupplied with European officers to train his army due to his reluctance to pay them enough money to make it worthwhile for them to travel to Constantinople. Consequently, the majority of officers lacked any formal training, and a deficiency of well-trained officers would cripple the Ottoman military for years to come.

In the last years of his regime, Mahmud dedicated nearly 70 per cent of his revenue to implementing Western military reforms within his army. On the exterior, the army appeared reformed due to the massive expenditure. Western uniform, armaments, and organization concealed the deficiencies that existed, principally in the number of well-trained officers and the poor quality soldiers. The wars in Syria during the 1830s unveiled these superficial reforms.

A well-trained and well-led Egyptian army of 30,000 soldiers under the orders of Muhammad Ali of Egypt advanced into Ottoman-controlled Palestine and Syria in 1831. In two separate battles, first at Humus on 2 July 1832, and then at Bilan on 29 July 1832, two Ottoman armies suffered defeats that allowed the Egyptians to advance towards the heart of Asia Minor. At the Battle of Konya, on 21 December 1832, Reşid Pasha's army of 53,000 attacked the undersized but entrenched Egyptian army of 15,000 under Ibrahim Pasha. Despite the Ottoman numerical superiority, the well-trained Egyptian artillery crews decimated the Ottoman ranks, while their cavalry sliced through their advancing infantry columns. The humiliating defeat destroyed the only major Ottoman army between Ibrahim's Egyptians and the Ottoman capital of Constantinople.

The Ottomans became so fearful of the occupation of Constantinople that they even pleaded for military assistance from their Russian neighbours. Great Britain diplomatically intervened to stave off the threat of occupation (not for the last time in the nineteenth century). The conclusion of the Kütahya peace agreements in May 1833 put an end to this threat, and the Ottomans handed over control of Syria to the Egyptians. Egyptian historian Dr Khaled Fahmy indicated the war demonstrated the ill-preparation and bad leadership of the Ottoman army, and that 'those thirteen years of military reforms initialed by Mahmud could not stand the first serious test posed to it.'

Muhammad Ali declared war for a second time six years later, dissatisfied with the Kütahya peace agreements. The two adversaries met again at the climactic Battle of Nisib on 24 June 1839. Ottoman soldiers took up defensive positions in a slow and disorganized manner over two proceeding days before the two sides met, allowing Ibrahim Pasha to manoeuvre into a favourable position to strike a death blow. The battle began with a ninety-minute artillery duel that allowed the Egyptians to establish their dominance, followed by an all-out assault. The disgust of the young Prussian Captain Helmuth Graf von Moltke supervising the Ottoman artillery that day resonated in a letter he wrote two days after the battle:

On the 24th of this month we threw away Syria. There was no special surprise, no surrounding of the wing, nothing of that kind, but a lively cannonade. The troops were so terrified, that first the brigade of Heyder Pasha, then the cavalry, and at last everybody took to flight.

The Ottoman capital was again vulnerable to Egyptian occupation. Military intervention by Great Britain, Russia, and Austria to counter the Egyptian aggression halted the outright collapse of the Ottoman Empire for a second time. Sultan Mahmud died in early July, before the disheartening news of the catastrophic defeat at Nisib reached Constantinople. Amid this chaos, his 16-year-old son Abdülmecid I (a reformer himself) assumed the role of sultan following his father's death. Mahmud's reforms helped to eradicate the Janissaries and emulate Western uniforms and organization, but the army remained far from a capable tool of war.

The Ottomans did not fare much better on the battlefield when war erupted with the Russians in 1853. Britain, France, and Sardinia intervened in the conflict in order to offset Russian expansion and lend the Ottomans military support. The Ottomans showed signs of minor success in the operations of the Balkans against the Russians from 1853–54, while under the command of Ömer Pasha, a transplanted Austrian officer in Ottoman service. Their dubious performance began to surface when a second front opened up in Crimea against the Russian fortress of Sevastopol.

The Crimean War, and later the Russo-Turkish War, demonstrated that the Ottomans suffered from the same chief handicap dating back to Mahmud's early reforms: the officer corps. The commander-in-chief of the French army in the Crimea, Marshal Saint-Arnaud, criticized the Ottomans as being crippled with 'no officers and even fewer NCOs'. The first class of cadets from the Military Academy in Constantinople graduated in 1847, and only ten officers received commissions by 1848. Not until the 1860s did more than fifty officers per year graduate from the academy. Trained Ottoman officers, or *Mekteblis* (from the school), at the senior and junior levels remained far too few to meet the demand.

The emergence of *Mekteblis* created an awkward relationship with the uneducated *Alaylis* (from the regiment). The *Alayli* officers lacked an understanding of waging modern warfare, and exhibited hostile behaviour towards any European influences on the strategy or tactics related to the war. One instance of this clash cited by Dr Candan Badem took place between Müşir Abdi Pasha and his chief-of-staff, Ferik Ahmed Pasha, within the second largest Ottoman army during the Crimean War. The Western-educated Müşir Abdi Pasha studied in Vienna during the late 1830s, while Ferik Ahmed Pasha was illiterate and lacked any formal military education. This educational rift created tensions and complicated collaboration between the two senior officers, commonplace even amid officers twenty years later during the Russo-Turkish War.

Mektebli officers did not succeed to infiltrate the army in significant numbers until the 1870s. Even by that decade, they failed to meet the demand required of them to fill commands on the eve of the Russo-Turkish War. Valentine Baker's brother of the 8th Hussars, James, published a book titled *Turkey in Europe* in 1877, which specified that one of the greatest 'defects' of the Ottoman Army remained 'a scarcity of good officers'. Out of the 20,000 regular officers in the Ottoman Army of 1877, only 1,600 of them were academically trained. Enmity and intrigue among officers further maimed the officer corps.

Favouritism and jealousy reigned supreme among both senior and junior Ottoman officers. In his 1905 book dedicated to the military operations of the Russo-Turkish War, Sir John Frederick Maurice revealed, 'The senior officers were generally appointed from the Mohammedan aristocracy and were dependent on favouritism and influence for their advancement.' James Baker declared that 'The higher grade officers, such as generals and the staff, are all appointed by favouritism, and without any regard to their military abilities.' Senior officers hindered the advancement of promising and deserving junior officers who demonstrated ability or ingenuity, generating jealousy. Baker indicated that jealousy existed to such an extent 'that it would require a perfect Marlborough to overcome it.'

Widespread corruption, bribery, and the embezzlement of supplies infested senior leadership. In some cases, officers robbed their men of rations, uniforms, and pay, debilitating their own commands from conducting military operations. Maurice concluded that a majority of Ottoman officers 'looked upon their commands merely as sources of income, and every form of peculation was rife.' One prime example is the reprehensible case of Ahmed Pasha that took place during the Crimean War.

Ahmed Pasha gained a notorious reputation for robbing his men of their supplies to line his own pockets. One disgusted observer noted:

> The fate of the miserable army under Ahmed Pasha is among the darkest records of war. His whole faculties were bent upon making money. He had in the first place to recover the sums he had already expended in bribes in Constantinople, and he had, besides, to make his fortune. I could not exaggerate the horrors of poor men suffered under

his command, for no chief can plunder without allowing a considerable licence to his subordinates, so that the poor soldier was fleeced by every officer higher than the major.

Ahmed Pasha was tried for his crimes in Constantinople, and found guilty in 1854, leading to his exile to Cyprus in 1855. The greedy officer received a pardon, and found himself back in a prominent administrative role governing Yemen from 1867–69. Negligent punishment was a standard occurrence in the Ottoman Empire.

The limited number of *Mekteblis* who managed to infiltrate senior commands – those not preoccupied with conniving against other officers or lining their own pockets – did not necessarily translate into officers cultivated in the art of war. Maurice judged that the 'higher commanders had little knowledge of war'. The Military University in Constantinople dedicated little attention to modern military theory and strategy, and instead focused on a semi-engineering curriculum. The emergence of Süleyman Pasha provided one example of an officer who made a grand bureaucrat and theorist, but was unable to implement these manoeuvres once placed in a field command. Valentine Baker complained that many of the senior Ottoman leaders spent too much time serving as administrators and bureaucrats:

There is no army in Europe so cumbered with reports, returns, and official correspondence. As a rule, a Turkish general spends the great part of his day entirely occupied with office work. He rarely visits his troops, and he seldom exercises them in the practical manoeuvres of a campaign.

Poor judgment and inflexible adherence to time-worn strategies and tactics encumbered senior leadership. This 'scattered deployment' strategy – named so by Dr James Reid – dated back to the sixteenth century, when the Ottomans used it to pacify conquered territories swarming with rebels and insurgents. The strategy had success against rebels and insurgents in vast hostile territories, but it proved to be impracticable when facing an organized and disciplined modern army. A proclamation made by Sultan Abdülhamid II in April 1877 best demonstrates the Ottoman devotion to this strategy: 'Let us preserve every stone of our fortresses, every inch of our territory, which has been purchased at the price of the blood of our ancestors or brothers, who fell conquerors or martyrs.' With the outbreak of war in 1877, Ottoman detachments were strewn over hundreds of miles in isolated pockets along the length of the Danube River facing the Romanian border to the north, crippling the Ottomans from synchronizing their attacks against the Russian passage at Sistova.

While foreign observers ripped into and criticized Ottoman leadership, the common foot soldier received praise from the same individuals for his obedience, durability, and bravery. James Baker wrote in admiration of the common Ottoman soldier that:

> The Turk may safely be said to be the finest material for a soldier that is to be found in any part of the world. He is strong, hardy, patient, brave, intelligent, obedient, and sober, and becomes easily attached to his officers.

Maurice concluded that 'he is sober, capable of enduring great privations, and a good marcher; a fatalist by religion, he is without fear of death.' One correspondent praised that:

> There are no soldiers in the world to compare with Turks. They possess the dash and enthusiasm of French troops, combined with the traditional stubbornness of British regiments. If led by good officers, their *morale* is indestructible. To crown all, they are as hardy as mules. I allude, of course, to full-aged and drilled troops; raw recruits are the same all the world over.

At the Battle of Balaclava in October 1854, four Ottoman battalions of 2,000 men validated this resolve when they held their redoubts against a furious Russian assault for two hours without any artillery support. When they fell back, they regrouped and attached themselves to the 93rd Highland Regiment, and took part in the stand of 'The Thin Red Line'.

Some contemporary military experts inaccurately typecast the common Ottoman soldier as lacking an 'offensive spirit'. James Baker viewed this as 'a most erroneous idea, and a want of appreciation of cause and effect'.

Baker perceived that the inability to conduct offensive operations should not be blamed on the common Ottoman soldier, but on the fault of poor leadership. 'No troops in the world will stand in the open field, unless they have confidence in their officers,' Baker illuminated. Lieutenant Herbert Chermside, assistant to the British military attaché Colonel Wilbraham Oates Lennox, indicated that 'man for man the Turkish soldier seems the better, but is very badly officered, which must tell in operations on a large scale in the open.'

All Muslim males were liable for conscription in the army from the age of twenty, beginning in the 1840s. Non-Muslim subjects were excluded from serving in the military, discounting thousands of prospective soldiers from serving in the ranks. A yearly poll tax, known as the *iane-i askeriye*, would be paid in exchange for service in the military. James Baker saw this form of conscription as one of the most serious limitations within the army, when he judged that 'it is next to impossible for Turkey to compete against a first-rate European power in a lengthened campaign.' A European style reserve system was initiated following a series of military reforms enacted in 1869 that divided the army into four major tiers upon mobilization.

The *nizam* made up the first tier. They served as the first line of defence of the Ottoman Empire, and received the best training. In comparison to the common infantryman of other armies of Europe, their training was below par, at best. After four years of service in the *nizam*, the soldiers passed into the *ikhtiat*, where they served for another two years. After a total of six years of service, the soldiers transitioned into the *redif*.

The *redif*, the equivalent to the Prussian *Landwehr*, formed the second tier. The former *nizam* soldiers, upon returning home, usually married and learned a trade or became farmers. Settling down and adopting a civilian lifestyle left them less inclined to take risks. During wartime, NCOs of the *nizam* were promoted to serve as field officers in the *redif*. The *redif* battalions rarely met the criteria of being armed and organized along the same lines of the *nizam*.

Two subdivisions made up the *redif*, requiring a total of six years of service. The first subdivision of the *redif* was the *redif mokadem*, made up of former *nizam* soldiers who had descended into the *redif*. The second subdivision of the *redif* was the *redif tali*, made up of men who escaped the first round of conscription and ended up in the *redif* battalions with little or no formal military preparation.

The *mustahfiz* (old guard) made up the third tier of the Ottoman reserve system. After twelve years of uninterrupted service in the *nizam* and *redif*, a soldier was considered to be at an advanced age (32 years old) and too old for active service. A majority of untrained civilians were intermixed with men who had served in the *nizam* and *redif* when called up in wartime. Service in the *mustahfiz* was required for nine years, or to the end of the conflict before emancipation. Valentine Baker criticized their overall performance during the Russo-Turkish War, having commanded some of these men at Tashkessen, declaring that the *mustahfiz* 'seized every occasion for deserting.'

The *bashi-bozuks* (broken heads) formed an extra tier only called up for service in wartime. These irregular cavalrymen possessed no collective uniforms or armaments, and lacked any formal training. Baker categorized them as no more than greedy brigands 'who follow the army in hope of plunder.' They indulged in theft and murder, leading to a number of atrocities committed against Bulgarian civilians and wounded Russian soldiers. Baker observed their poor performance in one specific battle as 'they pushed forwards into the line of battle at moments when they thought that all danger had ceased, and were the first to run to the rear directly [after] any firing recommenced.'

Nizam cavalry units proved competent in most instances. Valentine Baker stated that 'under good management I believe that the men are quite capable of rising again to the excellence of the cavalry of the early days of the Turkish Empire.' Their officers hindered their capability. Baker explained that Ottoman cavalry officers were 'not much looked up to in the Turkish army, and they are generally utterly deficient in all those qualities which tend towards the excellence of this branch of the service.'

The Ottomans lacked an efficient method for structuring divisions and brigades in their armies. Battalions were separated from their mother regiments and placed into single 'brigades', and intermingled into awkward formations with other detached *nizam*, *redif*, and *mustahfiz* battalions. This organization devastated any sense of *esprit de corps*. Author Henry O. Dwight noted the diverse makeup of an Ottoman brigade common during the Russo-Turkish War: 'There are negro soldiers, and Arab soldiers, and Kourdish

[Kurdish] soldiers – men speaking half a dozen dialects in any brigade.' The majority of the better trained *nizam* battalions guarded Constantinople in the rear, while *redif* and *mustahfiz* battalions endured the brunt of the fighting on the Balkan front during the Russo-Turkish War.

In 1826, Sultan Mahmud II introduced a mandatory dark blue uniform based on the European model to be worn by all Ottoman line and cavalry units for the next ninety years. The French inspired uniform consisted of a plain blue short jacket and baggy blue Zouave trousers tucked into the soldier's boots or gaiters. The infantryman carried his pack, or a bundle which represented a pack, attached by rawhide or threaded straps, a leather ammunition pouch that could accommodate eighty rounds, a water bottle, canvas haversack, and in some instances, wore a red sash around his waist. Typical headgear of the Ottoman soldier consisted of a red fez with a blue tassel attached to the top, and sometimes, a cloth turban could be wrapped around the fez in order to shade the soldier's eyes from the sun. The fez to Baker 'was a most inefficient headdress' and he complained that in the Bulgarian summer, sunstroke was 'commonly prevalent'.

Sultan Abdülaziz toured Europe in 1869, and stimulated by the sight of their armies, set out to arm his military with the most modern European firearms and artillery he could acquire. Large international loans allowed the Ottomans to place huge armament orders during the interwar years leading up to the Russo-Turkish War. This rapid expenditure of the national budget brought the Ottoman economy to the brink of financial collapse, but also led to a large majority of Ottoman soldiers being armed with better quality firearms than their Russian adversaries by 1877. The Peabody-Martini and the .577 Snider-Enfield were the two most imported breech-loading rifles carried by Ottoman soldiers during the Russo-Turkish War.

The American Peabody-Martini had a design almost identical to the British Martini-Henry, with the exception of more simplified mechanics. Maurice estimated that by 1877, 70 per cent (most likely overestimated) of Ottoman infantry carried Peabody-Martini rifles. The Peabody-Martini could hit its mark at 1,800 yards, which far outclassed any firearms the Russians could put into the field at the time. During the siege of Plevna in 1877, Osman Nuri Pasha employed at least 8,000 Peabody-Martini rifles and began to inflict casualties at the unfathomed distance of 1,800-2,000 yards.

The Snider-Enfield rifle was the second most prevalent weapon carried by Ottoman infantrymen during the war. In 1866, the British Army adopted its own conversion system for its stockpile of thousands of outdated, but serviceable, Pattern 1853 Enfield percussion rifles. The newly converted weapons became known as .577 Snider-Enfield rifles, considered only as an interim arm until superseded by the Martini-Henry in 1871. Though the rifle had only an effective range of 500 yards, it could stop a man in his tracks upon impact. The Ottoman Empire purchased about 600,000 Snider-Enfield rifles by 1875.

The Ottomans purchased and replaced a significant portion of their antiqued artillery arm with breech-loading weapons by 1877. A total of forty-eight modern breech-loading German manufactured Krupp guns were purchased. These steel guns had an accuracy of up to 2 or 3 miles, superior to any of the Russian guns. Outdated and short-range 4- and 9-pounder bronze rifled cannons made up the remainder of the artillery arm, akin to those used by the Russians. Also included in the army were quick-moving mountain guns, drawn by one-horse teams.

Though strides had been made in equipping their soldiers with modern firearms and Western uniforms during the 1830s, the Ottomans suffered from a number of obstacles that impeded their efficiency in their war against the Russians in 1877. Foremost, the Ottomans suffered from a deficient pool of resourceful and well-educated officers familiar with methods of waging modern war that haunted them since the destruction of the Janissaries in the 1820s. Corruption, favouritism, and jealousy among the officer corps crippled their war machine. Most foreign observers put faith in the common Ottoman soldier as 'fine material', but felt pitiful leadership, and the antiqued strategies and tactics better suited for fighting a war in the sixteenth century obstructed their ability to wage a modern war. Valentine Baker would have to cope with these strengths and weaknesses when he arrived in Bulgaria in August 1877.

The One-Eyed Russian

On the exterior, the Russian Empire appeared very similar to the other Western European nations during the eighteenth and nineteenth centuries. Despite this façade, it has always remained strikingly dissimilar in all of its social, economic, religious, and cultural aspects. The vastness of the Russian Empire, extending in length from the Baltic Sea to the Bering Sea, set it apart from any other country of Western Europe. The feudal-era system of serfdom remained a pillar in the foundation of the Russian economy well into the mid-nineteenth century. More similar to the Ottoman Empire than its European counterparts, the Russian Empire comprised a diverse religious and ethnic makeup, which included large populations of Polish Catholics, Caucasian Muslims, German Protestants, and Russian Jews.

A large portion of Russian subjects practised Orthodox Christianity as their official religion. Sir Richard Wilbraham explained that from the earliest days, Russia 'had to fight for her very existence as a nation against the enemies of her faith.' Upon the conversion of Prince Vladimir in 988 to Orthodox Christianity, the Russians fought a continuous holy war to defend the borders of their realm. Russia inadvertently served as a buffer between the East and the West, battling Mongolian, Tartar, and Ottoman invasions. It also battled fellow Christians, such as the Byzantines, Germans, Lithuanians, Poles, and Swedes.

Peter the Great introduced the first major modern military reforms in the Russian Army during the eighteenth century. In the years before the rule of Peter, the Russians secured their borders against undisciplined foes with armies composed of unorganized nobles and retainers. As Russia began to become embroiled in international politics towards the end of the seventeenth century, they clashed with well-trained modern armies of their European enemies, such as the Swedes. Caught in the midst of Peter's military reform, the Russians suffered numerous defeats during the Great Northern War against Sweden. At the Battle of Narva on 19 November 1700, the 18-year-old Swedish King Charles XII and his well-trained 8,000-man army struck and defeated the poorly led and trained Russian Army of 40,000, leading to a humiliating rout.

Peter continued on until he finalized his reforms, and shaped a well-trained and well-led army to contend with these professional European armies. From 1705 to 1713, 335,000 men were pressed into service through levies. The selected peasants received training on order and discipline, moulding them into obedient and reliable soldiers. Peter next turned to the Russian landowning sons of nobility for officers, issuing a decree in 1721 that required the military service of every able-bodied noble. A new military academy established in 1731 trained the new recruits in the art of war.

The first major test of Peter's established military reforms against a first-rate European army came during the Seven Years' War at the Battle of Zorndorf in 1758. Out of the total of 80,000 men engaged on both sides, 30,000 men fell as the Russian Army under the command of William Fermor exchanged blows with Frederick the Great and his world-renowned Prussian Army. Despite the battle resulting in a Russian defeat, Frederick the Great acknowledged that the Russians proved to be a worthy adversary. 'It was far easier to kill the Russians than to conquer them,' Frederick cautioned following the battle. The Russian soldier was recognized for his 'stubborn and enduring courage', and his loyalty, which endured well into the twentieth century.

Peter's 1721 decree that instituted no boundary between noble and officer on the exterior seemed genuine, but in reality its long-term effect had mixed results. The officer corps restricted deserving, but unaristocratic, officers from receiving promotion. Many senior officers of the noble classes regarded their positions as ceremonial by the late eighteenth century, and displayed little interest in learning the art of war. Russian senior officers performed less than stellar during the Seven Years' War, leading to three army commanders being replaced within three years.

A warrior emerged in the mid–eighteenth century who would influence the technique of waging war in Russia at a strategic and tactical level for over 100 years, and would fetch Russia sixty battlefield victories during his fifty years of military service. Generalissimo Alexander Suvorov entered the army at the age of eighteen in 1748, and forged a name while fighting along the Russo-Ottoman frontier. He led Russian armies to brilliant victories against the Poles, Ottomans, Tartars, French, and Prussians until his death in 1800. During the Battle of Rymnik in 1789, he met and defeated a force of 100,000 Ottoman soldiers with an army of only 25,000. His techniques for waging war would inspire Russian military and political leaders well into the twentieth century.

Suvorov attributed his victories on the battlefield to three elements: speed, assessment, and hitting power (*bystrota, glazomer, natisk*). Speed proved the most essential, Suvorov invoking that, 'Money is dear; human life is still dearer; but time is the dearest of all.' After assessing the enemy's position, Suvorov explained that an enemy force should be hit with all the strength that could be mustered, when and where he least expects it. 'The enemy sings, walks about, waits for you from the open field, and you hit him from beyond the steep mountains and silent forests, like snow on the head,' he proclaimed in another proverb.

Suvorov paid special attention to the welfare and training of the common soldier. He took special care of his men, and Dr Bruce W. Menning explained that Suvorov 'put his hand on the heart of the Russian soldier and learned its beat.' He never allowed his men to sleep directly on the ground, included a hefty amount of vegetables in their diets, and ordered that strict codes of sanitation were practised while in camp. He reminded his officers to 'converse with soldiers in their own language' in order to gain the trust of the men. He made sure his men received excellent training, declaring, 'If a peasant doesn't know how to plough, he cannot grow bread.'

Suvorov explained that the Russian soldier should always be on the offensive and should rely on the steel of his bayonet first and foremost in battle. Suvorov regarded the briefest mention of retreat as blasphemy. 'A step backward is death,' he warned. Dr Menning noted that Russian soldiers under Suvorov trained 'to bayonet the first, shoot the second and bayonet the third'. The poor quality of the eighteenth-century flintlock musket allowed Suvorov's bayonet-driven attacks to flourish on the battlefield.

In 1812, twelve years after the legendary Suvorov's death, Napoleon Bonaparte invaded Russia. Mikhail Kutuzov made a stand with a Russian army of 120,000 at Borodino, 60 miles from Moscow, against Napoleon's army of 130,000. Despite the fact that the Russians met defeat and Napoleon subsequently occupied Moscow, Napoleon could not induce the Russians to capitulate. Napoleon retreated back to France, losing the majority of his army. In 1814, the Russians victoriously marched on to Paris accompanied by a coalition of Prussian, British, and Austrian armies.

Most of the Russian senior officers demonstrated a mediocre performance during the Napoleonic Wars. No officer from the bunch rose to emulate the feats of Suvorov. The lethargic commander of the Russian forces that opposed Napoleon's invasion in 1812, the one-eyed Mikhail Kutuzov, never proved to be a master of the battlefield. Each senior commander reported directly to Tsar Alexander I, bypassing their superiors, complicating the chain of command. The struggle to establish a resourceful officer corps would be a recurring theme throughout the history of the Russian Army.

By the 1820s, the Russian Army needed a total makeover. Tsar Nicholas I, who succeeded to the Russian throne upon the death of his brother from typhus in 1825, fashioned himself as a soldier. Enamoured with splendor rather than talent, Nicholas chose to adopt pageantry over resourcefulness into the army. Officers sporting glittering uniforms with gold epaulettes and foot soldiers trained to conduct machine-like parade ground manoeuvres disguised the pitiable state of the army. Beneath the surface it was suffering from poor senior leadership, the absence of modern armaments, and the use of outdated strategies and tactics.

In December 1825, in what became known as the Decembrist revolt, disgruntled Russian officers revolted in an attempt to overthrow Nicholas. Young, imaginative, and well-educated officers made up the majority of the dissidents involved in the plot. Their demands included the emancipation of the serfs and the introduction of a number of military reforms within the army. The conspirators infiltrated at least forty Russian regiments on the eve of the coup. The loyal forces of the monarch managed to surround and massacre the organized resistance in Senate Square, St Petersburg, crushing the coup.

The failed plot left Tsar Nicholas paranoid and distrustful of the army for the remainder of his reign. Young and well-educated officers accused of culpability in the plot were banished to frontier posts in Caucasia, leading to the segregation of imaginative officers from Nicholas's inner circle. Favouritism, loyalty, and political connections steered officers towards the path of promotion, rather than military ability. Nicholas ordered unyielding obedience and drill within his army, ignoring other areas of needed reform, such as acquiring modern armaments or purging his army of old-fashioned military theories. Dr John S. Curtis stated that this paranoia held the Russian Army hostage to 'unthinking obedience and parade ground evolutions', for the next thirty years, until the death of Tsar Nicholas I in 1855.

The military success during a number of localized revolts and during the Russo-Turkish War of 1828–29 blinded Russian leadership to the decrepit state of the army. Stiff Ottoman resistance in 1828 initially halted the Russian advance along the Danube River at the fortresses of the Quadrilateral of Rushchuk, Silistria, Shumla and Varna, until General Hans Karl von Diebitsch defeated the Ottomans in the decisive Battle of Kulevcha, cumulating in the Ottomans suing for peace on 14 September 1829. British General Francis Rawdon Chesney saw through this hollow Russian victory. He reminded his readers in his book dedicated to the war that 'Although the bravery and passive endurance of the Russian soldier cannot be surpassed, the army of the nation cannot claim a first-rate place among European powers.' The Crimean War, the first major Europe war since the Napoleonic Wars, would provide the jolt to initiate reform.

Nicholas relied on the elderly and loyal but ineffective generals of his inner circle to lead his armies to victory in the Crimean War. The younger and more talented officers stayed banished to the fringes of the Caucasia frontier – ironically, they contributed to Russian military success in this region during the war. The senior officers fighting on the Crimean front were afflicted by sluggish movements and poor preparation that led to a series of devastating defeats. The 66-year-old Prince Alexander Menshikov, commander-in-chief in the Crimea, proved to be an inept leader for the Russians, leading his army to defeats at the battles of Alma and Inkerman.

Corruption ran rampant among Russian officers in a similar case to that of the Ottoman Army during the conflict, further hindering its ability to wage war. Regimental commanders used funds to buy substandard supplies for their men and pocketed the difference. In some instances of greediness, profiteering officers deprived their soldiers of firewood during the winter months, compelling them to battle the cold. The Russian Quartermaster Department and Commissariat gained a notorious reputation for issuing spoiled food, such as rotten biscuits, as well as second-rate equipment.

The Russians suffered from technological disadvantages in the war due to their addiction to obedience and drill, rather than upgrading their soldiers with modern armaments. The majority of Russian soldiers still lugged around smoothbore muskets with an effective range of only up to 200 yards. The British and the French provided their soldiers with far superior rifled muskets, which gave them an effective range of 500 yards or more. This superior range gave the British and the French the advantage on the battlefield, cutting up tightly packed Russian columns before even within range to exchange gunfire.

All of these factors contributed to a humiliating defeat during the Crimean War, and initiated a period of reform in Russia that continued well past the Russo-Turkish War. Tsar Alexander II ascended to the throne with the death of Nicolas in 1855, and endorsed significant social and military reforms. The reform-minded Alexander ended the feudal-era agricultural system of serfdom, emancipating 23 million serfs from their bondage in 1861. He appointed the scholar and former professor of the Nicholas General Staff Academy, Dmitry A. Milyutin, as War Minister in 1861 to initiate changes within the army.

Milyutin addressed the poor performance of the army during the Crimean War. He poured over the works of Suvorov while serving as a young officer in Caucasia, and later published a five-volume history of his 1799 Italian campaign. He reasoned that the Russian defeat could be attributed to the fact that it had drifted too far away from the doctrines preached by Suvorov. He believed the survival of Russia relied on reviving the 'spirit of Suvorov' within the establishment of the Russian Army. His reforms benefitted the army by improving army education, initiating administrative and structural improvements, and remedying the poor reserve system.

The Ukrainian soldier and military theorist Mikhail Dragomirov, also an advocate of Suvorov, played an integral role in restructuring the combat doctrines and infantry regulations of the common Russian soldier leading up to the Russo-Turkish War. Dragomirov favoured the soldiers to be trained as experts with the bayonet, and to obey orders with unwavering obedience. Dr Menning explained that in Dragomirov's approach, an 'unskilled but dependable soldier' was preferable 'to an accomplished but undependable one'. Dragomirov stripped the fluff and pageantry of the Nicholas regime from the army, but replicated doctrines that stressed instinctive obedience, and embraced Suvorov's reliance of the bayonet from the eighteenth century.

Dragomirov intended gunfire to play only a supportive role to what he saw as the unavoidable bayonet engagement. Dr Menning described that in the Russian regimental combat formations of Dragomirov's model, 'The prescribed assault formation placed four-fifths emphasis on cold steel and one-fifth on firepower.' Dragomirov feared the reliance on gunfire would 'break the flow of concerted energy' of an attack, as a common soldier was predisposed to stop to take aim and seek shelter while engaged in a firefight. Skirmishers were ordered to remain upright and face gunfire with a solemn disregard. Wholly ignored was proper training on the effective use of gunfire and adapting to terrain for cover.

An important aspect of Suvorov's bayonet doctrine remained forgotten to Russian reformers and officers in the nineteenth century. Although Suvorov had an infatuation with the use of the bayonet, he acknowledged the importance of the musket, stating in one instance, 'Infantry fire leads to victory.' He ordered his own soldiers to stuff 100 cartridges each in their pouches before they entered an engagement. Adopting this eighteenth-century tradition, without considering the technological advances in warfare over the last twenty years, would lead to catastrophic consequences for the Russians in 1877.

Fixed bayonet assaults had no place on the battlefields of the late nineteenth century. The rise of fast-firing and long-range breech-loading rifles and artillery made it nearly impossible for columns to penetrate an enemy position without being decimated before reaching their objective. An individual soldier armed with a weapon such as the Peabody-Martini would be able to drawn fire on the enemy at the range of 1,800 yards, and discharge about ten or more shots per minute. Most of the major Western European powers came to terms with the increasing role of firepower on modern battlefields, but Russian reformers chose to adhere to their outdated strategies and tactics.

If the Russian reformers did not recognize their archaic reliance on the bayonet by 1877, foreign observers certainly did. Maurice summed up the defective tactics in 1877 when he wrote:

The infantry tactics of the Russian Army were out of date in 1877. The strategical lessons of the Franco-German War had been carefully studied by the Russian General Staff, but its tactical lessons had been either misunderstood or altogether neglected. The traditions of Suvorov, whose favourite maxim was 'The bullet is a hag, but the bayonet is a queen', still had a strong hold upon the Russian infantry. They were trained to advance to attack in columns of companies, and to move to the assault while still at a distance from the position to be captured. The bayonet assault was looked upon as the one decisive feature in an infantry attack; no attempt was made to obtain superiority of fire over the enemy. In short, the possibilities of the breech-loading rifle were not understood.

The Russian officer corps of 1877 suffered from the same social inequalities that existed throughout its history. Men descended from wealthy and prominent families of Russia who received formal training in military schools made up the first class of officers, and usually received appointments in more prestigious Imperial Guard or Rifle battalions. Maurice observed that these officers reaped the benefits of social status, stating they 'rose rapidly through the lower ranks and monopolized appointments and commands throughout the army.' The second class of officers came from underprivileged backgrounds and had little education, which barred them from ever rising to command any formations larger than a battalion. Maurice noted that these unfairly treated officers 'were as a rule devoted to their men, but lived dull monotonous lives, and were without prospects or ambition.'

The army was embedded with royal appointments and favouritism, further afflicting the Russian senior leadership with a number of incompetent and unqualified generals. In all, twelve members of the Russian Imperial family commanded large bodies of soldiers when war commenced in 1877, abiding to the customary tradition of filling senior army positions with royal appointments. Tsar Alexander's oldest son, Grand Duke Alexander Alexandrovich (later Tsar Alexander III), commanded the army in the vicinity of Rushchuk, while his younger son commanded an Imperial Guard division. The Tsar's brother, Grand Duke Nicholas Nikolaevich, well known for his limited intelligence and ineffective leadership, commanded the Russian forces crossing the Danube. Such a large number of grand dukes served as officers that by the late summer of 1877, the war earned the tag 'the Grand Dukes' War'.

Tsar Alexander abetted in hampering his invading forces on the Danube front. A cumbersome caravan of 350 to 500 wagons loaded with his personal articles and edible delicacies, such as caviar, accompanied the tsar on the campaign to the south. Grand Duke Nicholas Nikolaevich, envied his brother's micromanagement, generating tension between the two. Officers were reluctant to take the initiative or voice their personal concerns for fear of gaining the displeasure or the contempt of Alexander. The battlefront was no place for Alexander, unqualified to make major operational and strategic decisions related to the war.

Universal conscription was first enacted in the Russian Empire in January 1874. Russian conscripts called up were required to serve six years in the regulars, followed by nine years in the reserves. Most reserve formations would form separate battalions dedicated to non-military tasks, such as conducting garrison or guard duty to relieve front line units. Some Russian subjects in the remote regions of the empire, such as in the Caucasus, were excluded from conscription.

The average Russian soldier forged a reputation dating back to the Seven Years' War for his loyalty, doggedness, and unquestioning obedience. Wilbraham hailed the Russian soldier when he wrote, 'We shall wonder rather that he should possess so many of the best qualities of a soldier,' despite the fact that he was brought up in a 'degrading system of serfdom' and 'trained to a blind, mechanical obedience.' He was also beset by dispiriting factors such as 'insufficient pay, the scanty and inferior rations, and severe discipline', but his religious faith allowed him to embrace misery with vigour. The correspondent Edward King noted the two prominent features he admired of the Russian character: 'democratic freedom from affection and perfect amiability', rationalizing that these 'are good qualities, especially in warriors'. Valentine Baker admired the Russian soldier's 'patience under hardship', which served him well while traversing the Balkan Mountains in freezing temperatures, or marching to his certain death against the entrenchments of Plevna.

The Russian soldier relied on his officers more than any other soldiers in the world. He was trained to advance with unfaltering obedience until he met the enemy with his bayonet, under the watchful eye and encouragement of his officers. Colonel L. Gaillard, French Military Attaché, observed that 'The officer can with confidence lead and keep him anywhere, but in general he needs to see or to sense his leader close to him.' In order to guarantee this cohesiveness, officers directed their men from the front line, leading to staggering casualties among junior and senior Russian officers during the war.

A military doctrine that embraced obedience over individual intelligence and initiative crippled the common Russian soldier. Lieutenant Greene claimed that, 'Deprived of their officers, a body of Russian soldiers may degenerate into a helpless, inert mass, and be slaughtered by means of their very cohesiveness.' Peasants made up three-fourths of Russian soldiers in 1875, and 79 per cent of Russian conscripts were illiterate. Valentine Baker explained that, 'Modern war, with the changes which it has compelled in military tactics, demands a higher standard of military intelligence from the individual soldier.' Russian soldiers lacked this intelligence and resourcefulness, a common requirement of soldiers in modern armies of the late nineteenth century.

In 1855, Nicholas approved an unadorned French-style uniform to be worn by all Russian soldiers, which looked dissimilar than it ever did in the previous centuries. In 1864, the army adopted the French style cloth kepi to replace the brass-tipped leather helmet, shako, and forage cap of the Crimean War. White linen cap covers known as havelocks, made famous by British soldiers serving during the Indian Mutiny, were also introduced. Beginning in 1872, officers were required to wear a stiff Austrian-style kepi, but most officers bent these regulations and wore the *furashka*. Soldiers wore green tunics and matching trousers in the winter, but in the torrid months they sported white blouses and white trousers, mimicking the uniforms worn by soldiers assigned to garrisons in Central Asia.

Stiff boards, or *pogoni*, were attached to the shoulders of the soldiers' uniforms beginning in 1871. These were used to indicate the number of the regiment assigned to each soldier. The battalion number of each soldier was stitched on the kepi for further identification and a colour band to indicate regimental seniority in the division assigned. These numbers helped Russian commanders to identify specifics units, but on the flip side gave the Ottomans the ability to identify the enemy regiments.

Russian soldiers were equipped with an array of other war articles. Soldiers wrapped their feet in cloths (linen in the summer and wool in the winter) rather than wearing socks. Loose fitting boots were worn, tucked into the trousers, allowing for room to pack straw into them during the winter.

Grey and dark beige greatcoats with hoods attached to them, or *bashlik*, kept soldiers warm in the winter months. Two cartridge boxes were worn on the front of the belt, while another sixty rounds were carried in a large haversack.

Cossack cavalry formed three-quarters of the Russian cavalry during the Russo-Turkish War. They were natural-bred horsemen and ferocious warriors, fabled for their exploits during Napoleon's invasion of Russia in 1812. Maurice noted their unique organization established 'a compromise between their national customs and the requirements of a modern army'. They provided their own horses and equipment and received little regular army training, while the government armed them with modern weapons and provided a blue jacket, trousers, and a fur cap to each man. King described his encounter with an animated Cossack detachment early in the war:

> The Cossacks were our chief delight. Dust and fatigue seemed to have no power to choke the harmony which welled up melodiously, as from the pipes of a mighty organ, whenever a Cossack regiment halted. On they came, now at dawn, now at dusk, thousands of lithe, sinewy, square-faced, longhaired youth, with shrewd twinkling eyes, small hands and feet, nerves of steel, and gestures full of utmost earnestness. The leader of each squadron usually 'lined' the hymn or ballad which was sung. Behind him hundreds of voices took up the chorus, and prolonged it until the heavens seemed filled with sweet notes.

The cream of the army, the Russian Imperial Guard, had a distinguished legacy that dated back to the eighteenth century. Russian's highest members of nobility served in the ranks of this superior clothed, fed, and equipped unit. Their uniform consisted of a double row of buttons attached to the tunic, stamped with an embossed eagle, red shoulder straps, bearing an imperial crown and embroidered with the title of the regiment, and dark green trousers with a narrow red strip down each leg. The *furashka* was worn by all ranks in the field, and in the winter months, a sheepskin coat known as a *polushubok*, reaching below the knees, was worn under their greatcoats. According to army regulations, the bayonets of this elite formation were to be fixed to their rifles at all times.

Russian Army reformers made an attempt to supply infantry regiments with cheap and mass-produced breech-loading rifles during the 1860s to replace the outdated muzzle-loading rifles of the Crimean War. In 1867, 200,000 outdated Russian muzzle-loading rifles were converted to the Karle breech-loading system. In 1869, the Russians purchased 800,000 cheap and fragile Pattern 1856 rifles and converted them to the Krnk system. The Krnk rifle only had an effective range of 500 yards. Parts of the original muzzle-loading rifles, such as the locks, stocks, and barrels, were recycled, and it gained a notorious reputation for its extraction issues.

Two Russian officers visited the United States in the late 1860s to find a breech-loading rifle model to adopt. Colonel Hiram Berdan, former commander of the 1st and 2nd US Sharpshooters during the American Civil War, won over the visitors by his innovative and well-priced design that could hit its mark at 1,250 yards. The Russians purchased several thousand copies of the rugged Model 1868 Berdan, or *Berdanka*, in 1875. Berdan afterwards altered his design and created a simpler and stronger rifle that was christened the Model 1870 Berdan. By 1877, only 232,000 copies of the Model 1870 Berdan were on hand, and in consequence, only the most exclusive units, the Guards, Grenadiers, and Rifle battalions, carried the *Berdanka*, while the other line units carried the cheaply made Krnk and Karle rifles.

Russian officers Axel Gadolin and Nikolai Maevsky designed a rifled breech-loading cannon in 1867 to replace the outdated Russian cannons of the Crimean War. The Russians embraced the use of bronze despite the fact that steel proved to be a sturdier material to adopt for manufacturing rifled cannon. The rifling in the barrel of bronze cannons wore out quickly, degrading accuracy and increasing the chances of premature detonation. The Ottoman-purchased Krupp guns out-ranged Russian artillery for most of the war. In some instances during the war, the Russians commandeered these guns and adopted them to their own use, as in the case at Shipka Pass in August 1877.

The Russians were far from finalizing their reforms initiated by Milyutin and fielding an up-to-date army on the eve of the Russo-Turkish War. Tsar Nicholas's taciturn attitude towards the army following the Decembrist revolt crippled the Russian's modern military advancement up until his own death in 1855. When reforms were initiated in the 1860s following defeat during the Crimean War, the overemphasized role of the bayonet by Russian reformers demonstrated the failure to appreciate the changing art of warfare. The Russian officer corps suffered for years from favouritism and social obstacles that barred deserving officers the chance for promotion, and placed inept royal appointments in high commands. Poor armaments and machinelike obedience afflicted the army, composed of soldiers praised for their enduring traits of facing hardship, but lacking in intelligence and resourcefulness.

The Ottomans and the Russians shared similar growing pains with initiating Western military reform in the nineteenth century. The Ottomans first saw success initiating military reforms in the 1820s under Mahmud, but had trouble establishing meaningful reforms that penetrated the foundations of the army. The Russians saw a period of successful modern military reform under Peter the Great in the eighteenth century, but exhibited a static period of reform until the 1860s. The greatest shortcoming of both armies remained the ability to mould a reliable and trusting officer corps to depend on, and their stubborn adherence to obsolete strategies and tactics to wage war. With the outbreak of war, neither side was wholly prepared to wage modern warfare, and these inadequacies primed the Russian and Ottoman armies for a grisly tournament in April 1877. The clash of these two ancient enemies would culminate in one of the most brutal wars of the late-nineteenth century.

Chapter 4

Discouragement along the Lom

I swear by the Prophet, that the Infidel who commands our cavalry fights with the courage of ten thousand tigers.

The words of an Ottoman artilleryman observing
Valentine Baker in the heat of battle.

The war had not been going particularly well for the Ottomans when Baker and his companions landed in the Black Sea port city of Varna on 16 August 1877. Since the Russians forced their way across the Danube in early July, the roads were cluttered with 'thousands of troops, grimly bending to their work, setting their faces sternly to the East', as observed by the war correspondent King. Baker was precise in his assessment that since the commencement of the war, it had 'been one of almost uninterrupted disasters and retreats.' Six Russian corps operated freely in Ottoman territory south of the Danube; the scattered Ottoman armies responded with confusion and immobility instead of action. Abdülkerim Nadir Pasha, the Ottoman commander-in-chief on the Balkan front, strangely did not conduct any offensive operations to halt the Russian advance, and chose to keep his scattered armies on the defensive.

The army of Osman Nuri Pasha proved the exception. Located to the far west at Widin, Osman relocated his army to intercept the Russians at the village of Plevna on 13 July 1877. After a non-stop march for six days tallying 110 miles, Osman's exhausted 11,000 men and fifty-four guns reached the outskirts of Plevna on 19 July 1877. A well-built road ran through the village and curled south through the Balkan Mountains towards Sofia, giving it strategic value to the advancing Russian Army. Osman's soldiers carved out an elaborate network of redoubts, fortifications, and trenches around Plevna, working in nightshifts illuminated by campfires. Osman surveyed the sturdy and fragile zones of his position as his men turned the sleepy village into an impressive stronghold.

The 45-year-old Ottoman officer was an excellent candidate to conduct a delaying action at Plevna. He graduated from the military academy of Constantinople in 1853, and forged a reputation over twenty-four years of service for his authoritarian demeanor, valour, and bold tactics. He generally sported a dirtied federal blue jacket that reached down to his knees, unadorned with any rank or insignia. While inspecting Ottoman soldiers in the 1890s, the American General Nelson Miles was impressed by Osman recording that 'Osman Pasha reminded me of General Grant more than any other man I saw on this side of the Atlantic. His manner is very much like that of Grant; a man of few words – in these expressing condensed thought.' Although a student who embraced Western military strategies and tactics, Osman was rightfully suspicious of the intentions of all European soldiers of fortune and entrepreneurs he encountered. He lived by the proverb spoken to General Miles: 'Persistency is the great secret of success in war. If an army is not successful one day, tenacity of purpose and persistency will in the end bring victory.'

A single Russian division appeared on the outskirts of Plevna on 20 July 1877. The 5th Division of Lieutenant General Nikolai Krüdener's IX Corps was composed of 8,600 men and forty-six pieces of field artillery, under the command of the 61-year-old Otto von Bismarck lookalike Lieutenant General Yuri Schilder-Schuldner. Schilder-Schuldner, well established for his mediocre leadership, launched an assault on the entrenched Ottoman defenders without making a thorough reconnaissance of their stronghold. Unknown to Schilder-Schuldner, Osman outnumbered him by nearly 3,000 men. The 5th Division was cut to pieces and repulsed within twenty minutes of the assault, at the cost of 3,000 men, while the Ottomans suffered a disproportionate fifty casualties.

General Krüdener moved with the remainder of his IX Corps, located 25 miles distance from Plevna, to aid Schilder-Schuldner's mangled division. General Krüdener and the men of the IX Corps marched towards Plevna with an air of confidence having captured the fortress of Nikopol with ease on 16 July 1877. Krüdener bolstered the decimated ranks of General Schilder-Schuldner's division, and brought the combined force to 35,000 men and 176 guns. Osman received reinforcements from Sofia, bringing his total force at Plevna to 22,000 men and fifty-eight guns. Krüdener and Schilder-Schuldner made preparations to seize the village.

On 30 July 1877, Krüdener ordered the second Russian assault on Plevna. Wave after wave of Russian infantrymen were cut down as they struggled to penetrate the intricate line of Ottoman entrenchments with sheer weight of numbers. The better-armed Ottoman soldiers blazed away with their Peabody-Martini rifles and Winchester lever-action rifles aimed at the exposed Russian soldiers. The Russian assault wavered by nightfall without making any significant progress, at the loss of more than 7,300 Russian soldiers to the roughly 2,000 Ottoman casualties. As other setbacks began to cast a gloom over the Ottoman armies in the Balkans, Plevna provided a beacon of hope to all the Ottoman soldiers south of the Danube.

The inability to dig out Osman's defenders at Plevna jeopardized the whole Russian offensive. The Ottoman stronghold threatened the weak supply lines and line of communication that stretched through Romania back to the heart of Russia. Some generals within the Russian high command considered retiring back across the Danube, fearful that a lengthy siege of the village was detrimental to bringing the war to a quick conclusion. Both repulses at Plevna placed most of the advancing Russian corps on a standstill, unable to progress much further into the Ottoman interior in strength until the obstacle was eradicated. The capture of Plevna was developing into the most important episode of the war.

Its capture not only provided strategic significance to the Russians, but it also became a matter of national prestige and of sanctified importance. Plevna embodied a struggle of race and religion; Russian vs Turk, West vs East, and Christianity vs Islam. The Russians viewed the war as a crusade to liberate the Christian Slavs of the Balkans from the infidel Turk. The inept army of the Ottomans – as judged by most Western experts early in the war – should have been driven back to the gates of Constantinople with ease. Plevna threatened both of these notions, and developed into an international embarrassment for Tsar Alexander II.

American and European war correspondents transmitted the news of Osman's two victories back home. The stout defence captured the romantic imagination of Western readers and turned the 'eyes of Europe' on the small village. Author Rupert Furneaux noted the popularity of the battle led to the christening of 'innumerable dogs, not a few cats, the son of an English peer, and a new type of lavatory pan' all after Osman. Portions of the British public who vilified the Ottomans during the 'Bulgarian agitation' transformed overnight into eager 'Turkophiles'.

Despite the severe handicap Osman had inflicted upon the Russian offensive, thousands of soldiers began to collect outside Plevna. In hindsight, Osman should have withdrawn and joined another army after his success, but his victory served as a rallying point to unify the multi-ethnic peoples of the Ottoman Empire. A 'sort of halo hung round the name of Plevna' to the authorities in Constantinople, and Osman received orders from Abdülhamid to hold the village at all costs. The window would not remain open for long for the remaining Ottoman armies in Bulgaria to aid the Plevna defenders and halt additional Russian gains.

While events at Plevna unfolded, a mixed Russian detachment from the VIII Corps composed of 16,000 light infantrymen and Cossacks swooped down to occupy Shipka Pass before the Ottomans could prepare a major defence. The capture of the pass would provide the best route for a major Russian army to advance through the Balkan Mountains and descend on Constantinople. Major General Joseph V. Gourko, in command of the detachment, divided it into two wings, with one subdivision composed of roughly 2,500 men under the command of Prince Nicolai Ivanovich Sviatopolk-Mirsky, and the remainder of the force under his direct command. Gourko left Mirsky to distract the Ottoman defenders at Shipka Pass, while he moved his own column to the east through the Hainkioi Pass and outflanked the Ottoman defenders from the south. The Ottoman guardians evacuated the imperative pass on 7 July 1877.

Gourko ordered his Cossack raiding parties to move down from the mountains and wreak havoc on the web of Ottoman railroad lines extending outwards from Adrianople. The Ottoman hero of the Serbian War, Süleyman Pasha, was ordered to transport an army of 30,000 veterans from Montenegro to Adrianople by the Mediterranean Sea to recapture Shipka Pass. On 26 July 1877, Süleyman disembarked his army at Adrianople, traversing the distance of 1,200 miles within twenty-two days by sea and rail. Maurice praised this feat, asserting that this was 'one of the most striking examples in military history of the value of sea power to operations on land'. Gourko was forced to recall the Cossack raiding parties and prepare to defend Shipka Pass against Süleyman.

Mehmed Ali Pasha arrived in Shumla on 19 July 1877 to replace the lethargic 70-year-old Abdülkerim Nadir at the head of the Ottoman units gathered at the Quadrilateral fortresses. Christian Jules Detroit was a transplanted German, born in Magdeburg, Prussia, in 1829. His father sent him out to sea at the age of fifteen to serve as a cabin boy aboard a vessel destined for the Mediterranean, restless for adventure. Detroit was ill-treated by the crew during the long voyage to Constantinople, instigating him to jump overboard and seek sanctuary aboard an Ottoman vessel anchored in the bay of the Ottoman capital.

As the boy floundered in the water to stay afloat, he came upon a vessel and pleaded to an Ottoman official to allow him to board. The Ottoman official happened to be Mehmed Emin Âli Pasha, destined to become an influential politician and reformer. Mehmed Emin Âli adopted Detroit and rechristened him Mehmed Ali. The boy received a formal military education, became fluent in Turkish, and adopted Islam as his official religion. He entered the army and served as an officer in the Crimean War, and fought in the Serbia and Montenegro wars as a subordinate commander to Süleyman Pasha.

The 48-year-old Mehmed Ali replaced Abdülkerim Nadir to invigorate some offensive spirit and raise morale within the major Ottoman armies acting to deter the Russian advance upon Constantinople. Before his removal, the slothful Abdülkerim Nadir Pasha rationalized to Abdülhamid II and the Sublime Porte (central Ottoman government) that he purposely allowed the Russians to ford the Danube River unattested, as this approach was part of his 'grand strategy'. His army gathered in the vicinity of the Quadrilateral fortresses to the east, so it is likely he planned to make a stand among the protection of its defences. As the Russians corps not held up at Plevna began to bypass the fortresses altogether and moved south in the direction of Shipka Pass, Abdülhamid II ordered Abdülkerim Nadir Pasha removed from command and replaced with the youthful and charismatic Mehmed. When Mehmed Ali arrived at the front, he brought with him a renewed spirit and the blessings of the sultan that Abdülkerim Nadir lacked.

The arrival of Mehmed Ali infused energy and elevated the depleted morale when he joined the Ottoman army aligned in the vicinity of Shumla. Wentworth Huyshe, a war correspondent of the *New York Herald* attached to the army, wrote that 'his spirit ran through the army like wildfire.' Mehmed Ali made a bold proclamation to his officers that he sought to promote individuals based on merit, to remove cowards or those unfit to command, and to execute those perceived as traitors. He had under his command 45,000 men dedicated to the Quadrilateral garrisons of Rushchuk, Silistria, Shumla, and Varna. Mobile subdivisions unattached to the garrisons, totaling 60,000–70,000 men, were restructured into two corps for a premeditated offensive.

Both corps commanders were political appointments inherited by Mehmed Ali. Ahmed Eyoub Pasha, in command of the I Corps, was described in one account as 'a fat, grey-headed, stout old fellow, very cheery and pleasant', criticized for his tardy movements during the Serbian War fortified in the upcoming weeks. The 23-year-old Prince Hassan, the third son of the Khedive of Egypt, known as the 'Soldier Prince', was in command of the II Corps. Hassan was educated in Britain and served in a Prussian cavalry regiment as a junior officer for a short time, but lacked any significant military experience. Hassan was recognized for his canary yellow gilded boots, large multi-ethnic staff, and pompous demeanor, rather than his military genius.

Mehmed Ali exercised limited control over Süleyman's 30,000 veterans at Shipka Pass and Osman's 20,000 pinned into the makeshift fortress of Plevna. Süleyman's and Osman's armies received orders directly from Constantinople, complicating the structure of command. Süleyman resented being placed under the command of his former subordinate. The limited exchanges between Süleyman and Mehmed Ali were strained, further complicating management and coordination of the war effort.

Baker arrived at Varna in the aftermath of these activities. A special train transported his party to Shumla to discuss their intended role with Mehmed Ali's army. Baker made his way to the large green tent where Mehmed Ali's headquarters was located for a personal audience with the charismatic commander. Mehmed Ali greeted him with 'warmth and geniality which has always made him so popular with officers under his command', and with courtesy invited Baker to dine with him and his staff. Mehmed Ali's own European roots and their shared energy led to a solid rapport that blossomed between the two. The transplanted German valued the military experience Baker presented, and offered him command of a small independent division in his reorganized army.

Mehmed Ali planned to conduct a bold manoeuvre to relieve the mounting pressure placed on the defenders at Plevna and theoretically derail the Russian offensive. The I and II Corps would make a strong demonstration towards a breach that existed between the Russian XII Corps and XIII Corps facing east opposite Rushchuk and Shumla. The foremost target would be the weak Russian right flank, anchored by outposts of the Russian XIII Corps outside of Eski Dzuma, 20 miles west of Shumla. The I Corps was to advance forward from Rasgrad in the direction of Katzelevo and Karahassankeui (pronounced Kara-hassan-keu), while the II Corps was ordered to occupy Eski Dzuma and eliminate any Russian opposition in the area.

Designated as the Army of Rushchuk, the Russian XII Corps and XIII Corps were extended in a strained 50-mile-wide arch facing Mehmed Ali's army. Its left flank was anchored on the Danube River outside the Ottoman fortress of Rushchuk near Pyrgos, and ran in a continuous line south to outside of the village of Eski Dzuma, near Sarnasuflar. The Army of Rushchuk was composed of 40,000 infantry, 5,000 cavalry, and 200 guns under the overall command of the heir apparent, 32-year-old Grand Duke Alexander Alexandrovich (future Tsar Alexander III). The XII Corps was made up of the 12th, 33rd, and 12th Cavalry divisions, while the XIII Corps was made up of the 1st, 35th, and 13th Cavalry divisions. Behind the extended line the Russian investment of Plevna was taking place, while further south, Russian soldiers occupied Shipka Pass.

The Army of Rushchuk was tasked with two objectives by the Russian high command. First, the army was to form a barrier against Ottoman thrusts to disrupt the Russian offensive from the direction of the Quadrilateral fortresses. The Russian defensive position along the Biela-Rushchuk line was well fortified, and one correspondent with the Russians judged it to be 'impregnable'. Second, if conceivable, the army had orders to besiege and capture the Ottoman fortress of Rushchuk.

On 21 August 1877, the same day that Mehmed Ali inaugurated his offensive, Süleyman Pasha began to launch his assault to recapture Shipka Pass. The assault initiated a five-day bloodbath as Süleyman hurled his 30,000 veterans against the 4,000 Russian soldiers dug into the rocky mountains. The two opponents fought furiously atop the heights. At one point in the action, the Russian defenders ran out of ammunition at a location known as the 'Eagle's Nest', hurling fragmented rocks and rolling large boulders down upon the Ottoman attackers, who dropped and rolled back down the hill.

Süleyman continued to order his battalions to certain death from the comfort of his telegraph tent. Minimal progress was made in the frontal attack, and Huyshe summed up the series of assaults appropriately when he explained that Süleyman 'banged his head against the Schipka [Shipka] Pass to no purpose.' Captain J.C. Fife-Cookson, accompanying Süleyman's army as an observer, estimated that Süleyman, having succeeded by using these same tactics against the untrained Serbian and Montenegrin rebels in 1876, 'probably believed that he must gain his objective eventually.'

Lieutenant General Fyodor Radetzky saved the day when he arrived with 20,000 men of the VIII Corps to reinforce Gourko on 23 August. Some of Radetzky's infantrymen hitched rides on the backs of Cossack horsemen in order to expedite their arrival. Süleyman continued to plunge his units forward in an attempt to reclaim the pass, hoping that his weight of numbers would prevail. When it was all over, Süleyman squandered the lives of 10,000 Serbian veterans in comparison to the 3,600 Russian casualties. Relief to defenders at Plevna would have to come from Mehmed Ali's army.

Mehmed Ali rode off towards Rasgrad to supervise the movement of Ahmed Eyoub and the I Corps, while the II Corps moved towards Eski Dzuma. The village of Eski Dzuma was in a state of complete pandemonium when the lead elements of the II Corps arrived. The village was swarming with 10,000 half-starving Muslim refugees, fleeing from their villages in the wake of the Russian offensive. Baker recalled that the refugees were in a 'state of terrible destitution', and 'told vivid and consistent stories of the brutalities they had endured at the hands of the Bulgarian soldiers and Cossacks.'

Russian outposts stood 13 short miles away from the village. Ottoman scouts confirmed that portions of the 1st Division of the Russian XIII Corps were located in the vicinity of Eski Dzuma. The forward units of the II Corps collected at Eski Dzuma consisted of Salih Pasha's 2nd Division, made up of thirteen battalions of infantry, three batteries of artillery, and nine squadrons of cavalry structured in two 'brigades' under the command of Assim Pasha and Sabit Pasha. Baker's brigade-sized division of three battalions, 1,000 irregular cavalrymen, and half a battery complemented the force. Prince Hassan was still travelling from Varna to Eski Dzuma with Ismail Pasha's mixed Ottoman and Egyptian 1st Division, leaving Salih as the senior officer in command.

Baker developed a close connection with Salih. Salih travelled extensively to both Great Britain and France before the war, and Baker recalled that their 'mutual visits were frequent'. Baker revealed that Salih was 'at all times a pleasant and interesting companion', and found him useful for providing 'information relative to Turkish habits, manners, and customs'. Salih shared the same consideration for conducting aggressive offensive operations as Baker.

It was oppressively hot on 21 August 1877 as the sweat-saturated Ottoman soldiers of Salih's 2nd Division crept forwards from Eski Dzuma. The soldiers stepped through a field of undisturbed Indian corn as it crunched beneath their feet, until they came upon a large plateau. Baker observed that 'a prettier or more rural scene it was difficult to imagine' after scaling the plateau, and forewarned, 'what a sad change the ravages of war would bring upon the fairy scene.' As Baker puffed away at his customary hand-rolled cigarettes astride his horse, he watched a large gap develop between the brigades of Assim and Sabit, making an old soldier uneasy. At least 2 miles of dense forest divided the two brigades, cutting off each formation from supporting one another if attacked.

Russian Lieutenant General Hahn, located at his headquarters in the village of Popkoi, grew anxious as he watched the Ottomans fortifying the position his men had evacuated only weeks before. The position was abandoned following the second repulse at Plevna. He feared the occupation of it would compromise his own right flank, so he decided to launch a surprise assault on Salih's men with a detachment of seven battalions, one squadron of cavalry, and sixteen guns.

On 22 August, the eruption of gunfire broke the stillness between the two forces. The Russian ambush fell upon Assim's infantrymen, cut off from supporting Sabit's Brigade. Despite the ambush, the Ottoman line held firm until a junior officer misinterpreted an order, and pulled his command from a commanding crest at the centre of the position. If the Russians managed to occupy the crest before the arrival of Ottoman reinforcements, the whole Ottoman position would fold.

Observing the potential chaos through his field glasses, Baker took it upon himself to act. He came to Bulgaria to assist the Ottomans to the best of his ability, and he did not intend to sit idle as a mere observer. After receiving permission from Salih to ride to the front, he dug his spurs into the ribs of his horse and dashed forwards at a fast gallop. He brought his horse to a halt when he came upon two retiring Ottoman companies, and ordered the terrified soldiers to about-face and follow close behind his lead.

With Baker mounted at the forefront, the cheering infantrymen plunged forwards towards the crest amid the spray of bullets and met the Russian infantrymen mounting the unoccupied ridge head-on. The Russians, caught completely off guard, were driven back down into the valley, and two Ottoman guns were brought up to the crest to rain iron upon them. This deed was completed in the nick of time, and the crest was recaptured by Baker and the Ottoman companies. The Russian detachment tasked with the ambush retreated back to Popkoi at nightfall with the loss of 400 men. Salih endured another furious Russian counter-attack in the concluding days, but secured the position.

Wentworth Huyshe was one of the many German, French, British, and Austrian war correspondents, 'amateurs', and military attachés cluttering Baker's homely bell tent in the early phases of the operations near Eski Dzuma. Huyshe was impressed in the manner Baker carried himself in the aftermath of the action at Eski Dzuma. He remembered the taciturn Baker was never a braggart, modestly 'unwilling ever to talk much about his success,' but when he did speak he was 'so quiet, so self-possessed, so unconscious of his own skill and his own valor'. In Huyshe's eyes, Valentine Baker was 'every inch a soldier and gentleman' regardless of what individuals whispered about his humiliation and subsequent banishment.

Mehmed Ali returned from Rasgrad on 28 August, and summoned together Prince Hassan, Salih, and Baker for a council of war at the village of Sarnasuflar. Infantrymen and cavalrymen of the Russian XIII Corps were strongly entrenched at the village of Popkoi, while the village of Karahassankeui was weakly defended, and with the rear of the village facing the Lom River. The Russian left flank, situated at Karahassankeui, was held by 3,500 men under the command of Major General Leonov, composed of a mixed force of cavalry, infantry, and three field guns. A single wooden bridge provided a passage across the river. The feebler position at Karahassankeui was selected for the next point of attack, scheduled to take place on 30 August 1877.

A strange cry rang out one night in the Ottoman camp, which alerted Baker's curiosity. He recalled:

> A given sound on the bugle was repeated by all the buglers in camp, and then all the troops broke out into a shout of 'Allah', repeated again and again, each time that the buglers sounded. The result was something very like a British cheer.

This peculiar chant was revived after being first instituted by Mehmed Ali during the war against the Montenegrins. Baker fixated on the high-pitched chant, and Mehmed Ali told him how this battle cry was used in a number of engagements to inspire the Ottoman soldiers to do their duty and fight with limitless courage, initiated by this trumpet call. He assured Baker that it could be used to 'produce a most dispiriting effect upon the enemy', even in the most dismal situations.

Huyshe (as many other correspondents) was restless to find out when and where the Ottoman assault was scheduled to take place. To his frustration, Huyshe felt that 'Baker was a little less non-committal' than he would have preferred, refusing to reveal the details of the operation, kept secret among the members of Mehmed Ali's council of war. Huyshe planned to travel 30 miles to Shumla to transmit his reports to his employer before the anticipated engagement. He feared the battle could take place any day, and he would miss the action if he left the front for even a short period of time.

He rather bluntly asked Baker if there remained time to travel back to Shumla, and still return to witness the battle. He recorded his dialogue with Baker:

'Yes,' said Valentine Baker, with his quiet smile, in answer to my anxious questioning, 'I think you will have time to ride in to Shumla and post your letter; but I should be back here on or about the 30th, if I were you.'

With Baker's words of advice, Huyshe rode off and made sure to return back to camp before 30 August. He came back to the sound of Jacques Offenbach's familiar hymns from the opera *La belle Hélène* (*The Beautiful Helen*) being played in front of Mehmed Ali's tent. There he witnessed Baker, Prince Hassan, Mehmed Ali, and their staff officers relishing in the serene melodies, forgetting for a few hours the bloody business scheduled to commence in the morning.

The battle for Karahassankeui opened early next morning with a fierce artillery duel between the Russian and Ottoman gunners. This duel lasted for a few hours as Mehmed Ali and Baker tranquilly observed the Russian position through their field glasses from an elevated hill. Stationed next to the officers were three Krupp guns lobbing shells on the Leonov's men in an attempt to dwindle their defences. The ivory minaret of the mosque jutting above the thatched roof homes of the village provided a target for directing artillery fire and coordinating the infantry attack.

The main infantry assault on Karahassankeui was to be conducted by Nejib Pasha's 3rd Division of the I Corps moving south from the direction of Rasgrad, supported by Salih's 2nd Division of the II Corps. Nejib misinterpreted his orders and assumed the assault was 'only a reconnaissance in force', moving his division into position with no sense of urgency to drive the Russians from the village. The attempt to push the Russians back across the river was destined for failure as Sabit's Brigade of Salih's 2nd Division bore the brunt of the assault alone. Meanwhile, 300 Russian infantrymen arrived as reinforcements from Popkoi at 2.00 pm to help cushion the Russian defence of the village. Both Sabit's Brigade and Nejib's 3rd Division were forced back, followed by an inexcusable lull in the battle.

Baker's frustration intensified as no sounds of battle came from the direction of Karahassankeui. Beyond Sabit's Brigade, the majority of the II Corps remained uncommitted, further irritating Baker. He could no longer tolerate the lethargic nature of how the battle was being conducted by the Ottoman commanders:

> It was perfectly maddening to remain a spectator on our point of observation, and to see a battle so completely thrown away. I could stand it no longer, and begged Mehmed Ali to let me go down and order a general advance upon the village.

Mehmed Ali permitted him to take a single battalion to investigate the stillness, and to reinforce Sabit's Brigade. Baker collected his English staff of 'fire-eating Englishmen', composed of Allix, Briscoe, Jenner, and Sartorius, disappearing into the wooded forest leading to Karahassankeui.

After exiting the woods into an open plain, the party stumbled upon an idle Ottoman battery and four squadrons of cavalry. Baker shouted to both of the respective commanders of the units to immediately advance towards the village. The dismayed ex-colonel of Hussars observed the core of Sabit's Brigade disengaged and cowering in a cornfield about 3,500 yards from the village. Sabit was nowhere to be found, as he had ridden towards Nejib's 3rd Division 2 miles away in an attempt to locate the division commander to coordinate a renewed assault. Baker felt that the men of Sabit's Brigade 'were immovable', having become dispirited that 'the day had gone adversely, and no one appeared willing to make an effort to retrieve', and pleaded with the soldiers to renew the assault: 'It was in vain that we urged forward the line of skirmishers to the attack. A general depression seemed to have set in among the men of Sabit's Brigade.'

Baker ordered Allix to locate Sabit, and the Turkish-speaking Jenner to ride back and invigorate Mehmed Ali to order a general advance. Baker, Briscoe, and Sartorius galloped up and down the Ottoman skirmisher line posted to the front of Sabit's Brigade within 1,200 yards of the enemy, as the prone Ottoman infantrymen exchanged rifle fire with the entrenched Russian infantrymen. The mounted Englishmen attracted Russian artillery fire as they galloped up and down the line, and a Russian shell exploded within close proximity, slinging particles of dirt into their faces. A second shell exploded and hit its mark, lobbing fragments into the air that tore open the abdomen of Briscoe's horse, killing it instantly, and tossing Briscoe to the ground. A few seconds later, a third shell exploded nearby and Baker and his mount collapsed into the dirt.

Neighboring Ottoman skirmishers briefly halted their sporadic fire, presuming the 'Inglese Pasha' had been killed or mortally wounded. To their astonishment, he rose up from the ground dirtied but unscratched, and straightened his crooked turban-wrapped fez upon his head, shortly after commandeering a new horse. His horse – seriously wounded by the shell in the hip – had been purchased in a hurry before his departure from Constantinople. Before the battle, Baker had removed his saddle from his favourite horse Imaum and had left him behind, saving him from this deadly fate.

Leonov's Russians soon after launched a furious counter-attack on Sabit's idle battalions. The Russian line of battle extended for 1 mile, with their right flank resting on the Lom River. Unbeknown to the Russians, the Ottomans held the advantage on the defensive. The battalions armed with superior-ranged Peabody–Martini rifles allowed them to remain 'practically untouched' against those Russian infantrymen armed with their inferior Krnk rifles. Huyshe recalled the Russians 'found out that the clumsy Kranka [Krnk] rifle of the "Moscov" was no match for the Martini-Henry [Peabody-Martini], and that while the Russian fighting distance was 400 yards, they could come into action with deadly effect at twice that distance.'

The Ottoman cavalry squadrons and the battery of artillery Baker previously ordered forwards arrived during the climax of the battle. The gunners unlimbered their guns and began to spew shrapnel on the Russian infantrymen at a close range, tearing lanes through their lines. Thanks to Jenner's pleas, reinforcements arrived from Mehmed Ali to bolster the Ottoman battalions engaged outside of Karahassankeui. The Russian defence began to disintegrate with the mounting pressure to their front. They gradually withdrew through the village and crossed over the Lom River to escape being surrounded and cut off.

Baker saw this as a 'golden moment' to overrun and capture all of the Russian guns and infantrymen in one swipe. He hoped that he could cut off the remnants of Leonov's battalions before escaping across the river. Baker rode up with his staff towards the wooded forest not far from the village, and discovered two motionless Ottoman cavalry regiments under the command of Kerim Pasha. Limbered Russian artillery guns intermingled with infantrymen could be observed falling back in panic. Baker pleaded with Kerim to give chase with his immobile regiments, but the stubborn officer refused to leave his position without direct orders from Mehmed Ali.

The indifferent response of the Ottoman cavalry commander sent Robert Briscoe into a frenzied rage. Briscoe's 'Irish blood was roused' as his cheeks reddened and his eyes came alive, and the Gaelic soldier drew his large Hussar sabre from its steel scabbard, brandishing the blade in the air above his head, calling for the bravest of the Ottoman cavalrymen to follow him to glory or death. Clusters of motivated Ottoman horsemen began to break ranks, and the enthused cavalrymen, including the commanders of both regiments, followed Baker and Briscoe 'down the ravine at a headlong speed into the valley' while Kerim remained behind, speechless and humiliated.

As the cavalrymen galloped forwards, Briscoe joined in the shouts of 'Allah!' alongside the charging horsemen 'in a stentorian voice, and with a shade of brogue'. The hesitation of Kerim allowed for the majority of the limbered Russian guns and fleeing soldiers to escape across the river. The 'golden moment' slipped away. The pursuers did not leave empty-handed, for they managed to capture some slow-moving ammunition wagons to corroborate their efforts.

Flames seared the ivory-coloured buildings as Leonov's infantrymen departed the village. Ottoman infantrymen rushed down the blackened streets and into the charred remains of the village by 7.00 pm, chiefly due to the forceful leadership of Baker. Ottoman pickets were placed all along the river's banks and soldiers slept in the skeletal remains of buildings for the night. The Russians suffered roughly 1,800 casualties in their spirited defence, while the Ottomans sustained 1,000 casualties before the day came to a close.

The aftermath of the engagement left a grim scene on the surrounding landscape. As Baker travelled back to the village with his staff, the Englishmen passed a specific spot where the fighting was particularly fierce:

As we passed near the wood, the Russian dead were lying thickly around, nearly all killed by the enfilading fire of Sabit's battery. The whole vicinity of the wood was strewn with arms, knapsacks, and every sign of a hasty and disordered flight.

Huyshe, less exposed than Baker to the horrors of war, recalled as he toured the battlefield that 'in the gullies by which the cliffs were broken lay many of the unburied dead, stripped naked, their backs riddled with bullet holes.' An Ottoman cemetery caught in the middle of the battle was desecrated as pulverized fragments of the monuments lay strewn in the grass, and tombstones lay toppled over. As he continued along the edge of the heights, Huyshe observed:

a long line of shallow graves contained those who had found hasty burial; the bodies were scarcely covered. Everywhere – in the woods, in the fields, in the village, even up on the hillside behind it, the horrible stench of a battlefield poisoned the air.

Baker and his staff rode back to Mehmed Ali's headquarters at Sarnasuflar, guided by the rays of the moonlight. Rumor spread like wildfire throughout Mehmed Ali's army that the valiant 'Inglese Pasha' had been killed or captured during the heat of battle. The news of his horse being shot from underneath him earlier that day led to the embellished report. A telegraph sent to Constantinople chronicling the victory publicized he was missing in action, presumed to be dead.

Huyshe was one of the first to discern this rumor to be untrue. He instantly recognized Baker, despite the layer of powder and smoke caked on his face when he returned to Mehmed Ali's camp, and recounted the few words exchanged between the two men: 'You are not hurt, Colonel, are you?' Baker responded, 'No – my horse is wounded, but those guns got away! Got clear off! – and I could have taken them with a single squadron of English cavalry.' Baker steamed off in a rare show of frustration without speaking another word to Huyshe.

The Battle of Karahassankeui 'gave rise to very serious reflections' for Baker concerning the capability of Ottoman leadership. He criticized that 'scarcely a single error had been left uncommitted in carrying out the carefully considered plan of attack' during the battle. Seven Ottoman brigades were acting in the vicinity of Karahassankeui, but most failed to make any significant impact. Battalions were fed into the battle piecemeal, while a majority of the II Corps was held uselessly in reserve. Baker's discontent with the lack of urgency displayed by fellow Ottoman commanders, and their reluctance to take the initiative when favourable opportunities developed, would only continue to mature in the coming weeks.

Praise was heaped upon the head of the 'Inglese Pasha' following the engagements at Eski Dzuma and Karahassankeui. Mehmed Ali signalled out his unqualified respect for Baker after the battle in his report, stating that he 'greatly distinguished himself', and presented him with the green enameled Order of Osmanieh. Foreign war correspondents attached to Mehmed Ali's army reported tales of him braving the racking fire and his battlefield successes to their Western audiences, detached only by two years from being vilified by the same newspapers. One war correspondent left a perhaps slightly exaggerated account of him at the Battle of Karahassankeui:

> I saw a shell explode within a few yards of Baker Pasha; his brave horse fell and down he came. That was the end of the grey Arab, but not of his master, for Baker was up in a moment, on the charger of a common trooper, in the middle of his men hacking like a very Hercules.

The Hornet specified that these engagements provided clear evidence that, 'Baker is not merely a dashing hussar officer, as is usually supposed, but an "all-round" soldier of no ordinary merit.'

Baker was a unique example of a resourceful soldier of fortune, not blinded by selfish and materialistic considerations as other adventurers in Ottoman service. His unrelenting search for redemption unconsciously fuelled his dedication and genuine concern for achieving success in the war. The engagements at Eski Dzuma and Karahassankeui demonstrated his aptitude to not only successfully lead large formations of soldiers, but to also inspire Muslim soldiers under his command despite being an Anglican by religion and an Englishman by birth. One author recorded that, despite being unable to speak a word of Turkish, 'His tact and popularity have completely broken down the barrier of jealously to the foreigner in the army.' His bold and aggressive tactics provided a spark that the senior Ottoman leadership badly needed.

Baker and his staff halted the morning following the battle at Karahassankeui to share in some Turkish coffee being simmered over a fire under the care of a junior Ottoman officer. The Englishmen relished the moment to be able to take a short break from the previous day's busy activities and sip on the refreshing fluid. This moment of harmony was interrupted when an Ottoman officer came back frantically waving his hands up in the air and yelling for them to stop downing the substance. Taking a moment to catch his breath, the officer revealed that the water used to brew the coffee came from a contaminated well filled with Russian corpses dumped in after the battle. 'Some of our party grew pale with horror and disgust,' Baker remembered observing the expressions of his companions, and they decided to unanimously make a 'mental vow not to touch the seemingly harmless fluid during the remainder of our stay at Karahassankeui'.

Mehmed Ali held a council of war at his headquarters in the aftermath of Karahassankeui to determine the second phase of the offensive. He appeared somewhat reluctant to continue with the operations, satisfied with his success thus far, but allowed his subordinate commanders to decide the next course. He asked his senior commanders to freely voice if the army should remain on the defensive in order to meet a possible reinforced Russian counter-attack (which he favoured), or if it should continue with its offensive operations to further exploit the dispirited condition of the Russian XIII Corps. All of the senior commanders present were unanimously of the opinion that to allow the demoralized Russian troops to recover 'would be a fatal mistake'. It was decided to cross the Lom River and continue with the offensive towards the village of Biela.

The Ottoman offensive would continue to drive a wedge between the disordered segments of the Russian XIII Corps and the XII Corps. Major General Arnoldi, with five battalions and eight guns, was the only major opposition located in this breach at the heights of Katzelevo, while Lieutenant General Baron Driesen held Ablava on his right with seven battalions, and thirty-two guns of the 12th and 33rd divisions, in total, 10,000 men. In order to preoccupy the left flank of the Russian XII Corps near Rushchuk,

Mehmed Ali ordered Kayserili Ahmed Pasha of the Rushchuk garrison to make an aggressive sortie. The main thrust would come from Ahmed Eyoub and his 30,000 men, made up of his three divisions of the I Corps from Rasgrad, and Nejib's division at Karahassankeui, towards Katzelevo. The II Corps, under Hassan, would advance in unison towards Popkoi and threaten the Russian units near Cerkonva to prevent the XIII Corps from supporting their companions at Katzelevo.

Baker saw this as an exceptional opportunity to collapse the whole Russian offensive and hurl the Russians and Romanians back across the Danube once and for all. He reasoned that 'a bold and decisive blow struck on any part of their long and badly protected line might turn the tide of the campaign completely in favour of the Turkish arms.' A major success would compel General Radetzky's force at Shipka Pass to fall back with their line of communication exposed, and allow Süleyman and his army to freely occupy the pass he sacrificed so much to try to capture. The united armies of Mehmed Ali and Süleyman could then move to the aid of Osman and his defenders under the Russian pressure at Plevna. Baker appreciated the impact of these offensive operations on the war and calculated that 'It was clear to me that the movement of the next day must, in one way or the other, entirely decide the whole fate of the campaign.'

On 11 September 1877, the third Russian assault to capture Plevna was scheduled to take place in honor of the anniversary of Tsar Alexander's baptism. Alexander, accompanied by his brother, the Grand Duke Nicholas, arrived with their glittering entourage of finely dressed staff officers to spectate what they anticipated would be the final assault. Alexander requested (more like ordered) the village to be in Russian hands by nightfall as a fitting baptismal gift. A large wooden platform was constructed for him to view the anticipated storming of the Ottoman entrenchments, with a table of fine delicacies such as Russian vodka, French wine, caviar, and fresh game arrayed for the spectacle.

For four preceding days, 424 Russian guns pummeled the Ottoman defenders with more than 30,000 shells before 84,000 Russian and Romanian soldiers would launch a three-pronged assault. The faint roar of the Russian cannonade on Plevna could be heard by the men of Mehmed Ali's army. Baker wrote that, despite the battle being 'upwards of 100 miles', the cannonade in some instances was 'distinctly audible'. This was not improbable; it was likewise recorded that the Confederate bombardment at Gettysburg, Pennsylvania, could be heard in Washington, DC – a little less than 100 miles away – during the prelude of Pickett's Charge on 3 July 1863.

11 September consisted of a wholesale day of bloodshed and carnage as the Russians and Romanians bore down on the Ottoman entrenchments. The 'White Russian', General Mikhail Skobelev – sporting his ivory uniform and mounted on the same colour charger – personally led one assault towards the southern redoubts with sword in hand. Edward King chronicled the events of this feat:

Skobeleff [Skobelev] rallied the stragglers and carried them forward into the very enemy's lines; his own sword was cut in two in the middle, while he was leaping a ditch; his horse shot dead underneath him; and he rolled into the ditch, but sprang to his feet with a shout, and finally led the mass of men over the ditch, scarp and counterscarp and parapet, and into the redoubt.

Skobelev's column was the only one of the three that made any headway, as the other assaults stalled due to poor coordination and withering fire from the entrenchments. Despite gaining a foothold within the Ottoman entrenchments and beating off repeated Ottoman counter-attacks, Skobelev 'came out of the final fight with his clothes covered with mud a filth, his sword broken, his decorations twisted on his shoulders, his face black with powder and smoke, his eyes bloodshot, and his voice broken,' after his men retired under orders from the Russian headquarters, unable to spare reinforcements to exploit his breech.

Rather than attempt a fourth bloody assault to capture Plevna by storm after suffering 15,000 casualties in the most recent failure, Alexander chose to barricade and starve the defenders into submission. In the coming weeks, he summoned the hero of the defence at Sevastopol during the Crimean War, General Eduard Totleben, to the front. By mid-November, 120,000 Russian and Romanians would enclose the village, cutting them off from the outside world. The defenders had defied the odds for a third time, but as the number of casualties began to increase, Osman could not compensate for the losses of manpower. Ratios inside Plevna dropped down to a half a pound of bread and a lump of meat for each man per day; only soup was available for the wounded, supplemented by anything that walked or crawled, including cats, dogs, and even rats.

The effort of Mehmed Ali's army in September would dictate the outcome of the war. Mehmed Ali's heart was not behind the offensive and lost his vigour from when he initially took command. He saw his army's movements only as a simple demonstration to disrupt Russian operations, and of secondary importance to the greater scheme of the war – the first sign of this timid demeanor surfaced during his council of war after Karahassankeui. Baker felt quite the opposite, and could clearly visualize the havoc an aggressive movement could generate for the Russians. 'The flippancy and want of interest shown in all the military arrangements for the coming struggle were absolutely disgusting to anyone having the true feelings of a soldier,' thundered Baker.

Part of this hesitation may have developed due to the fact that Mehmed Ali could rely on few of his colleagues in the army, as intrigue among senior Ottoman commanders 'proved stronger than patriotism.' Ahmed Eyoub and Süleyman were model cases of troublesome subordinates causing setbacks to the Ottoman war effort to satisfy their own gains by sending defaming messages back to Constantinople in regard to their commander. Mehmed Ali had sent a message to Süleyman requesting part of his army to be detached and sent to aid his scheduled offensive towards Biela. No reply was ever received from the envious Süleyman. Instead, he launched a second frontal assault on Shipka Pass from 13–17 September that was repulsed at the cost of another 3,000 Ottoman soldiers.

Baker was further displeased with the confusing and complicated manner orders were issued throughout the army. Division commanders in both corps received all of their orders from Mehmed Ali's staff, rather than from Prince Hassan or Ahmed Eyoub. In similar instances, brigade commanders regularly received orders directly from Mehmed Ali's staff, circumventing the authority of their division commanders. Baker described the members of Mehmed Ali's staff as 'utterly incompetent', yet they held this 'unbounded and undue authority' to issue vital decisions in his stead during the next few weeks of the campaign.

Ahmed Eyoub advanced his I Corps at a lumbering pace, and did not attack the strongly entrenched Russian detachment at Katzelevo until 5 September 1877. Eyoub's battalions moved through the ravines and streams of the surrounding landscape to form a 7-mile half-circle in front of the Russian position. The Ottoman artillery bombardment commenced at 7.00 am to soften up the Russian position before the infantry assault. For four hours, General Arnoldi repulsed seven times his number at Katzelevo, while the Ottoman attack on his right at Ablava did not commence until 11.00 am. Mehmed Ali arrived around midday and assumed command of the operations, and by 3.00 pm, the Russians were driven back across the Lom, at the loss of roughly 1,300 men on each side.

Hassan's II Corps moved to outside the village of Popkoi on 6 September 1877. An assault of the village proved unnecessary, as the Russian defenders vacated it and withdrew towards Biela without a fight. Prince Hassan was criticized by Baker and Salih for allowing the fleeing Russians to evade capture, losing a grand opportunity to bag a portion of the Russian XIII Corps. The whole of the Russian XII Corps and XIII Corps were reeling backwards by 8 September 1877. Mehmed Ali's line now stretched 35 miles with 30,000 men of the I Corps at Katzelevo, and 20,000 men of the II Corps at Popkoi.

Mehmed Ali rode back to confer with Baker, Salih, and Prince Hassan to reveal that the main thrust in the direction of Biela would come from Ahmed Eyoub and the I Corps. All three officers disagreed with the manoeuvre, arguing that an attack would expose the Rushchuk garrison, and that the northern segment of the Russian line protecting Biela was too strongly fortified to be assaulted. Rather, they argued that a thrust should be made by the II Corps from the south at Verboka outside of Cerkonva, where Russian defences were reported to be much weaker. Mehmed Ali relented to their guidance, and a general advance towards Cerkonva began on 12 September 1877, under a torrent of rainfall. Ahmed Eyoub was rumoured to be unhappy with the diminished role of his I Corps, and chose to delay his movements out of spite.

The Russian defenders occupied a stripe of rifle pits and trenches on the surrounding heights near the village of Verboka. The Russian detachment consisted of a mixed force of 10,000 cavalrymen and infantrymen under the command of Major General Tatischev of the 11th Cavalry Division.

In addition to two regiments of cavalrymen and six batteries, Tatischev commanded two regiments of the 32nd Division (XI Corps), one regiment of the 1st Division (XIII Corps), and one regiment of the 26th Division. The 102nd Regiment was on its way from Biela to reinforce Tatischev.

The high-water mark of the war came on 21 September 1877. Mehmed Ali's senior officers were at odds over where to launch the assault on the Russian position; Baker and Salih wanted to drive a wedge between Kopritza and Verboka in the centre of the Russian line, while Mehmed Ali's staff, led by Rifaat Pasha and Prince Hassan, wanted to push through the broken and thickly wooded country to swing around the Russian right flank, akin to the familiar crushing manoeuvre conducted by Confederate General Thomas J. 'Stonewall' Jackson at the Battle of Chancellorsville during the American Civil War. Mehmed Ali chose to adopt the plan that would in theory incur the least number of casualties, i.e. the second option. The Ottomans collected thirty-five battalions – 20,000 men – and fifty guns of the II Corps. Ten battalions of Egyptian infantry of Ismail Pasha's Division were held in reserve to support the sweeping movement on the Russian right flank.

Rainfall, followed by a heavy fog, draped the Ottoman camp in the early hours of dawn as the battalions of the II Corps prepared for the day's battle. Baker rose at 3.00 am, and Huyshe remembered that the 'merry men' of his staff were ready in their saddles at the break of dawn for the clash he described as the 'eventual day for the destinies of Bulgaria'. Ottoman artillery crews opened up on the Russian position at 11.00 am, not commencing the battle until late in the day. The bombardment inflicted minimal damage on Tatischev's defenders and alarmed the Russians of the imminent threat. To further denote the lack of urgency of some officers within the Ottoman camp, Baker discovered one of the brigade commanders leading the main assault sound asleep in his tent.

The Ottoman effort to outflank the Russian right began at 2.00 pm and failed to live up to 'Stonewall' Jackson's famous assault. Prince Hassan's column got bogged down in the dense timber and essentially removed itself from the fight, while the Ottoman diversion on the Russian centre and left flank commenced as scheduled. Despite this setback, a breakthrough in the Russian line appeared conceivable as two Ottoman battalions occupied the village of Verboka. Mehmed Ali ordered the ten Egyptian reserve battalions forwards to support the breakthrough, but they moved at such a sluggish pace along the muddy roads that they never actually made it up to the front. The Russian 102nd Regiment arrived at 4.00 pm after a forced march from Biela, and General Tatsichev hurled them into the Ottoman line, forcing the Ottoman battalions from Verboka in confusion through the woods towards Cerkonva.

The battle from the beginning to the end was a masterful display of Ottoman inefficiency. The assault failed due to a 'consecutive series of errors' including poor coordination, bad troop deployment, and the lethargic demeanour of some of the Ottoman commanders. Out of the thirty-five Ottoman battalions present on the field, only nine were actually engaged during the battle. The Ottoman II Corps suffered three times the number of casualties compared to the 500 Russian casualties.

Baker was not timid about articulating his displeasure of the squandered opportunity at Verboka. He forewarned Mehmed Ali on numerous occasions:

> that the crisis of the war had been reached, and that if within a few short days we did not take advantage of the great opportunities which circumstances had given us, the last chance of a victorious campaign must be lost for the Turkish army.

Mehmed Ali ignored his subordinate's passionate pleas, arguing that the actions fought were 'mere trifles in the general course of the campaign'. Baker remembered that he helplessly watched as 'the last gleam of hope' to drive the Russians back across the Danube evaporated.

On 24 September, Mehmed Ali called off the offensive and ordered a general retreat of his army, ending the only major chance of disputing the Russian offensive in Bulgaria. He lost all taste for battle, and had been reluctant to initiate a major offensive towards Biela in the first place after gaining success at Karahassankeui, regarding his movements as an 'offensive reconnaissance'. He was also anxious over the underhanded actions of his subordinates – the scheming of Süleyman's and Ahmed Eyoub's underlings – feeding smearing reports of his performance back to Abdülhamid II and the Sublime Porte in Constantinople.

The I and II Corps retraced their steps back across the Lom under a relentless downpour, vacating the majority of the territory captured in the preceding weeks. The dirt roads leading to Sarnasuflar became a 'sea of mud', and sunken wagons stuck in the quagmire loaded with cases of ammunition, tents, armaments, and provisions were discarded along the sodden roadside. Morale in the Ottoman ranks plummeted, as many cold and wet soldiers were disappointed, having sensed the nearness to victory.

By 1 October, Mehmed Ali's army was back across the Lom. Russian pickets followed close behind and reoccupied the original posts vacated only a few weeks beforehand. Huyshe wrote that Mehmed Ali's army, 'which had swept down like a tornado and scattered the infidel like chaff, was slinking back to the fortresses, baffled and broken, never again to reappear as an army in the field.' The American military observer, Lieutenant Francis Greene, labelled the events of the campaign in a nutshell as a 'complete fiasco'. The Ottoman armies around Sarnasuflar would not conduct another meaningful offensive in this region for the remainder of the war.

Within days of Mehmed Ali's return to Sarnasuflar, a sealed telegraph awaited him addressed from Constantinople. The telegraph revealed that he was to be immediately relieved of command. He was ordered to return to the capital, and to hand his army over to his rival, Süleyman Pasha.

A deep depression hung over the army in response to this news. Despite his failure in the most recent campaign, Mehmed Ali was still celebrated for the inspirational direction he gave the army, and was held in high regard by the common soldier; he held a McClellan-like aurora over his men. Word travelled in the ranks of Süleyman's useless sacrifice of his men at Shipka Pass, and many feared or refused to serve under his command. Prince Hassan was one of these officers, and he trekked to Varna with his Egyptian battalions for transport back home to Cairo.

Baker paid one last visit to his ousted commander before his premature departure. He found Mehmed Ali alone in a small house, 'much depressed and discouraged'. Despite their emerging differences on the objective of the campaign, Baker had no hard feelings for his commander: 'I parted from the Marshal with the greatest pain and regret … his kindness of heart and general good nature had much endeared him to all the officers by whom he was surrounded.' A carriage waited to transport Mehmed Ali back to the capital, but not before he was scheduled to make a stop to hand over his command to Süleyman in person.

Baker reluctantly met with his new commander upon his arrival to Sarnasuflar. He was familiar with the tensions that existed between Süleyman and Mehmed Ali. He favoured Mehmed Ali, and was aware of the poor performance displayed by Süleyman in his struggle to recapture Shipka Pass. Süleyman did not leave a noble first impression on Baker, who viewed him as an incompetent toady:

> His appearance and manners were certainly not prepossessing. There was nothing of the soldier about him, but his features gave the impression of considerable shrewdness and cunning. He wore a dilapidated suit of clothes, lined with fur, which would certainly have been rejected by any Israelitish London dealer, and was without an approach to uniform of any description.

Some inconclusive engagements, followed by a period of stagnation, beset the Ottoman army after Mehmed Ali's departure. The army remained in its position in November as it hunkered down in a static defence. Süleyman had no intention of initiating another campaign so late in the season, and was content holding the defensive line.

Those of Baker's original staff who had landed in Varna began to dissipate. His animated Irish companion, Briscoe, was stricken with dysentery during the retreat, and had to be transported back to Constantinople. Sartorius, only on temporary leave, received letters that 'compelled him to return to England.' Jenner, who had been attached to the staff of Mehmed Ali earlier during the offensive, also vacated the party. Only Allix and his servant Reilly remained.

Baker settled down in a modest two-room cottage in Sarnasuflar as he prepared for the coming Bulgarian winter. Life was dull outside the normal task of killing scorpions or preventing the choking dust from getting inside his living quarters. Reilly and his other Ottoman servants occupied another room of the small cottage. Holes cut in the cottage walls represented windows but had no glass inside, and were instead covered by a loose layer of paper in an attempt to keep out the elements. Baker could barely stand in the Spartan structure without hitting his head on the beam of the ceiling.

Reilly kept Baker humoured for a short while during this period of inactivity. He only spoke 'about three words of Turkish', reported Baker, while his Ottoman soldier-servants did not speak a single word of English. The stubborn Reilly 'never would believe that they did not understand him.' He was amused in one specific incident when Reilly sat down next to a Circassian cavalryman, and talked to him for half an hour 'without stopping'. The Circassian was oblivious to what the strange Englishman spoke to him, but the long-winded Reilly continued to fill his ear with his gossip.

By early November, Baker had had enough of Süleyman's inactivity and lack of urgency to relieve the defenders in Plevna. 'The apathetic way in which Osman's army seemed likely to be left to perish for want of effective aid was distressing to me,' Baker explained. He heard rumours that a force was being assembled in the vicinity of Sofia under command of his former commander, Mehmed Ali (he had been reinstated as the Ottomans were short on commanders), with the objective to liberate the defenders of Plevna. If this proved true, he could not pass up the opportunity to distance himself from Süleyman and get back into action. On 11 November 1877, he bid farewell to Salih and left the dreary camp at Sarnasuflar and set out southwards for Constantinople.

Calm before the storm. Valentine Baker around the time of his trial. (*Illustration by Zsuzsanna Hajdu* (*www.facebook.com / zsuzsihajduarts*))

Prefented to Cap^N VALENTINE BAKER by the Merchants & Infurers of Briftol for gallantly defending the Ship Cæfar againft a French Sloop of War greatly Superior in Force to his own Ship and beating her off on June 27^{tb} 1782

Rendition of the inscription on the ornate silver vase awarded to Captain Valentine Baker in 1782. (*Illustration from Douglas T. Murray and Arthur S. White*, Sir Samuel Baker: A Memoir, *Macmillan, London, 1895*)

Celluloid pin badge of Major General Hector 'Fighting Mac' MacDonald. MacDonald was glorified for his exploits on the battlefield, but met a similar fate to Baker. He instead chose suicide over dishonour, after accusations of homosexual behaviour threatened to derail his illustrious military career. (*Author's collection*)

Suleiman (Süleyman) the conqueror, Metcalf & Co printers, Northampton, Massachusetts, advertising card. Süleyman Pasha is pictured in the foreground in a glorified pose. Notice the discarded Russian *furashka* beneath the hooves of his horse. He was portrayed in a very different light by the end of the Russo-Turkish War. (*Author's collection*)

A modern overview of Shipka Pass and the Monuments of Freedom. Süleyman hurled his battalions forwards with reckless disregard in an attempt to capture this position. (*Courtesy of the National Park Museum Shipka-Buzludzha*)

Ambush! A detachment of Ottoman soldiers armed with Peabody–Martinis are surprised by a Cossack cavalry patrol. (*Illustration by Zsuzsanna Hajdu (*www.facebook.com/zsuzsihajduarts*))*

The Russian Imperial Guard trudges towards Plevna under a heavy rainfall. (*Illustration from Edmund Ollier*, Cassell's Illustrated History of the Russo-Turkish War, *2 vols, Cassell, Petter & Galpin, London, 1879*)

Ottoman leadership in 1877. Pictured in this print are the principal Ottoman leaders during the Russo–Turkish War. (*Illustration from* The Pictorial World, *11 May 1878, author's collection*)

A section of the Panorama Pleven (Plevna) depicting the Russian assault. Major General Skobelev is faintly pictured on the white horse in the centre of the painting leading an assault on the Ottoman entrenchments. Known to his soldiers as the 'White General', the flamboyant Skobelev rode into battle clad in a full dress white uniform matching his horse, and possessed a knack for compelling his men to phenomenal feats in a similar manner to Baker. (*Courtesy of the Panorama Pleven* (*www.panorama-pleven.com*))

Another section of the Panorama Pleven (Plevna) depicting Russian soldiers storming the Ottoman entrenchments. (*Coutesy of the Panorama Pleven* (*www.panorama-pleven.com*))

Russian infantrymen from Gourko's flanking column cocooned while asleep to protect themselves from the freezing temperatures of the Bulgarian winter. (*Illustration from Edmund Ollier*, Cassell's Illustrated History of the Russo-Turkish War, *2 vols, Cassell, Petter & Galpin, London 1879*)

Gourko's flanking column files through the Balkan Mountains under a heavy snowfall to outflank the Kamarli line. (*Illustration from Edmund Ollier,* Cassell's Illustrated History of the Russo-Turkish War, *2 vols, Cassell, Petter & Galpin, London, 1879*)

Members of Baker's staff during the Russo-Turkish War. One war correspondent labelled Baker's companions as his 'fire-eating Englishmen'. From top left: Radford, Burnaby, and Briscoe. From bottom left: Sartorius, Baker, VC, and Allix. Depictions of his other companions could not be located. (*Illustration by Zsuzsanna Hajdu (www.facebook.com/zsuzsihajduarts)*)

Baker holding a meeting with some of the members of his staff at Tashkessen. Fred Burnaby is in civilian attire sporting the bowler hat. (*Illustration from John Cookson Fife-Jackson, John Cookson, With the Armies of the Balkans and at Gallipoli in 1877–1878, Cassell, Petter, Galpin and Co, London, 1880, courtesy of the US Army War College Library and Archives, Carlisle, Pennsylvania*)

Ottoman soldiers deploying: Valentine Baker supervising the deployment of his battalions during a heavy snowstorm. (*Illustration by Zsuzsanna Hajdu (www.facebook. com'zsuzsihajduarts*))

Gourko's triumphant entry into Sofia. The war correspondent Edward King recorded that the victorious general 'was met by thousands of citizens led by priests with banners, crucifixes and lanterns.' (*Illustration from Edmund Ollier,* Cassell's Illustrated History of the Russo–Turkish War, *2 vols, Cassell, Petter & Galpin, London, 1879*)

Baker Pasha's Egyptian column at El Teb met disaster in its attempt to relieve Tokar. The illustration is from a sketch by Major G.D. Giles, who was one of the fortunate survivors of the rout. Baker is pictured in the top left, mounted on the white horse, calmly issuing orders amid the chaotic retreat. (*Illustration from* The Graphic, *1 March 1884, author's collection*)

Labelled as the 'Supreme Master of Irregular Warfare' during Queen Victoria's Little Wars, Dr Joseph Lehmann noted that 'Wolseley believed the best possible way to get ahead in the army was to try to get killed every time he had a chance.' This belief enabled him to rise from an ensign to a field marshal, but at the cost of the sight of one eye and countless wounds. Field Marshal Lord Wolseley remained a staunch supporter of Baker throughout his lifetime. (*Author's collection*)

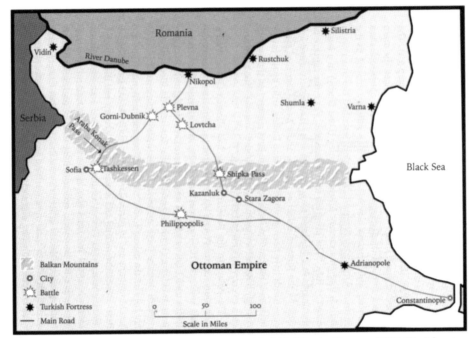

The major battles and fortresses during the Russo–Turkish War in Europe, 1877–78. (*Courtesy of Dr Nicholas Murray, who retains this map's copyright*)

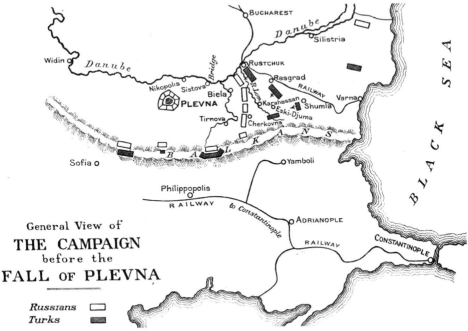

Operations leading to the siege of Plevna. Spelling discrepancies between the map and the text include: Karahassankeui (Karahassan), Eski Dzuma (Eski-Djuma), Rustchuk (Rushchuk), Widin (Vidin), and Cerkonva (Cherkovna). With Russian forces stalled at Plevna and Shipka Pass between the Danube River and the Balkan Mountains, Mehmed Ali had an opportunity to derail the whole Russian offensive. (*Map from Huysche, Wentworth,* The Liberation of Bulgaria: War Notes in 1877, *Bliss, Sands and Foster, London, 1894*)

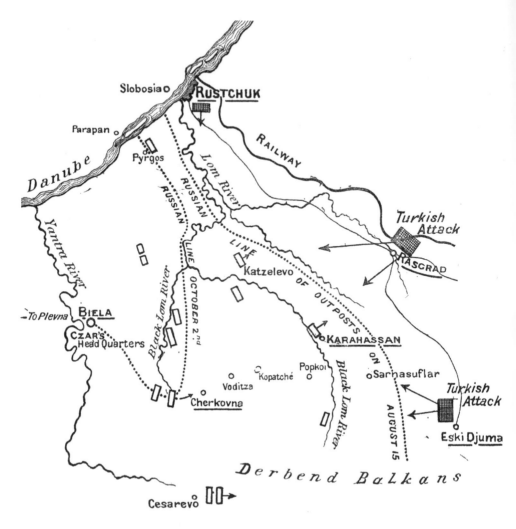

Map to illustrate
MEHEMET ALI'S ATTACK
on the
ARMY OF THE CZAREWITCH.

Turks...... ▨
Russians... ▭

Mehmed Ali's Lom offensive in August 1877. (*Map from Huysche, Wentworth,* The Liberation of Bulgaria: War Notes in 1877, *Bliss, Sands & Foster, London, 1894*)

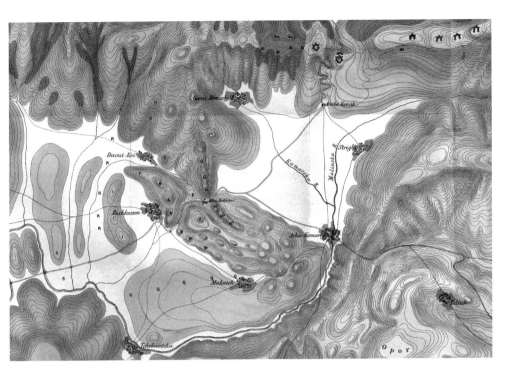

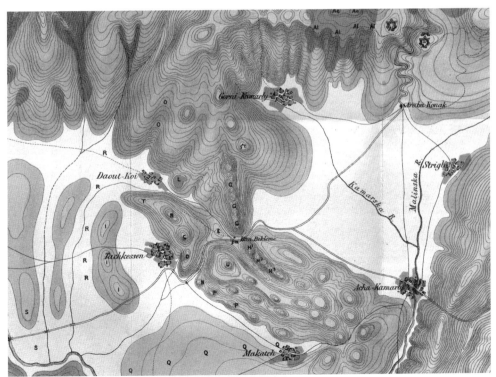

Geography near Tashkessen and the Kamarli line. Spelling discrepancies between the map and the text include Kokantia (Tchokantcha). The Kamarli line is denoted by the black star symbols located to the north-east. (*Map from Valentine Baker,* War in Bulgaria: A Narrative of Personal Experiences, *2 vols, Sampson Low, Marston, Searle & Rivington, London, 1879. Courtesy of the Combined Arms Research Library (CARL) of Fort Levenworth, Kansas*)

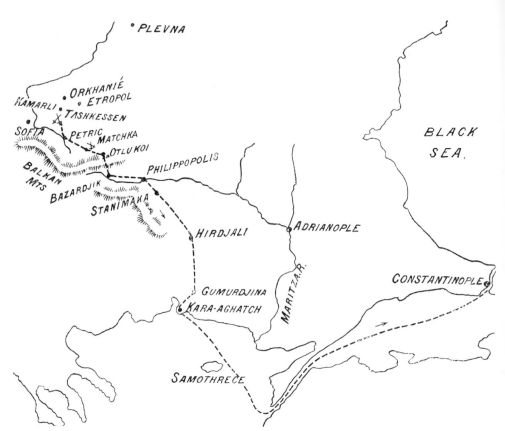

A sketch of the route of Süleyman's retreat following the Battle of Tashkessen. (*Map from Thomas Wright,* The Life of Colonel Fred Burnaby, *Everett & Co, London, 1908*)

Chapter 5

Ottoman Misfortunes

It was evident that the Tashkessen Pass must be held to the last.
Valentine Baker in *War in Bulgaria.*

Valentine Baker scheduled a prompt audience with the top officials of the Sublime Porte upon his arrival in the Ottoman capital. He implored them to act now and march to the relief of Plevna before it was too late. 'I urged that everything should give way to the relief of Osman,' he pleaded. He explained that the units stationed along the Lom River sat idle, bogged down by the incompetence of Süleyman. His pleas to the officials did not fall on deaf ears.

The Englishman received wonderful news. Ottoman officials had already begun preparations to organize a separate army for the sole purpose of relieving the Plevna defenders. The relief army was placed under the command of the reinstated Mehmed Ali, and had already begun its advance from the city of Sofia located to the west. From Sofia, the army would march north through the Araba Konak Pass and fall on Plevna. Had the Ottomans finally embraced the offensive vigour that Baker ardently urged all along?

On 27 November 1877, Baker departed Constantinople aboard a train headed for Tatar-Bazardjik – located 5 miles to the west of Philippopolis – to join Mehmed Ali in Sofia. Allix and Reilly remained as the only original members of Baker's staff. Allix brought an aged Frenchman named Charles who served as a horse artilleryman during the Crimean War and 'had seen better days'. He was joined by a new face, Charles George Baker, of the Imperial Ottoman gendarmerie – known as Baker, VC to distinguish him from his superior. Baker, VC was a shipwreck survivor and earned the Victoria Cross in 1858 during the Indian Mutiny as a lieutenant of the Bengal Police Battalion when he charged and routed 1,000 Indian mutineers with only sixty men.

The train's fi rst stopover from Constantinople was at the city of Adrianople, formerly the Ottoman capital until it was moved in 1453. A line of half-finished fortifications surrounded the strategically located city, while rolling plains ran for miles in each direction as far as the eye could see. The magnificent 296-step Mosque of Selim, completed in 1574, was located at the city's centre. Baker and his party spent the night in an American-owned hotel, described by a visitor to be 'the last place of decent entertainment' between the city and the Danube River.

Baker was ecstatic when he bumped into an unusual visitor at the railway station in Adrianople. A towering man wearing a civilian overcoat and bowler hat stepped off the train and on to the station's platform. It was Baker's pal from the Marlborough Club, Captain Fred Burnaby, accompanied by his familiar companion, George Radford, sporting his impressive Balaclava whiskers. The two adventurers exited the train with an air of self-confidence, but appeared out of place and befuddled. After an exchange of greetings, Burnaby revealed to Baker what brought the outsiders to Bulgaria.

Burnaby and Radford had a bold, but foolhardy, scheme. They intended to gain access in the Russian camp outside of Plevna in order to make a dash through no-man's-land to join in the defence. The three repulses Osman exacted against the Russians turned the Ottoman defenders into international celebrities. Fred Burnaby – the thrill seeker and the embodiment of a Victorian paladin – found the heroic aura radiating from the defence irresistible. He could not help but be drawn to the same promises of immorality Plevna would hold if it continued its resistance, comparable to the legacy that the martyrs of Lucknow already held.

Burnaby's plot, though romantic, was a candid plan at best. Baker later wrote: 'Even if, by a miracle, he was successful in penetrating them [the Russian entrenchments], he would, in all probability, be shot on his advance towards those of the Turks.' Burnaby did not normally back down from a challenge; instead he embraced adversity. Burnaby and Radford decided to accompany Baker at least to Sofia, where they would confer with Mehmed Ali before setting out on their audacious trek to Plevna.

The remainder of the journey from Tatar-Bazardjik to Sofia would have to be navigated by horse. Baker attempted to achieve comfort along his rugged travels down the ancient Roman road. He took with him two packhorses loaded with camp furniture – made up of a bedstead, a table, and a folding chair. This was just enough furniture to snugly fit into his small bell tent. He spent countless hours under candlelight at the small table issuing orders and chronicling his experiences of the war.

Baker discovered that Mehmed Ali's headquarters and his army were located further to the north upon his arrival to Sofia. Mehmed Ali's army was entrenched amongst the Balkan Mountains to foil a Russian attempt to force their way through the Araba Konak Pass. The Kamarli line consisted of six redoubts connected by entrenchments that extended east to west for 4 miles, erected on a wooded ridgeline to command the road that ran from Orkhanie (about 16 miles to the north) through the Araba Konak Pass. The highest redoubt rose at an elevation of 4,500 feet above sea level. A foggy mist regularly shrouded the ridgeline, hindering the line of sight for artillery crews and infantrymen.

Baker and his staff rode through the small Bulgarian village of Tashkessen on their way to the Kamarli line. Tashkessen in Turkish translates to 'the cut rock', named after a corridor cut in the rocky ridge located to the rear of the village. The ridge at the head of the pass sat at an elevation of roughly 1,000 feet, which then descended into the Kamarli plain. The village contained a conspicuous mosque, and only about fifty thatched-roof homes. Three prominent knolls speckled with timber ran in a straight line behind the village.

The party continued on from Tashkessen for another 4 miles until reaching Araba Konak, located at the foot of the Kamarli heights. From this point, they made an upward ascent running into Mehmed Ali's picket line. Baker located Mehmed Ali in redoubt No. 6, who 'in hope of encouraging his troops, was exposing himself immensely,' as Russian shells showered the road and the surrounding entrenchments. Baker and Mehmed Ali shook hands and congratulated one another at their reunion, but the celebration came to an abrupt end when a shell hit the corner of a parapet, throwing a pile of earth upon the heads of both officers and their amassed staffs.

It did not take long for Baker to comprehend that Mehmed Ali's army was 'quite inadequate' to undertake the relief of Plevna, or to even advance further than the Kamarli line. Most of his army was composed of ill-trained Mustahfiz battalions. This was the first time these raw recruits had handled a weapon in their lives, and most lacked exposure to any kind of formal military training. Many were reluctant to leave their families behind to serve in a war that the Ottomans appeared to be losing.

Mehmed Ali cultivated distaste for the hopeless position in which he felt he had been placed by the ministers in Constantinople. It would be impossible for him to make a major demonstration towards Plevna with his trifling army of 20,000, against a Russian army of no less than 30,000 detached from the siege of Plevna to hinder his advance. The opposing sides were momentarily content with entrenching, exchanging sporadic gunfire, and lobbing projectiles into each other's defensive positions to compensate for the dormancy. The defenders of Plevna would be left to fend for themselves.

Mehmed Ali agreed to meet with Burnaby to give his appraisal of the planned escapade to join the defenders of Plevna. In his now standard gloomy temperament, Mehmed Ali gave a blunt assessment of the plan, advising the odds of succeeding 'are more than a hundred to one against you'. He told Burnaby that his bold enterprise 'would be simply throwing away your life for no useful purpose.' Burnaby yielded to Mehmed Ali's counsel, and decided to attach himself to Baker's staff instead of undertaking the reckless feat.

Baker meanwhile busied himself with assisting Mehmed Ali in restructuring the amalgamation of Ottoman battalions holding the Kamarli line into a more efficient command. The 20,000 men of the army were divided and organized into three separate divisions, each composed of two brigades, and a dedicated reserve. The three divisions were respectively placed under the command of Shakir Pasha, Redjib Pasha, and Baker Pasha.

Baker was pleased with his colleagues in command of the two other divisions, dissimilar to his experience in Mehmed Ali's Lom army. Shakir 'spoke French very tolerably,' which allowed Baker to converse with him, while he also described him as 'an excellent scribe, and a man of great intelligence'. Despite his previous background serving in civil desk positions that led to a portly frame, he struck Baker as a man of 'very considerable military acquirements'. As for Redjib, Baker described him as an 'an active little man, of only about 34 years of age, of very pleasant and genial manners'. Redjib had recently been promoted after he had distinguished himself at one of Süleyman's futile assaults on Shipka Pass.

The bulk of the men under his command were another story. After a general inspection, Baker concluded that the majority of the soldiers were 'an encumbrance and a source of weakness'. Most of the battalions in his division were pitifully understrength. Major William G. Knox, a British officer acting as an observer, described these men as 'the last drain of the population'. Knox continued in further detail that the soldiers in the Kamarli line were, 'old, worn-out, small, ill-bred men', and that 'they could not be spoken of in the same breath as the men of Plevna or the men buried at the foot of Shipka.'

A few respectable battalions from the Bosnian and the Serbian frontiers complemented the untrained material in Baker's division. A Bosnian battalion from Touzla and a battalion organized in Uskub were intermixed with the rabble. The two battalions proved to be 'composed of admirable material', of which Baker could 'place implicit confidence'. He also assumed command of an Albanian battalion organized in Prizrend, which came from a regiment that forged a rare reputation earlier in the war for its fighting abilities.

These three efficient battalions were consolidated to create one resourceful regiment-sized formation. Baker placed them under the overall command of Islan Bey, whom he described as a 'fine old Turkish lieutenant colonel, who, by his energy and decision, had already won my confidence'. He also took on as his chief-of-staff a man by the name of Shakir Bey. Baker described Shakir Bey as 'a most intelligent officer of the Turkish Staff', and found him a favorable candidate for his staff, having been formerly a military attaché in Paris with extensive battlefield experience.

Life in the entrenchments felt comparable to standing in an ice chest by early December, and Baker's men suffered severely while positioned in the No. 6 and No. 7 redoubts. 'The cold was now so intense that one could not ride along the different positions without having one's face completely muffled up,' Baker remembered. A graduate of the University of Glasgow and volunteer English surgeon with the Ottoman forces at Kamarli, Richard Burns Macpherson remembered that 'the men were supplied with coarse grey cloaks and hoods, but their sandal-shod feet, and their bare hands, suffered greatly, a large number of the cases we were now receiving being frostbite of the hands and feet.' On average, forty men per night were found dead from hypothermia while stationed in the Kamarli line. Baker, VC, became so sick that he had to be evacuated to the village of Strigli, a mile from Araba Konak, and placed under the care of English surgeons.

Sentries were swapped by day and night by Allix and Baker, with the intention to ease their suffering and decrease losses due to exposure. Russian and Ottoman sentries stood only 20 yards apart at the closest point, and suffered equally from the cold and damp snow. Warm winter quarters for the Ottoman soldiers were constructed behind the line, insulated by tree branches and covered with turf. While on the front line away from the huts, the soldiers had little protection from the elements. Macpherson documented the unfortunate condition of the soldiers as they were transported to hospitals set up in the villages of the Kamarli plain, such as in Strigli:

> It was the long hours of duty in the trenches which did the mischief, frostbite and chest complaints disabling a large number of the men, about 100 coming down to our hospitals daily. So far reduced were many of these poor fellows that it was not uncommon to see mules walking into the village with lifeless frozen bodies on their backs, the short journey having been sufficient to extinguish the small spark of vitality remaining.

English and Ottoman surgeons set up provisional field hospital tents to serve those wounded in the daily firefights and bombardments on the front line. Many surgical operations were conducted under the dim light of a candle wedged into a bayonet socket, with the floors of the tents strewn with straw to soak up blood. Macpherson recalled the grim work he was tasked:

> Our work here was very disheartening, a large proportion of the cases being severe shell wounds, which were quite hopeless without operation, but such was the aversion of the soldiers to this that many would persistently refuse consent, though told there was no other chance for them.

Those men severely wounded were transported back to three large horse stables employed as hospitals in Tashkessen, until healthy enough to be transported to Sofia.

Baker formed a special bond with one of these altruistic volunteer English surgeons while serving on the front line. Dr John Gill, a transplanted surgeon from Great Britain, had left his practice in Shropshire to offer his services to the insufficient medical department of the Ottoman Empire. He was described in one account as of a most 'cheerful disposition' and 'always had a kindly word for the poor,' and in another version as 'cheerful, marvellously unselfish, and unremitting in his attention to all who suffered'. Gill earned the degrees of Membership of the Royal College of Surgeons (MRCS) in 1865 – winning a gold medal in clinical surgery the same year – and Licentiate of the Royal College of Physicians (LRCP) in 1866.

The selfless act of Gill tending to a wounded man while under fire caught the attention of Baker, and he afterwards persuaded him to join his staff. Gill carried a plethora of remedies in a large haversack that hung by a cord over his shoulder and wrapped around his back, which helped to keep Baker and his staff in the saddle on more than one occasion. Baker recalled: 'He seemed to carry with him – a magic bag, which could produce at any moment all that was required to relieve distress.' Baker exclaimed one day in a moment of sarcasm after being reduced to feasting on rock-hard biscuit rations, 'Now if we had even a few sardines, what a luxury they would be.' In response to this remark, Gill dug his arm deep into his haversack and pulled out a small tin box containing preserved sardines, which he presented to his commander.

The coolness displayed by Baker and his staff while under fire in the entrenchments endeared them to the common soldier. Macpherson described Baker as 'a great favourite with the soldiers' but revealed his unpretentious demeanor, remaining 'very reserved and quiet'. Captain Herbert Kitchener, while paying a visit to the Kamarli line, noted that 'an enthusiastic admirer of the Pasha [Baker]' pointed out the locations where he demonstrated his coolness under fire:

He pointed out a very warm place in one of the batteries where the Pasha had stopped for some time while the shells were coming thick about him: one lodged in the edge of the parapet, about 2 feet from the general, who never moved, but went on giving his directions.

In another instance, the Ottoman artillery officer pointed out another location vivid in his memory: 'Close by he showed me where a shell had burst over Colonel Alex's [Allix's] head, killing men right and left of him, but leaving him unscathed, smiling, as cool as ever.'

Macpherson recalled that 'no one was a greater favourite in camp' than the affable Fred Burnaby. One night, Burnaby retired early after not feeling well, and the next day woke reinvigorated. He declared to Macpherson's amusement when asked how he was feeling: 'Oh! All right, thanks. Took a Cockle's pill last night.' A few Cockle's antibilious pills appeared to remedy any aliment for Burnaby, who paid tribute to their miraculous effects on numerous occasions during his lifetime.

The forlorn position in which he had been placed, coupled with mounting pressure from Constantinople to advance to Plevna's relief, left Mehmed Ali fearful of dismissal. He had been ousted from command once before, and could not stand to bear the disgrace of it a second time for factors out of his control. He was stimulated by the thought that he might either be killed or wounded in the Kamarli line, absolving him of the dishonor of being dismissed. 'He certainly did his best at this time to accomplish the wish,' Baker explained, witnessing his commander 'thrust himself in every little attack of infantry.' A glorious death in battle was denied to Mehmed Ali, and instead he seemed to live 'a charmed life, and neither shells nor bullets appeared to have any effect upon him.'

Mehmed Ali's intuition was correct. He received a telegraph from Constantinople on 9 December 1877, in the same manner as two months before, relieving him of command and ordering his return to the capital, leaving Shakir in command. A popular presence among the men, his removal was camouflaged as a necessity to prepare for the defence of the capital. Mehmed Ali could be labelled as one of the most hapless figures of the war. Shortly after the conclusion of the war in September 1878, he was brutally murdered by Albania rebels while serving in an administrative role.

The army had dwindled down to 13,000 from the original 20,000 by the time of Mehmed Ali's departure. It experienced similar conditions to those suffered by George Washington's army at Valley Forge during the winter of 1777–78. According to Baker, the army of Shakir 'melted quickly away under the terrible stress which was imposed upon it,' hardly able to maintain the redoubts and the line of entrenchments due to effects of enemy bullets, famine, and sickness. The hillside was peppered with the hastily dug graves of soldiers killed in firefights and from artillery shells lobbed upon the sheltered defenders. Mismanagement of supplies from Sofia had become the norm, leaving the men 'ill-clad and ill-shod', and disease continued to wrack the army exposed to the harsh elements of the Bulgarian weather, not witnessed on this scale by Baker since the Crimean War.

Morale was at an all-time low during this period. Sentries were posted at the foot of the mountain with their bayonets fixed to deter desertion. In some instances, dispirited men opted to shoot their own fingers off, most commonly the forefinger of the right hand (the trigger finger). To further obliterate the morale within the army, the most dispiriting news of the war was received at Shakir's headquarters. Baker received an urgent telegraph from Shakir only intended for his eyes, printed in French:

> News has just reached us that Plevna has fallen. Osman Pacha [Pasha] and all the garrison are prisoners. Be good enough to mention this to no one, as it is important to maintain as much as possible the morale of the troops.

Monday, 10 December 1877 was the darkest day of the war for the Ottoman Empire. After 143 days of spirited resistance, Plevna capitulated. By mid-November, the 50,000 defenders were boxed into the village and the surrounding entrenchments by a combined army of over 100,000 Russians and Romanians complemented by hundreds of guns. Pressure from daily bombardments, a dwindling food supply, and irreplaceable casualties, left Osman with no other choice than to surrender or attempt to break out by early December. With no viable hope of Mehmed Ali's relief column reaching him, Osman decided to force a breakthrough rather than surrender.

Osman concentrated a large portion of his army to one sector of the Russian line in an attempt to overrun the defenders. The initial Ottoman surprise assault successfully penetrated the first line of the Russian entrenchments. They lost momentum, however, and stalled at the second line of entrenchments due to well-directed Russian artillery fire and fresh reinforcements from other sectors. The climax of the battle came when a bullet tore through Osman's leg, inflicting a serious wound. Rumour spread that he had been killed, and the determination that held the defenders together for months melted away.

The Russians counter-attacked from all sectors, and by midday, the defence collapsed, leaving Osman with no choice but to surrender. The Ottomans lost nearly 6,000 in the attempted breakout to the 1,300 Russian casualties. Over 40,000 hungry, sick and barefooted Ottoman soldiers remained as prisoners of war, but only 15,000 of this number would reach captivity in Russia due to a Bataan-like winter death march. With the fall of Plevna, the chances of success in the war became dubious for the Ottomans. Over 100,000 Russian and Romanian soldiers were freed from the siege, and able to renew the offensive towards Constantinople.

Plevna served as the last beacon of hope to stall the Russians from advancing any further into the Bulgarian interior. That optimism was crushed within the Ottoman armies. Word travelled rapidly of the surrender, and it only took two days for this heart-wrenching news to circulate throughout the Ottoman camp at the Kamarli line. The news had a debilitating effect.

Süleyman, entrusted as the commander-in-chief following the final battle of Plevna, had orders from Constantinople to constrain the Russians to the north of the Balkan Mountains. A considerable portion of his stagnant army stationed along the Lom River was transported to Sofia, where he set up his new headquarters, leaving the remainder of his men in the fortifications at Rushchuk and Shumla. He instinctively intended to secure the mountain passes of Shipka and Araba Konak against this coming onslaught with his isolated detachments now gathered around Sofia. He refused to abandon the traditional Ottoman tendency of scattering their armies to retain as much territory as possible despite the inadequate strategy.

Baker saw this as a mindless tactic to protect territory essentially already lost. He had his own plan of how to defend against the renewed Russian offensive. He felt it would be best for the scattered Ottoman armies to concentrate on Adrianople, where they could utilize the fortifications of the city and make a Plevna-styled stand as a unified army, rather than as segmented subdivisions. Extending their supply lines over the mountains for hundreds of miles, and facing the prospect of another prolonged siege, the Russians would have no choice but to negotiate a peace. Shakir approved this proposal when Baker presented it to him, and relayed the details to Süleyman, which came to no avail, to no one's surprise.

Russian military success hinged on a rapid thrust to the gates of Constantinople to bring a quick conclusion to the war. The Russian high command was divided about whether it would even be feasible to undertake a campaign during a fierce Bulgarian winter. The more conservative Russian generals argued in favor of waiting until the snow melted and the roads dried before continuing their southern offensive. Bolder and more aggressive officers, such as Gourko and Skobelev, felt they should follow up with their success at Plevna while the Ottomans were in disarray, and finish the task at hand. The more aggressive faction feared that a prolonged war would allow time for the British to consider military intervention, and also allow the Ottomans time to recuperate from their setbacks and blunders.

A number of daunting obstacles made such an operation on this scale a frightening thought for even the most iron-willed of officers. Russian supply lines would be strung out for hundreds of miles down battered Bulgarian roads and through the mountain passes, forcing officers to rely on meagre rations and forage in enemy territory to feed their soldiers. No sufficient railway line extended through the mountains, and the advancing armies would encounter none until they reached Adrianople or Tatar-Bazardjik, producing a logistical nightmare. A Bulgarian winter presented conditions that an army would plunge into and never reappear: treacherous plummets in temperature to below freezing; deep snow and ice mounded at 10 feet high at times, blocking the only available mountain passes and roads; and thick Danube fogs that shrouded the visibility of any man or beast trapped under its veil. Tsar Alexander supported the bolder factor despite these obstacles; sensing the end in sight, he intended to bring the war to a swift conclusion.

Russian soldiers released from the fall of Plevna would be redirected to reinforce both armies facing the major mountain passes of Shipka and Araba Konak on the path to Constantinople. A portion of the reinforcements would move south and reinforce General Joseph Gourko's 30,000 assembled in the vicinity of Orkhanie facing the Kamarli line, while other reinforcements would join General Fyodor Radetzky at Shipka Pass. The reinforced Radetzky – with seventy-four battalions of 56,000 men, 2,000 cavalrymen, and 252 guns – had orders to push forwards and crush the

Ottoman army facing him at Shipka Pass, while Gourko – with eighty-four battalions of 65,000 infantry, 6,000 cavalrymen, and 280 guns – would force his way through the Araba Konak Pass, capture Sofia, and move down the ancient Roman road towards Philippopolis. Together, the united wings, over 100,000, would march upon Adrianople, while the Grand Duke Alexander Alexandrovich remained behind with 54,500 men to guard the Quadrilateral fortresses.

Gourko drafted a bold plan to defeat Shakir's army and capture Sofia. With Shakir's army occupied along the Kamarli line by a comparable Russian force to its front, Gourko planned to cross with a strong column over the mountains located further west, outflanking Shakir's men and exiting through a small corridor near the village of Tchuriak. Gourko's columns would then make a 2,000-foot descent on to the Sofia plain, and move down the Sofia road to strike the flank and rear of Shakir's army firmly locked in the Kamarli entrenchments. Once he had crushed Shakir's army, Gourko could then move on and capture Sofia and its garrison of 10,000 men, rumoured to be stockpiled with an abundance of provisions. Once he was finished with the Ottoman armies in the west, he would turn east, and continue his drive towards Adrianople to unite with Radetzky's army.

On 24 December 1877, Baker urged Shakir to allow him to take a small detachment and make a reconnaissance to divulge any Russian efforts to outflank the Kamarli line. Shakir consented, and Baker took a squadron of cavalry in the direction of the village of Tchuriak. When he arrived with the small patrol, he could clearly observe a regiment of Cossack cavalry and the men of the Preobrazhensky Regiment of the Imperial Guard already stirring in the village as advance units of Gourko's flanking columns. On his journey to Shakir's headquarters from the Tchuriak valley, Baker and his reconnaissance party moved down the Sofia road through the Tashkessen Pass, and arrived back by nightfall. He hurried back to report to Shakir that a Russian effort was taking place on his extreme left flank.

Baker pleaded that a detachment should be sent to protect their flank at Tashkessen Pass before 'a storm would burst upon us.' Shakir reasoned that he could barely fill the Kamarli line with his skeleton units, and was too weak to even detach a small portion of his men. Lieutenant General Baron Krüdener's units still faced Shakir, made up roughly half of Gourko's army, composed of thirty-four battalions and ninety-five guns under detachments commanded by Lieutenant General Schilder-Schuldner, Count Schouvaloff, Prince Oldenberg, and Major General Bock. If Krüdener made a significant attempt to press their front, the whole Ottoman line would likely cave in.

On Christmas Day 1877, Baker, his staff, the English doctors from Strigli, and foreign military attachés in the vicinity of the Kamarli line, set aside time despite the worrying circumstances to celebrate the birth of Christ. The makeshift Christmas dinner celebration took place under the supervision of George Radford in the village of Strigli. One of the men retrieved three fowls, two small sheep, and a pig, all at the cost of about twelve shillings, for the dinner meal. To compensate for the absence of a dessert, Radford concocted a plum pudding made up of ambiguous ingredients.

The same day as the Englishmen sat down to their crude Christmas dinner, a general advance of Gourko's detachment began under a thick black fog, vindicating Baker's fears. Gourko's flanking column – composed of three separate detachments, under the command of Generals Rauch, Kataley, and Kourloff, with Gourko in the vanguard – made last-minute preparations to funnel through the treacherous mountain defiles to the left of Shakir's army. One column, under Lieutenant General Wilhelminoff, was tasked with shielding the right flank of Gourko's three detached columns from a surprise Ottoman assault. Another column, under the command of Major General Dandeville, moved to outflank the right flank of Shakir's army by advancing into the Kamarli plain.

Known as 'little Papa' to his men, General Joseph Gourko had risen from a lowly Hussar ensign to an army commander through his thirty years of military service. Never afraid to share in the hardships of his men, Vasily Vereshchagin, painter and war correspondent accompanying the Russians, noted that 'His troops stood in some awe of him.' He described him as 'a good fellow, and a great favourite in the army', but it must be admitted that he was 'a bit of a martinet'. Notorious for his fierce temper, Vereshchagin remembered that 'everyone knew that there were moments when it was prudent to keep out of "Papa's" way.' Archibald Forbes, British war correspondent of the *Daily News*, came to admire Gourko, whom he respected for his resolve and reckless abandon for his own welfare:

As he rode in front of the cortège, that iron man was visible to us in strictly correct military attire — the dark-coloured frogged surtout, which an officer told me was the undress uniform of the Guard Cavalry, buckskin gloves and cavalry boots. He rode along apparently unconscious that the hoar frost was whitening his beard and covering him and his horse with frozen crystals. I wondered beyond measure that the cruel cold did not strike him to the bone. But he did not seem to feel it in the least.

The abovementioned depiction of Gourko showcased the fortitude essential for the commander of this bold flanking manoeuvre. The distance between Orkhanie and the Sofia plain was not more than 20 miles – but this was mid-winter in Bulgaria, unveiling the harshest conditions in the world. The temperature would unexpectedly plunge to 15 degrees below zero, which 'seemed to freeze one's very vitals,' and hours of blinding snowfall made travel perilous. Forbes recorded that it was so cold in one instance that, 'My teeth were chattering already and I could not have written my name, so numbed and dead were my fingers, if the simple signature would have made me a millionaire.'

Blended with men, guns, and supply mules, Gourko's columns inched forwards single file through the icy defiles of the snow-capped mountains. These pathways cut into the mountainside served as the only highways, and officers, bundled in heavy overcoats, pleaded with their men to continue onwards through the blizzard conditions. At night, men huddled together around small fires for a brief respite of warmth, and slept in clusters inside craters scooped out of the snowdrifts. Many men never woke again, freezing to death during the night, while others were left frostbitten and exhausted from exposure to the extreme cold. British war historian Henry Montague Hozier claimed Gourko's crossing was 'one of the most marvellous feats of human energy, and deserves to rank with the crossing of the Alps by Hannibal and Napoleon.'

Gourko's trek was a colossal risk, but it had fruitful rewards. The Ottoman high command, with Süleyman as the forerunner, imprudently viewed such a crossing as an impossible enterprise during the winter months. When Gourko's columns miraculously appeared descending on the Sofia plain after three days, the Ottomans were caught completely off guard. The entrance leading to the Sofia plain at the village of Tchuriak had been left virtually unguarded.

Gourko proclaimed upon peering across the horizon of the Sofia plain, 'Now we can say, in all conscience, that we have crossed the Balkans, in every phrase of the undertaking,' and turned to shake hands and congratulate his entourage of surrounding staff officers. Gourko then called for his orderly, who retrieved a small tin box from his horse's saddlebag. The richly ornate box had the appearance of a container that would be used to store some kind of Orthodox icon. Gourko removed three small nuggets of chocolate. He gave a piece each to General Rauch, General Maglovsky, and the Prussian military attaché, Major Liegnitz, who all joined in his celebration of the successful enterprise.

Gourko's chief of staff, General Maglovsky, allegedly remarked upon gazing down on the Sofia plain, 'We may make another Sedan of the business!' He was making reference to the Prussian pincer movement at the Battle of Sedan in September 1870, which led to the encirclement and decisive defeat of a French army. Most of the Russian soldiers that caught sight of the oval-shaped Sofia plain perhaps viewed it as an oasis, for it signified the end of one major obstacle and the start of a new one. Gourko had successfully placed his three columns between Süleyman's headquarters in Sofia, and the rear of Shakir's army protecting the Araba Konak Pass. He was in an excellent position to isolate and destroy each army in detail.

The opportunity to encircle a whole army was too alluring for Gourko, and he chose to close in first on Shakir. Gourko was self-assured that he could easily sweep down on the rear of Shakir's army moving down the Sofia road through the pass at Tashkessen, destroying him before turning to the south-west on the prized city of Sofia. The destruction of Shakir's army and the capture of the garrison at Sofia would virtually eliminate all opposition before Adrianople. This confidence was validated once Gourko entered the Sofia plain, as he made no attempt to conceal his movements.

The telegraph communication between Shakir and Süleyman in Sofia was severed by Cossack raiding parties. It would be a matter of hours before Gourko's three columns fell on the rear of the Kamarli line, as the Sofia plain was only about 10 miles in length. Shakir, at first, was reluctant to send Baker to delay this advance without direct orders from Süleyman. Shakir relented, with his communication cut and scouts confirming Gourko's movement, and allowed Baker to take a small detachment to Tashkessen to confront this threat. He opted to remain in the Kamarli line with the remainder of his army to hold Krüdener's units at bay.

Shakir was unwilling to part with his best battalions, although they would be necessary to delay Gourko. He initially selected the six worst Mustahfiz battalions of his army to accompany Baker to Tashkessen. Baker was furious, and he reiterated to Shakir that he would not be held responsible for any disaster that would befall the column due to Shakir's restraint. Baker felt entitled to at least take with him the three resourceful battalions of his command over these useless battalions. Shakir yielded, and with these dependable battalions Baker promised to hold the Tashkessen Pass to 'the last extremity'.

The Uskub (350 men), Prizrend (580 men), and Touzla (450 men) battalions were made ready to march out that night sometime after 9.00 pm. The three battalions left their tents standing in order to cloak their departure to the Russians, which would cause them much suffering in the succeeding days. The Edirne battalion, known for its 'very bad fighting reputation', being made up of Mustahfiz troops, arrived to accompany the battalions to Tashkessen. Baker, wanting to rid himself of these poor soldiers, ordered it to stay behind. Baker also took two field guns and two mountain guns stationed at Araba Konak.

A few observers sensing a grand contest attached themselves to Baker's column. Captain Fife-Cookson, the military attaché of Great Britain temporarily staying in Strigli, joined Baker as an observer. The 55-year-old author, angling expert, and correspondent of *The Times*, Francis Francis (yes, the same first and last name) also joined Baker. When the column was ready to march out, it moved off silently into the darkness down the Sofia road towards the village of Tashkessen.

The column marched about 4 miles under the winter's moonlight towards the village. Along the road, they were confronted by fleeing administrative and medical officials frantically avowing that the village had been already occupied by the Russians. If this was the case, the column could at least occupy the rocky ridge overlooking the village near the head of the pass.

Continuing further down the Sofia road, a British observer, Captain Thackeray – who had been staying with the English surgeons at Tashkessen – rode out to inform Baker that neither the rocky ridge nor the village had been occupied. To his relief, Baker evoked that, 'It was a case of life and death for the whole army as to whether that crest was lost.'

The Ottoman infantrymen came upon a two-story mustard-coloured *han*, or hotel, upon their arrival to the rocky ridge. This strongly built stone building, peppered with many windows, would be, in Baker's words, 'well adapted for defence'. Baker concluded that if he lost the village, the elevated ridge would provide a superb location to delay the Russian advance. The last desperate hours of the battle would take place here.

The column continued downhill to the sleepy village. The descent down the Sofia road was so slick from ice that the Ottoman infantrymen struggled to stand upright without falling, while the officers had to dismount and lead their horses. Francis described the scene as he accompanied the column through the night: 'It was bitterly cold, and a driving wind bore with it clouds of frozen snow. There had been a slight thaw during the day, succeeded by a sharp frost; consequently the sheep tracks and road were like glass.' Hundreds of Russian camp fires flickered in the distant countryside visible throughout the Sofia plain. Baker estimated by the number of Russian camp fires that he would soon be opposing nearly 20,000 men with his less than 2,000 men.

Baker knew that the Tashkessen Pass must be secured if Shakir's army were to survive nightfall, and began to make preparations to defend it. A road branched off from the Sofia road to the right at the village leading towards the village of Daoudkoi. The Touzla battalion was positioned on this fork in the road. The Uskub and Prizrend battalions encamped in the village square of Tashkessen. Baker's column was joined by three squadrons of Arab cavalry on reconnaissance in the region that acted as a screen to the Russian advance. With his troops in position, Baker decided to ride back to Shakir's headquarters to make a report of the cataclysmic situation in person.

Baker was exhausted, dreading the fact he would have to make a second journey through the bone-chilling weather and back up the treacherous path he had already travelled. But he understood the importance of emphasizing to Shakir the strategic significance this village would play in determining the fate of his army. 'The prospect of a night journey was not cheering, yet, so urgent did I consider the importance of a personal interview, that I determined to accomplish it,' he afterward declared.

He started back uphill in an ambulance wagon, leased by the English doctors tending to the wounded in the village. The wagon jerked and jolted as it progressed down the road as Baker dozed off. The wagon halted at Araba Konak, and the remainder of the uphill journey had to be made by horse and on foot. 'Our horse slipped at every step, constantly sliding off the pathway, and rolling over with us,' Baker remembered as he made the precarious uphill ascent. Despite these struggles, he continued on: 'Battered and bruised, it seemed as if we should never reach the headquarters, yet time was all important, and we pressed on.'

He arrived at Shakir's quarters two hours after departing Tashkessen and burst through the doorway. He roused Shakir, and explained to the dreary listener that roughly 20,000 Russians were on his exposed left flank, and were within a few hours' march of the Kamarli line. Shakir explained that he had not heard from Süleyman since his last order to remain in his current position, but Baker reminded him that it was his foremost duty to look after the welfare of his army. Shakir gave his word that if he had not received word from Süleyman by the morning, he would begin an orderly withdrawal towards the village of Acha Kamarli, located in the Kamarli plain, and would send support to Baker at Tashkessen. Baker was content with the lukewarm pledge, arranged for a telegraph line to be opened up with Shakir's headquarters, and headed back to join his men.

Baker led his horse back down to Araba Konak, and hopped into the ambulance wagon as it patiently waited for his return. Along the return journey, one of the horses attached to the wagon slipped and fell to the ground, and the wagon began to slide out of control towards a precipice, with its terrified human cargo loaded in the back. The frantic horse dug its hooves into the ice and snow, halting the sliding wagon within 3 inches of tumbling over the precipice. Baker, unnerved and fatigued, returned back to Tashkessen an hour before daybreak. He had no time to rest, and began his last-minute defensive preparations before a Russian advance at first light.

Chapter 6

Baker's Spartan Stand at Tashkessen

To have witnessed the battle of Tash-Kessan is one of the proudest recollections of my life, and one that I never recall without some glow of the old enthusiasm that animated us on that day recurring to me.

Francis Francis of *The Times,* in his book
War, Waves, and Wanderings, a Cruise in the Lancashire Witch.

28 December 1877: The First Encounter

The defensive arrangement made on the three knolls by Baker was a daunting obstacle. The Touzla battalion and the two mountain guns occupied the rocky knoll to the right of the village (B), the Uskub battalion the centre knoll (C), and the Prizrend battalion the left knoll (D). The Prizrend and Uskub battalions busied themselves by burrowing into the frozen ground with their shovels and pickaxes to build a line of entrenchments. The Touzla battalion was unable to excavate due to protruding rocky boulders projecting from the ground, so instead they piled fragmented stones chest high for protection.

The three squadrons of Arab cavalry gathered on a range of low hills a mile in front of Tashkessen to monitor the Russian advance (I). The two field guns unlimbered on a little hill to the left of the Sofia road (N). The well-built road would allow the guns to move quickly to redeploy or withdraw if needed. The Edirne battalion (300 men), whom Baker had left behind at the Kamarli line, was sent by Shakir as his first promised reinforcements and arrived at the front. After a few cursing words, he placed the Edirne battalion on the centre knoll in reserve, where it could do the least damage.

An hour after sunrise on 28 December 1877, Baker peered through his field glasses and observed four densely packed Russian infantry squares streaming over the hills in the distance headed in his direction. Clusters of mounted Cossacks fanned out to protect the flanks of the squares. The forest green Russian uniforms and grey greatcoats radiated off the white slopes, inspiring Baker to comment that 'it was impossible to imagine a more beautiful scene of war.' As the snake-like column of squares drew nearer to his main position, Baker calculated it to be made up of sixteen Imperial Guard battalions, identified by their distinct *furashka* caps. The four squares were headed in the direction of the village of Daoudkoi, but the men on the three knolls diverted their attention.

Baker intended to conceal his true strength to the advancing Russian squares. He ordered his two mountain guns to unleash a salvo upon the advancing Cossack patrols at the extreme range of 5,550 yards, and ordered the two field guns to do the same when within range. He hoped this liberal use of artillery fire would give the impression that his position was held by a plethora of guns; a force stockpiled with surplus ammunition, and a large quantity of guns, would only be bold enough to encourage fire at such an extreme range. He ordered clusters of soldiers to ostentatiously march back and forth to create the deception that he was receiving a continuous flow of reinforcements – similar to Confederate General John B. Magruder's tactics during the Siege of Yorktown in 1862. This scheme had the desired effect, as Russian accounts later inflated his strength to 5,000 men and ten guns.

The catastrophic volume of Russian casualties suffered around Plevna earlier in the war left some Russian officers too timid to launch frontal assaults near the end of December 1877. Thousands of lives had been thoughtlessly thrown away against well-entrenched positions to no avail. Gourko was one of these officers that had learned firsthand the costly lesson of relying too heavily on Russian bayonet-driven shock tactics, having been reprimanded for squandering the lives of the 100 officers and 3,200 men of the Imperial Guard at the Battle of Gorni Dubnik on 21 October 1877. Tsar Alexander delivered a humiliating rebuke on him for directing this gory battle, which nearly cost Gourko his command. He would not make the same mistake.

Some officers chose to adopt a more practical doctrine of rapid flanking movements to substitute for traditional frontal assaults. Gourko had already utilized this doctrine successfully by brilliantly bypassing the strong Ottoman defensive position at the Kamarli line, outmanoeuvring them instead of assaulting their well-entrenched position head-on. He chose to implement the same strategy when faced with his strongly entrenched enemy at Tashkessen. The four Russian squares that appeared on Baker's front on 28 December 1877 chose to halt in response to his projected strength. They instead proceeded towards high ground 6,000 yards to the front of the knolls and began to entrench and await the arrival of reinforcements from Tchuriak.

The only action came from a lone Cossack patrol sent on a reconnaissance mission into the village of Daoudkoi. Baker ordered a single detached company from the Touzla battalion to drive the assailants out of the deserted Bulgarian village, which they accomplished with ease. He then ordered the company to return to the right knoll, as he could ill afford to jeopardize the company becoming isolated from his main position. His strength depended on his ability to keep his command draw together. The company returned to camp with a few head of cattle from the village, butchered them, and distributed the meat among Baker's hungry men.

Preparations were made to remove the Ottoman sick and wounded from the village of Tashkessen under the care of the volunteer surgeons. The majority of the surgeons accompanied the wagons filled with the wounded southwards, but a few devoted individuals of the Red Cross and Red Crescent Societies remained behind with those men too seriously wounded to be removed. Baker sent a squadron of his Arab cavalry to cover the withdrawal of the encumbered ambulance wagons until they reached the safety of the village of Ichtiman, roughly 30 miles to the south. The evacuation proved to be a practical decision since a significant portion of the village would be demolished from artillery fire in the forthcoming battle.

Late afternoon, much needed reinforcements arrived from the Kamarli line. The first battalion to arrive, the El Bassan battalion (320 men), was made up of reliable Albanian Redif soldiers. On the contrary, the Eski Cheir battalion (220 men) was made up of inexperienced and untrained Mustahfiz soldiers. Baker loathed this battalion, stating they were 'miserable recruits that could not be trusted'. Three field guns also arrived to bolster his artillery firepower.

Baker integrated the reinforcements into his current defensive position. The El Bassan battalion moved into the village of Tashkessen, located to the front of the centre knoll. The battalion whittled out loopholes in the outer walls of the village's buildings with their bayonets to provide an opening to fire. The Eski Cheir battalion joined the two field guns on the small hill to the left of the Sofia road, where they would have a commanding field of fire to cover any approaches that came down the road.

Baker feared the Russians would try to occupy the right rocky knoll and overwhelm the Touzla battalion in a surprise night attack. He chose to provide more artillery support by bringing up a field gun to the position. Moving the field gun up the steep knoll covered in an almost bottomless layer of snow and peppered with boulders was a daunting task. With the help of two devoted companies of the Touzla to drag it uphill, the field gun was into position before nightfall.

Baker and his staff occupied a deserted house in the village to get a few hours of sleep. The accommodations in the home were primeval at best. Baker crammed into a single room with three of the closest members of his staff: Allix, Burnaby, and Shakir Bey. Reilly and Radford lay on the hardwood floor at the doorway. A heavy snow fell upon the Ottoman entrenchments that night, layering the soldiers bundled up in their overcoats and huddled together for warmth having left their tents behind at the Kamarli line.

29 December 1877: Winter Veil

Extreme snowstorms and unexpected drops in temperature played a significant role in hindering military operations in December 1877. On 29 December, a sudden and fierce snowstorm generated a grey veil between the opposing units at Tashkessen. The blizzard produced such a darkening effect that it made it tough to see more than 300 yards in the distance. Movement on a large scale was nearly impossible, eliminating any possibility for the Russians to launch a full-scale attack on Baker's position. Baker nonetheless ordered his officers and men to remain on the lookout as best they could.

The Russians could ill afford every moment wasted in front of Tashkessen. Fred Burnaby appreciated the importance of the delay, afterwards writing, 'Every moment gained was so much time lost to the enemy.' Baker grew stronger with each passing day as a slow stream of reinforcements arrived from Shakir and the Russians hesitated to dislodge him from the three knolls. Gourko's ability to quickly envelope Shakir's army would never come to fruition as long as Baker's units remained wedged in front of the Tashkessen Pass.

Despite the delay initiated thus far and the imposing Ottoman position, the prospect of success appeared grim for Baker and his units. Gourko possessed three distinct advantages when his vanguard began to arrive at Tashkessen: numerical superiority, superior troop quality, and a technological edge. The Russian units at Tashkessen were receiving a continuous stream of reinforcements over the subsequent days, and would soon outnumber the Ottoman defenders nearly eight to one. The well-trained and well-disciplined Russian Imperial Guard battalions that made up the majority of Gourko's units at Tashkessen were armed with superior-ranged Berdan I and II rifles, described by Baker as 'far better than the Schneider [Snider]'. Only about half of the Ottoman soldiers at Tashkessen were armed with the Peabody-Martini rifle, while the battalions that Baker relied on most – the Touzla, Uskub, and Prizrend battalions – were all armed with surplus .577 Snider-Enfield rifles.

Despite these clear Russian advantages, the Ottoman units held some significant gains at Tashkessen. Baker was facing an overconfident foe that was self-assured of victory, which leads to carelessness in battle. The relentless march through the Balkan Mountains combating subzero temperatures, frostbite, sleep deprivation, and the hazardous terrain left most of the Russian soldiers drained when they arrived at Tashkessen. Baker handpicked the field of battle for his rearguard operation, and oversaw the construction of strong defensive arrangements that made his position a formidable obstacle. The defenders were well aware of the significance that their stand at Tashkessen would play in saving Shakir's army.

The likelihood of an Ottoman success in the wake of Gourko's advance had mixed reviews among the foreign observers. Captain Fife-Cookson considered the defence of the Kamarli line and Tashkessen as hopeless endeavors. He had orders from the British government to avoid being captured, which would be viewed as an international embarrassment to Great Britain: he detached himself before the fighting commenced while there was still a road open. On the contrary, Francis of *The Times* decided to remain with Baker despite the threats of annihilation, and may have been mindful that he had the opportunity to chronicle a gallant story for British readers. Captain Thackeray, having met Baker earlier as he advanced towards the village, also chose to remain, despite the fearful odds.

Reports came into camp that 300 Circassian cavalrymen were in the vicinity of the village of Makatch, located on the extreme left flank of the Ottoman position. Baker sent a dispatch rider in that direction through the snowstorm, in the hope that the irregular horsemen could at least assist him in some capacity during the upcoming battle. An eccentric looking Circassian colonel arrived soon after to camp, trailing the dispatch rider. The colonel proudly swore to Baker that his command would help in any way possible, and would challenge all Russian efforts to outflank Baker's position to the left.

Something about the Circassian colonel left Baker uneasy. He had dealt with plenty of swindlers and deceivers though his life to know when he was confronted with one. The Circassian colonel returned to his command and led them out on patrol. As Baker feared, the colonel and his cavalrymen were never heard from again. Under the colonel's direct orders, the 300 cavalrymen headed south, as far away from the action as possible.

A telegraph from Shakir's headquarters arrived that morning, asserting that he was sending more reinforcements to Tashkessen despite the menacing weather conditions. Baker, though content to receive any support, was aggravated when the reinforcements appeared in the Ottoman camp that afternoon. The Tchengueri battalion (320 men) was viewed by Baker to be at best 'indifferent' as soldiery material. He placed the battalion on a hill in the rear of his position that connected the three knolls to the rocky ridge at the head of the Tashkessen Pass (E). The hill was wedged between the Sofia road and the road that ran into the village of Daoudkoi.

Late that afternoon, the winter blizzard began to subside and Baker got a quick glimpse of the Russian position before darkness fell over the open plains and hilltops. He observed thousands of infantrymen to his front relentlessly entrenching, an indication that a continuous flow of Russian soldiers had been funnelling towards Tashkessen since the previous day. Baker had managed to delay his foe for two whole days, reducing their probability of a quick victory, but his achievement would be hopeless unless Shakir proceeded to withdraw from his exposed position towards Acha Kamarli. Baker sent a stern telegraph warning Shakir of the mounting size of the

Russian force in his front, and to pressure him to begin the preparations to withdraw from the Kamarli line before it was too late.

30 December 1877: Final Preparations

During the morning hours of 30 December 1877, the Russians continued to bolster and lengthen their exterior lines around Baker's position. At 11.00 am, a botched Russian order threatened to overrun the village of Tashkessen. A large detachment of Russian cavalry appeared in a single column on the Sofia road and proceeded to move forwards towards the village at a slow trot. Awaiting them was the El Bassan battalion, shielded in the village's buildings. Baker prepared his artillery to meet this bold, but careless manoeuvre.

Orders sent to the Ottoman artillery crews directed them to hold fire until the exposed cavalrymen were within the close proximity of 1,800 yards. As the horsemen drew closer to the village, the Ottoman guns thundered. Their raking fire was concentrated on the centre of the Russian column, tightly packed in a double line. The rapid burst of fire caught the cavalrymen unprepared and cut gaping holes in their ranks, sending them in frenzied retreat to the rear.

The three squadrons of Arab cavalry were lying in wait behind the large hill located to the front of the village. As soon as the Russian cavalrymen began to break in panic, the Ottoman cavalrymen let out an enormous cheer, and plunged forwards in pursuit. Baker's infantrymen on the surrounding hills could clearly observe the three little squadrons chasing after the much larger Russian foe. The Ottoman defenders on the three knolls cheered them on. The act – though possessing little tactical value – had a morally uplifting effect on the whole command, helping to temporarily alleviate the reminder of the task ahead.

Baker worried that Russian scouts would soon discover an alternative route around his well-defended position. On his extreme left flank, an undetected road existed that branched off from the village of Kokantia towards the village of Makatch, and then skirted around the Tashkessen Pass through a mountain gorge that led to the Kamarli plain. If Russian patrols discovered and took this route, it would render Baker's current position untenable. It would put the Russians in the rear of Baker's position, initiating a nineteenth-century Cannae – stalling Baker's front while the Russian cavalry moved in a sweeping movement around his flank and in his rear. It would also allow the Russians to completely cut off Shakir's line of retreat at the village of Acha Kamarli.

His fear became a reality when a detachment of Cossacks moved into the village of Kokantia. Bulgarian civilians came from the sanctuary of their homes and pointed out to an inquisitive Russian officer the road leading in the direction of the village of Makatch. Baker dreaded that 'if this cavalry officer were moderately intelligent, he would push on a party to explore this road through the hills.' He knew that he must disrupt the reconnaissance mission or all would be lost, and detached four companies of the Prizrend battalion down from the left knoll to deter any approach made towards Makatch. The Russian patrol immediately bolted when they saw the approach of the four companies, not intending to initiate a general engagement.

Baker sent another hasty telegraph to Shakir, urging him to provide his verdict for evacuating the Kamarli line in response to these recent occurrences. He gave the estimate that nearly 50,000 Russians had already crossed over the mountains on to the Sofia plain, and was faced by about half that number. Soon after, Baker received a reply from Shakir confirming his intention to inaugurate the withdrawal to Acha Kamarli. Gossip that Süleyman was cut off and the garrison at Sofia was under siege helped to spur Shakir to this decision.

Shakir requested Baker to hold at least for another day if possible. If able, he would initiate the withdrawal that night. It would be necessary for Shakir to first withdraw all of his slow-moving guns and provisions towards Acha Kamarli, making sure the roads were cleared before his infantrymen could begin to vacate their entrenchments. The Ottoman infantrymen would be withdrawn the following night.

The withdrawal would have to be conducted with delicate precaution during the evening hours to conceal the movement from the Russian sentries. At the closest point, the sentries of Lieutenant General Krüdener's units stood only 20 yards from the Ottoman sentries, and the disputed territory between the Kamarli line and the Russian entrenchments stood only 400 yards in width. If the sentries were alerted, it would jeopardize an all-out assault from Krüdener in an attempt to disrupt Shakir's retreat. Shakir deployed a detachment of the brigade of Mehmed Zekki Pasha, first to Acha Kamarli to cover the passage to the village for the remainder of his army. Baker was ordered to disengage the Russians and join the main column once all of Shakir's units had been safely withdrawn to Acha Kamarli.

That night, the last of the Ottoman reinforcements arrived at Tashkessen. They arrived in the form of the crack Chasseur battalion (250 men), all armed with modern Peabody-Martini rifles. This undersized battalion, under the command of the reliable Hadji Mehmed, was made up of light infantrymen trained for rapid manoeuvres on the battlefield. The battalion was the most reliable of all of the reinforcements, and would play a vital role in the upcoming battle. The arrival of the Chasseur battalion brought the Tashkessen force to a grand total of 2,790 infantrymen, 180 Arab cavalrymen, five field guns, and two mountain guns, on the eve of 30 December 1877.

Final preparations were made to meet the anticipated Russian assault the next day. The Touzla battalion and one field gun were reinforced by the Uskub battalion and two mountain guns on the right knoll, placed under the overall command of Islan Bey, a 'fine old Turkish lieutenant colonel', as described by Baker. He placed much faith in Islan for his energy and judgment. Baker and his faithful staff occupied the centre knoll alongside the unreliable Edirne battalion. Four companies of the Prizrend battalion (half), placed under the command of Hadji Mehmed of the Chasseur battalion, remained on the left knoll.

The other four companies of the Prizrend battalion (half) and the crack Chasseur battalion acted as a reserve to plug any breaches in the line or counter any outflanking movements. The Eski Cheir battalion remained on the small hill to the left of the Sofia road, with the four field guns adjacent to it. The El Bassan battalion remained in the village of Tashkessen in front of the main position. Packhorses loaded with reserve ammunition were placed near the Sofia road on the reverse side of the knolls to easily distribute ammunition to the men to the right or left flanks. Nothing was left unprepared.

Baker knew he would only be able to hold his current position for a short time against the mounting Russian strength and an outflanking effort, so he devised an exit strategy. The current position of his battalions was intended to be his 'false position'. The rocky ridge near the entrance of the

Tashkessen Pass was about half a mile distance from the three knolls, and was at a higher elevation of 1,000 feet. It was much better suited for a strong defensive action and harder to outflank. In the centre of this position stood the mustard-coloured *han* (F), with the face of the building peppered with large square windows that could provide a platform to fire down on both the Daoudkoi and Sofia roads.

A fighting withdrawal to the ridge would be conducted when pressure became too great or when the three knolls were outflanked. Baker anticipated that the Russians would attempt to bypass his position rather than risk heavy casualties in a frontal assault. If able to entice the Russians to attack his 'false position', the Russian units would become disorganized and fragmented in the wooded terrain after scaling the abandoned knolls, forcing them to launch a second round of lumbering assaults on his sturdier second position. Baker explained:

> It seemed likely, therefore, that instead of benefiting by their immensely superior numbers to penetrate the mountain range on either flank, both divisions would close in upon our first position after we had abandoned it, and would then find themselves massed and disordered in front of the main crest.

If this manoeuvre could be enacted, it would help to buy the time needed for Shakir's withdrawal, and force the Russians to devote all 25,000 men congregated in front of the knolls to drive a force of less than 3,000 men from the entrance of the Tashkessen Pass.

The plan was not without its risks. The withdrawal to the second position would have to be conducted with precision and discipline. Any breach in the Ottoman line could be mercilessly exploited by the Russians, leading to mayhem or a complete rout. Nothing is more complicated than realigning formations of soldiers in the heat of battle. Baker would have to rely heavily on the discipline of his battalions and the composure of his officers to enact an orderly withdrawal while under attack. Baker understood the flawlessness necessary to conduct this manoeuvre, stating it 'had to be executed with the precision of parade.'

31 December 1877: The Spartan Stand

Baker rose before dawn on the dull winter morning of 31 December 1877 after only a few hours of sleep, anticipating an eventful day ahead of him. Allix made sure all of the Ottoman battalion commanders woke their men before first light, and cautioned to keep a clear lookout for enemy activity. He saddled and retrieved Imaum, bringing the horse to the door of Baker's quarters. Reilly and Radford roasted cups of cocoatina – a chocolaty concoction of sugar and water – and casually shared among Baker's staff, 'without which they never suffered their masters to depart for a long day's work and precarious meals.' By 7.30 am, the guns were exchanging shots, initiated by Russian batteries.

Artillery fire could be heard thundering in the distance from the direction of the Kamarli line about the same time that Russian guns opened up the unequal duel at Tashkessen. Baker directed one last telegraph to be sent off to Shakir before the Russian assault commenced. He soon discovered the civilian telegraph operator in the village had panicked and already taken flight from his telegraph office. With his line of communication incapacitated, he sent a mounted orderly to request last-minute reinforcements from Shakir.

Baker stood erect and at ease on the centre knoll with his staff as they received the Russian bombardment. They appeared indestructible. A fusillade of shells fell upon his sheltered men as three Russian columns advanced forwards as far as the eye could see. 'The odds indeed seemed desperate,' Baker afterwards recalled as 25,000 Russian soldiers advanced forwards over the snowy plains. Despite these daunting odds, he proudly observed:

> The enemy outnumbered us by more than twelve to one [eight to one]. But I was delighted with the behaviour of the Turkish troops. Every man could see the grave nature of the position, for the whole Russian force lay plainly visible. We were now under rather a heavy shellfire, yet every face looked cool, calm, and determined. Even the Edirne lying down amongst the stones were steady enough.

The main objective of Gourko was to distract the soldiers on the three knolls with two of his columns, while the remaining column moved towards

Makatch to outflank the Ottoman position. Gourko had assembled an impressive force of thirty-two battalions, two cavalry brigades, and thirty-six guns in front of Tashkessen. Major General Rauch led his column of ten battalions and eight guns to demonstrate against the right and centre knolls (R). Lieutenant General Vasily Kataley's column – composed of twelve battalions and twenty guns – was held back about 2 miles in the rear and acted as a general reserve, fanned out in a line across the Sofia road (S). The main flanking thrust was to be conducted by Major General Kourloff, who led ten battalions, eight guns, and two brigades of cavalry past the left knoll towards Makatch, and in the direction of the Kamarli plain in the rear of Baker's position (Q).

The first effort to dislodge Baker began with Rauch's column in the direction of the right knoll (T). General Rauch and his veterans waded through the deep snow and moved cautiously forwards to the foot of the knoll. The Russian battalions easily drove off a handful of Ottoman scouts in the village of Daoudkoi. Three battalions and a single gun under the command of Colonel Vasmund were detached and occupied a small hill in the rear of Daoudkoi (L). The occupation of this hill posed a direct threat to the right knoll, but it was far too distant from the general Ottoman position for Baker to counter its occupation. Vasmund ordered the gun to open fire on the rear of the Touzla and Uskub battalions.

An enormous gap developed between Rauch's column on the right, and Kourloff's column on the left, as they moved off in opposite directions. For a moment, Baker's thoughts drifted to the possibility of leading his outnumbered battalions through this breech towards Sofia before he was enclosed by the Russian pincher movement. Evacuation of the knolls could have conceivably saved his command, but it would have meant abandoning Shakir and his men to extermination. Baker was a man who stuck by his word despite the futility of the situation, and decided to remain and fight it out.

On the left, Kourloff's column attempted to push rapidly past the left knoll and march on towards Makatch. Baker observed this movement and soberly remembered, 'Then it appeared as if all my forebodings would be realized.' Unless Kourloff's column could be stalled from pushing around his left, Baker's stand at Tashkessen would be a forlorn hope. To counter this threat, a bold manoeuvre was conducted comparable to Colonel Joshua L. Chamberlain and the men of the 20th Maine at Little Round Top. The reserve units composed of the four companies of the Prizrend and the Chasseur battalions were ordered to lengthen the left flank of the Ottoman line, and extend it to a stripe of drawn-out hills, hoping the salvo from the Ottoman riflemen on the hilltops would entice the Russian column to reroute and assault the position (P).

As the lead Russian battalions drew within range of the Chasseurs, they opened a fierce barrage of fire down from the hilltops as they rammed cartridges into the chambers of their Peabody-Martini rifles and fired, hitting the tightly packed infantrymen at the range of 1,800 yards. Soldiers began to collapse into the snow from the accurate and rapid fire, including General Mirkovitch of the Volhynia Regiment. Disobedient soldiers and officers halted to return fire. General Kourloff impulsively allowed his men to deviate from their mission, and the whole division halted and changed front, and now faced the defiant Ottoman defenders on the drawn-out hilltops. 'A gleam of hope shot through my breast,' Baker remembered when he observed the rerouting of the whole column away from Makatch.

The Russian officers hurled their formations forwards in an attempt to drive the outnumbered defenders from the hills with their sheer weight of numbers. Lieutenant Francis Greene described how:

They were obliged to advance very slowly, the men running forwards a few yards and then lying down in the snow, as they were entirely exposed in the open plain to the fire of the Turks concealed behind rocks on the mountain.

The Russian line of infantrymen burst out in a jackal-like roar as they surged forwards like a furious wave with bayonets fixed to their rifles towards the peaks. The rifle fire exchanged between the two sides became deafening as the smoke accumulated over the battle lines. Casualties mounted on both sides with the sporadic exchange of gunfire, as the few hundred Ottoman defenders drew fire from thousands of Russian soldiers.

Baker was determined to give his men the confidence boost they desperately needed, remembering advice that Mehmed Ali had once given him. He grabbed his trumpeter by the sleeve of his uniform and pointed to his bugle and shouted, 'Sound the Turkish cry – the appeal to God!' The sounds of the trumpet resonated from the centre knoll. The shouts of 'Allah! Allah!' thundered from the parched throats of the outnumbered defenders, surpassing the sounds of battle – taken up by the defenders on all of the knolls – challenging their adversary's battle cry. The soldiers of the Prizrend and Chasseur battalions sprang to their feet, and the steel on steel clicks echoed on the hilltops as they fixed bayonets to their rifles.

Baker was stirred by his men's gusto. 'It was a glorious sight to see the confidence of the scanty little band of Turkish troops, as the great Muscovite wave rolled up against our position,' he later recalled. Also inspired by these events, Fred Burnaby later remarked:

It was a sensation worth feeling; it was a moment worth ten of the best years of a man's life; and a thrill passes through my heart at the time – that curious sort of thrill – the sensation which you experience when you read of something noble and heroic, or see a gallant action performed. It was grand to hear these 2,400 Mohametans, many of them raw levies at the time, cheering back in defiance of those thirty picked battalions, the choicest troops of the Czar.

The outcome of the next moments would dictate if the left flank could hold.

The men of the Prizrend and Chasseur battalions plunged forwards with their bayonets secured to their rifles and a grim look of fury on their faces. They crashed into the stunned Imperial Guard battalions scaling the slopes. The two sides hacked, stabbed, and discharged their weapons in vicious close quarters combat. Taken aback by this fearless charge, the Russian assault faltered and had 'to fall back again exhausted and with thinned and demoralized ranks from Turkish fire,' reported Hozier. Baker sent special thanks via a courier to the battalions on his left, promoting Hajdi Mehemet on the spot, and ordered them to be ready to withdraw towards the second position.

The Russian commanders made two fatal mistakes in the initial manoeuvres against the Tashkessen position. Firstly, instead of making it a priority to march towards Acha Kamarli and cut off both Baker's and

Shakir's line of retreat, Kourloff allowed his command to become drawn into a costly struggle against Baker's extended left flank. Secondly, there was a complete lack of coordination between the three columns, characteristic of Russian strategy throughout the war. If Gourko's Russians could have only managed to utilize their numerical superiority in a simultaneously coordinated attack, the sheer weight of numbers would have overwhelmed Baker's small command. The columns of Kataley and Rauch instead sat idle while Kourloff hurled his column against the Ottoman left flank.

This poor coordination allowed Baker to skillfully deploy and rearrange his soldiers to concentrate on the zones most threatened as he began preparations to withdraw to the second position. He first withdrew the Touzla battalion from the right knoll and placed it back alongside the Tchengueri battalion to the left of the *han*, moving the El Bassan battalion from inside the village of Tashkessen to supplant it. The El Bassan batallion moved adjacent to the Uskub battalion and prepared to meet the Rauch's assault on the right.

Rauch's column finally abandoned its cautious 'halting and hesitating attitude' and launched its own full-scale assault on the right knoll. The lead Russian brigade advanced directly up the sloping knoll near the village of Daoudkoi and struck the flank and front held by the Uskub and El Bassan battalions. The Russian gun that had been dragged up the hill by Colonel Vasmund's three battalions proved to be ineffective. The shots from the gun instead flew wildly over Baker's men's heads and instead hit friendly Russian soldiers. The Russian battalions fell back into the plain at the base of the knoll after suffering severely from the intense barrage of gunfire unleashed from behind the manmade wall of fragmented stones.

Fortunately for Baker, three more Arab squadrons of cavalry (180 men) arrived to benefit his arranged withdrawal. Baker ordered all six of his cavalry squadrons to move down in front of the village of Tashkessen, shielding the withdrawal of the units from the centre knoll to the second position. The commander of the Arab cavalry recoiled, unwilling to take his mounted men into what he viewed as a suicidal barrage of Russian artillery from Rauch's batteries. Without hesitation, Baker called out to Allix to personally lead them forwards in his place. Francis recorded Baker saying, 'Allix, will you take the cavalry down on to the plain again? Spread the men out; give the movement as much importance as possible. It will make our line look stronger – fill up a gap, as it were.'

The valiant Arab horsemen, with Allix in the lead – accompanied by Captain Thackeray, who decided to fasten himself to the cavalrymen's ranks – dashed out on to the open plain to the front of the village in the face of Rauch's and Kataley's columns. This gave Baker time to commence the withdrawal of his centre. In *Czar and the Sultan*, Archibald Forbes recorded the words spoken to him from a Russian artillery major ordering his batteries to fire on the line of bold cavalrymen:

> It is merely a demonstration to cover your friend's retirement to the main crest. Very neat dexterous business I call it. I wish your Baker Pasha belonged to us, then one day our cavalry might do something that men would talk about. Well, we've emptied a few Turkish saddles; and that long-legged Englishman [mistook Allix for Baker], having arrested events for half an hour or so, is shouting 'Three about!' and going up the hill again. I will make it hot for him as he goes!

When their mission was completed, the Arab cavalry squadrons moved to the rear into the Kamarli plain to screen for any Russian movement on the extreme left.

With Rauch's column driven back down into the snowy plains, and with the success of Allix's delaying manoeuvre, Baker initiated a general retirement to his second position. He ordered the two mountain guns and one field gun from his right to move to the second position, which caused him 'much anxiety' as the guns had a difficult time moving downhill over the broken terrain. All of his guns were eventually concentrated around the *han*. Baker in succession withdrew the El Bassan and Uskub battalions from the right knoll, the Edirne battalion from the centre knoll, and the four companies of the Prizrend battalion from the left knoll. The Uskub battalion and the four companies of the Prizrend battalion formed the reserve of his second position.

Archibald Forbes admired Baker's grit. He felt he had already accomplished more than what was required of his outnumbered command: 'It seemed to me that Baker had already done a good day's work, and that the time had now surely come when he was amply justified in retiring from the unequal struggle.' Forbes's enthusiasm radiated from his prose in his praise of Baker's realignment to the ridge:

It was truly beautiful, the quiet cool deliberation with which he withdrew his little command up on to the main upper crest of the ridge, into a position which I could easily discern was infinitely stronger than the one which he had previously been holding. He had befooled the Russians to some purpose in letting them imagine that they were outflanking him on both right and left, whereas they had been doing this as regarded only his initial position; and now they must go right at the front of his new and stronger position, or recommence from the beginning a fresh series of flanking movements. I could scarcely contain myself from cheering as the skillful tactics gradually dawned on me; and how I wished that I had a fellow Briton by my side with whom to take pride in the brilliant military genius of our brave unfortunate countryman!

Baker's withdrawal was not without its kinks. The Eski Cheir battalion suddenly broke and began to stream towards the rear down the Sofia road after taking heavy artillery fire. The four field guns positioned nearby also limbered up and began to withdraw without orders, after their commander was decapitated by a well-directed Russian shell, leaving the artillerymen shaken. Burnaby remembered the exploits of Baker to halt the retreat of the gunners:

General Baker saw this at a glance, and, sticking his spurs into his horse, he galloped down the slippery height – his animal now up to the haunches in the snow, then sliding down the steepest of declivities – the loose stones and pebbles flying like hail in the faces of those who attempted to follow him. He rode up to the retreating artillerymen, made them return with the cannon to the original position, and remained there for more than an hour, in the most exposed part of the field – his presence so encouraging the gunners that they redoubled their exertions, and fired so fast and accurately that for a time they completely paralyzed the Russian movements.

Baker rallied the Eski Cheir battalion and the field guns, and supervised their orderly withdrawal to the *han*.

In one instance while falling back to the second position, Burnaby's life nearly came to an abrupt end. His saddle became loose when his breastplate broke, and his mighty frame toppled in the snow from atop his undersized horse. The fall inflamed a sprained ankle Burnaby had suffered a few days before; he was unable to stand upright or mount his horse with the severed breastplate. As Russian bullets directed from infantrymen at 500 yards ricocheted around the immobilized warrior, Francis sprang from his horse, undid a long sash from his waistcoat, mended Burnaby's breastplate, and then helped Burnaby back on to his horse. Through his efforts, both managed to escape under a hail of gunfire.

The four companies of the Prizrend battalion and the Chasseur battalion were the last to join the other battalions on the ridge. Baker indicated that 'Hadji Mehemet [Mehmed] was fighting gloriously, holding every inch of ground, and only abandoning each successive peak when it was impossible to hold it longer.' At one point, Baker received a frantic message from Hadji Mehmed stating that, 'We could hold our ground longer, but are short of ammunition.' The ammunition from their Peabody-Martini rifles was not compatible with the Snider-Enfields' ammunition used by the four companies of the Prizrend battalion. The ground over which the Chasseur battalion fought was so broken and hilly that the packhorses with reserve ammunition crates bundled on their backs had no feasible way to scale the hill and resupply the soldiers.

The danger of having various battalions armed with dissimilar calibre weapons was a widespread problem in both the Ottoman and Russian armies. Days before Tashkessen, Baker went so far as to propose that the poor quality battalions at the Kamarli line should be stripped of their arms, which should be redistributed to the better quality troops of the army. This idea was rejected because 'it was considered that the men at least knew their weapons, whereas there might not be time to instruct them in the new arm before some emergency would arise.'

But on this day, he wished his words had been heeded. Baker sent runners to Tashkessen to search for any spare Peabody-Martini cartridges that may have been left behind. Fortunately, a skeleton batallion of sixty men had been broken up and assigned to escort duty only a few weeks before the battle. They had been armed with Peabody-Martini rifles, and their surplus ammunition remained stockpiled in an abandoned building within the village. The spare ammunition was immediately conveyed to the Chasseurs. The besieged battalion was replenished before they were forced to resort to fighting with shovels, their bare hands, or hurling stones in a similar manner as the Russian defenders at Shipka Pass.

Russian infantrymen of the three columns flooded over the three knolls as all of Baker's battalions fell back and realigned on the ridge (G, H). The Russian units became a disorganized throng of men in the wooded and hilly terrain as they advanced forwards, causing units to funnel piecemeal towards the Ottoman-held ridge. The Russian battalions were forced to renew their assault with little artillery support; the guns were unable to traverse the terrain and get into position. It was no longer viable to conduct a flanking movement around Baker's second position, as this movement could not be completed until nightfall. Night would be the deciding factor for victory in this battle; to Baker's battalions it meant salvation, and to the Russians it meant defeat.

The Russians managed to gain a foothold on a high, round-topped hill located to the left of the Sofia road, only 700 yards from the front of the *han* (U). Baker ordered the Edirne battalion to occupy the windowed *han*, where they would have a line of sight to fire down on enemy soldiers moving along the Daoudkoi and Sofia roads. However, the battalion wavered for fear of being trapped inside, jeopardizing the Ottoman centre. Baker witnessed 'only about a dozen more adventurous spirits' creeping forwards to the corner of the building, but all were unwilling to enter. Islan Bey and Burnaby made their way among the gutless soldiers, and eagerly lashed the skulls and backs of the men with long wooden sticks they carried 'that served as an emblem of discipline and justice,' ordering them inside the building to no avail.

Russian officers observed the anarchy taking place in the centre and sprung to action. They attempted to exploit the disorder and occupy the building by conducting a general assault on the weakened position. Berdan rifle fire at the close range of 200 yards ripped into the bodies of the exposed soldiers of the Edirne battalion huddled around the *han*. It had a devastating effect, causing the green soldiers to panic and flee down the Sofia road towards the rear.

In the process of their flight, they crashed into four reserve companies of the Uskub battalion, who had just arrived to reinforce the centre under Baker's orders. For a moment, the sturdy soldiers of the Uskub companies grew anxious as the soldiers of the Edirne battalion pressed and thrashed their way through their ranks in terror. Baker rode amid the four Uskub companies and called to them to stand their ground, while he 'hurled opprobrious Turkish epithets' at the fleeing soldiers of the Edirne battalion.

Baker ordered all seven of his guns to concentrate their fire on the Russian assault near the *han* to stabilize his crumbling hold on the centre. The Ottoman artillerymen unleashed canister shot on the advancing Russian battalions concealed in brushwood at 200 yards' distance. Return rifle fire from the Russian infantrymen led to heavy casualties among the artillerymen, but the iron balls of the shotgun-like canister shot maimed and decapitated the Russian soldiers. The ferocity around the *han* earned the label as the 'Second Hougoumont' by Hozier, drawing a comparison to the large farmhouse of Waterloo fame. As the two sides savagely battled, Baker coolly sat astride Imaum, untouched in the hail of rifle fire that sliced through the air, reassuring his men to remain resilient for a little while longer.

Four companies of the Uskub battalion pushed forwards to occupy the *han*. From inside the structure, they brought effective rifle fire down upon the Russians, bobbing in and out of the windows to discharge their rifles. Baker and Burnaby managed to rally the Edirne battalion, and herded them back into the fight to support the centre. The heavy casualties inflicted on the Russians brought the assault to a grinding halt and forced them back. It was about 12.30 pm, and the battle still seemed far from over to the Ottoman defenders as the number of casualties mounted.

A dispatch rider arrived from Shakir during a short lull in the assault. The message 'heaped blessings on my head for the resistance that we had offered,' Baker recalled, but begged him to hold on as long as he could. The dispatch said nothing of reinforcements, or of Shakir's progress with the withdrawal to Acha Kamarli. Baker sent a stern reply explaining the magnitude of their situation, and urged that a few good battalions must be sent to bolster his line against these repeated Russians blows.

How much longer could he feasibly hold the ridge? Most of the men of the battalions remained unwavering in their dedication to Baker, but the superior strength of the Russians and the mounting casualties began to take a toll. Baker afterwards evoked that:

The men of the five good battalions were fighting so splendidly that I had absolute confidence that they would die at their posts. But the odds were so overwhelming, the fighting so incessant, and our consequent losses so great, that it seemed highly plausible that we might all die.

Baker's men barely hung on from being swept away by the Russian tidal wave.

The Russian assault recommenced on the centre and right of the Ottoman-held ridge. Baker concealed two mountain guns behind a small crumbling building near the *han*, where they managed to keep up an intense rate of fire. He was forced to commit four companies of the Prizrend battalion to strengthen his line. This left him with only four companies of the Uskub battalion as his last reserve. The battle raged without intermission for about an hour.

It was about 1.30 pm, and Baker's battalions were exhausted, but still straddled the ridgeline. He persistently glanced at the hand of his pocket watch to check the hour. 'I looked at my watch from time to time; the hand seemed to stand still,' he later remembered with anxiety. At times, the gunfire slackened along his front, but it never ceased. The battle had been raging for several hours, and in another few hours darkness would intercede to bring the engagement to a close, liberating his command from certain destruction.

By 2.30 pm, the afternoon sky began to turn hazy, an omen of the perils still to come. Only a faint roar of intermittent artillery fire could be heard in the direction of the Kamarli line. The Russians continued to used their foothold near the left centre of the Ottoman line as a point to spring further assaults. Baker hoped for a momement that the hazy mist would thicken and shroud the battlefield, which would save his men 'from almost certain destruction'.

Baker sent Allix to personally check if the last part of Shakir's orchestrated withdrawal would take place that night. An Ottoman courier soon returned with a scribbled message from Allix. 'Just then an event occurred which made my situation tenfold more anxious than before,' Baker evoked. Allix pleaded in the note for Baker to evacuate the ridge, certain that the Shakir's army was in full retreat from the Kamarli entrenchments, signifying he had betrayed Baker and his command to their unfortunate fates. The only possible way for Baker to save his besieged command would be to immediately order a retreat towards Acha Kamarli before being cut off.

Baker trusted Shakir to hold to his word as much as he trusted the words of Allix. Allix was one of Baker's most loyal confidants, having accompanied him since landing at Varna in August. When Baker received this distressing news from Allix, he took it into deep consideration. This placed him in a nerve-racking predicament that would tear any ordinary man in two. Should he abandon his position on his trusted aid's word, or stick by the flimsy arrangement made with Shakir?

He rotated towards the direction of Acha Kamarli, and scanned the Kamarli plain through his field glasses. In the distance, he could clearly observe dark clusters of Ottoman soldiers moving down from Araba Konak in the direction of Acha Kamarli. He verbally arranged with Shakir that the evacuation of the infantrymen was not to commence until nightfall, and the provisions and guns were to have been evacuated the previous night. Why were his men then moving in broad daylight? Had Shakir given up all hope and abandoned the Kamarli line as Allix indicated? If so, Baker would not only have to contend with the three Russian columns on his front, but would also have to oppose thousands of Krüdener's soldiers soon to be in his rear. Baker afterwards wrote when confronted with this news:

The situation was distressing to say the least. 'It seemed so hard to sacrifice the lives of the brave men under my command who had behaved so magnificently. We had been fighting for hours to save this Kamarli army. They had sent no reinforcements, and now they seemed to be quietly sacrificing us in order to save themselves by an unnecessary and treacherous retreat before the time agreed upon.

Baker would have to make a decision, and do it fast. Another frantic message arrived from Allix, imploring him to retreat at once and save what was left of his command.

Baker chose to follow his gut instinct. He would hold his ground to the last bullet or man, whichever came first, even if this meant sacrificing every man to save the 12,000 retreating soldiers from the Kamarli line. The same sense of duty must have overcome King Leonidas when he gave the steadfast final order to his Spartan warriors at Thermopylae to fight to the death. Baker recalled with dignity that 'I determined to remain and hold on to the last.'

Both messages from Allix were concealed from the officers and men in fear that this disheartening news would shatter their morale. Meanwhile, Gourko's officers were able to see 'their prey was escaping before their eyes', as Shakir's men evacuated the Kamarli lines. In response, they furiously renewed their assaults on Baker's position 'that exceeded the others in violence.' The Ottoman field guns suffered fearful casualties, and had so little ammunition remaining – rendering them virtually useless – that Baker sent them to the rear to protect his left flank if the Russians attempted to turn his position.

It was now 3.00 pm; his left flank was under assault. The morale of the battalions stationed in the centre hinged on his mere presence, hindering him from personally vacating the centre to check on the flank. He had to rely heavily on his capable subordinates, Hadji Mehmed and Islan Bey, to act independently on each flank. Captain Thackeray volunteered to bring a report to Baker on the wellbeing of his left flank. He returned with the good news that no major demonstration had been made towards Acha Kamarli, and the left was holding strong despite it 'dissolving away so rapidly under the terrible strain.'

Gourko's three columns still had little over two hours left of daylight to break through Baker's defences. The engagement dragged on 'as if the day would never end' and exhausted men on both sides struggled to overcome it to finalize the bloody contest. Burnaby best embodied the struggle by declaring the battle for both sides was what 'the Yankees would call most particular hell'. By 3.30 pm, it appeared as if Rauch's column had given up all hope of forcing the Ottoman line to the right of the *han*. Baker reluctantly left the centre, and rode down to the hard-pressed position on his left, leaving Islan Bey in temporary command.

Baker and Burnaby had nothing but praise for those fighting to defend the ridge. Baker heaped laurels on Islan Bey, who he stated 'behaved admirably all through the day'. Of Shakir Bey of his staff, he stated that he 'stuck to me like a shadow, and wrote every order which I gave with such clearness that everything worked perfectly.' Burnaby remembered that Gill performed 'the duties of a good Samaritan' tending to the wounded along the firing line 'in the thick of the fight throughout the day'. Baker was concerned about the safety of Baker, VC, when it became necessary to evacuate the ridge – Baker, VC was still bedridden in the village of Strigli – and sent orders for an ambulance wagon to evacuate him to Acha Kamarli.

It was about 4.00 pm, and darkness would shroud the field in the next hour or so. Baker knew the Russians only needed one direct and well-coordinated stab to puncture his line and push the defenders off the ridge. The last of the Ottoman reserves, four companies of the Uskub battalion, were ordered to a semi-detached hill to protect the extremity of his left flank. The number of Ottoman soldiers unwounded or dead were few, but those that remained still gripped the stocks of their rifles with determination in anticipation of one last assault. A glare of terror could be seen in their eyes – a stare only seen when a wild animal is backed into a corner and fighting for its survival.

Gourko's Russians readied themselves for one final effort to dislodge the persistent Ottoman defenders and unravel the left flank. Bringing up lightly engaged troops to reinforce them, the Russian soldiers moved forwards over the bloodstained snow littered with the bodies of their dead and wounded comrades. The flash of every rifle could be seen as the sunset fell away behind the hills around Tashkessen. The Peabody-Martinis and Snider-Enfields bellowed once again and bullets reigned down upon the Russians as they advanced in column, but those who remained able to fire were too few to make a significant impact.

The Russians surged forwards to the top of the ridgeline with wild excitement, sensing the nearness to victory. Once more, the call of 'Allah!' rang out from the trivial number of exhausted Ottoman infantrymen's throats. The Ottoman defenders sprang to their feet with a renewed sense of vitality, and engaged the Russians in a brief, but wild, hand-to-hand combat. One final time, the Russians were involuntary driven back down the hill. The repulse was decisive, and Baker recalled the exhilaration his men displayed beating back this final assault:

> Pale, and exhausted with the long-continued fight, they climbed up the rocks, their faces fierce with the light of battle; bloodstained and wounded as many of them were, they waved aloft their weapons in the air, and hurled defiance at the retiring foe. And many dying man raised himself up with an expiring effort, and spent his last breath in that loud shout of victory.

Darkness followed and concluded the ten hours of continuous combat as hundreds of Russian and Ottoman corpses littered the countryside. The Russians were drained, and all attempts to capture the ridge ceased, 'having well-nigh reached the limits of endurance with the terribly fatiguing work of the past seven days,' professed Lieutenant Greene. Russians soldiers were so tired that many collapsed in place, and Gourko's columns failed to post sentries that night. Francis overheard Baker whisper to himself under his breath following the final repulse, 'We win,' and recalled, 'His face had never betrayed a trace of emotion all day, but now he smiled a little contentedly.'

Baker's defence of Tashkessen bought the time that Shakir needed to escape to Acha Kamarli. Baker afterwards discovered that the withdrawing soldiers viewed by Allix and with his own eyes were detachments from Mehmed Zekki's Brigade, in the process of escorting Shakir's provisions and guns to Acha Kamarli. The provisions and guns were significantly behind schedule, originally planning to depart the night before. Shakir went ahead and sent the provisions and guns during the day so he would not hinder the departure of his infantrymen from the Kamarli line that night. Shakir had stuck by his word after all.

All of Shakir's command marched safely back to Acha Kamarli that night. No losses were suffered, with the exception of a few guns that had to be left behind due to their damaged carriages impeding their trasportation. Despite the fact that a successful departure was enacted under the nose of Krüdener, a scene of anguish overwhelmed the army when it departed, captured by Hozier's account:

It was a terrible scene! Men eager in flight stumbled along, sinking into the snow at every step; the cutting winds blew up the icy particles of snow, which penetrated the thin and tattered garments of the luckless Turks and burnt their skin like red-hot iron.

This was only the beginning of the despair that would dampen the spirits of Shakir's army in the coming weeks.

Baker began preparations for the withdrawal to Acha Kamarli under the cover of darkness with his mission completed. The sick and wounded were removed first under Gill's care, followed by the guns. Skirmishers slipped out of the outlying posts and filled their place with dummy sentries. The weary, but unbeaten battalions were pulled from their positions and marched down the Sofia road through the Kamarli plain to join the remainder of Shakir's army. Two companies of the Uskub battalion had to be ordered to withdraw twice, unwilling to give up the position they had fought so hard to maintain.

The Battle of Tashkessen was a costly struggle for both sides. Sten Anders Wallin, a Finnish soldier serving in Gourko's ranks, recorded in his post-war memoirs that the Ottomans caused the Russians 'rather great losses'. The Russians lost roughly 1,000 men, and thirty-three officers as casualties. More than 800 Ottoman soldiers gave up their lives in the defence, about 25 per cent of Baker's column – the Touzla and Prizrend battalions lost half of their strength. Baker recorded that the men of the Prizrend, Touzla, and Chasseur battalions each expanded at least 260–300 rounds per man in the desperate firefight, demonstrating the ferocity of the engagement.

When the vanguard of the Tashkessen defenders finally arrived to Acha Kamarli with Baker in the lead, they were congratulated in person by Shakir. Shakir detailed Mehmed Zekki's Brigade to relieve Baker's tattered command of the rearguard duties for the protracted retreat south through the mountains towards Otlukoi. Shakir amiably expressed that the stress of the day had caused him to lose 3 inches from around his waistline, and that he was forever thankful for the service Baker's men did on that day. Had this not been a war fought under another country's banner, and the laurels won by a man with a checkered past, it is not inconceivable to think that a Victoria Cross would have had been pinned to the breast of Valentine Baker for his actions that day.

Baker inspected his command when it was mustered for roll call. He had nothing but admiration for his men, writing that the behaviour of his 'five good battalions had been simply grand.' The frozen bodies of their comrades had been left behind on the field of battle, and few voices responded to the names methodically called out during the roll call. 'Bosnia and Albania had a right to be proud of the way in which their sons had conducted themselves through that trying day,' Baker wrote. The sight of what remained of his force nearly brought him to tears:

The little column stood in the darkness on the white, snowy road. My heart bled as I inspected their sadly diminished ranks. They were but the wrecks of those fine battalions that had stood on the hillside when the morning light had broken. But they were brave wrecks still. They had sacrificed themselves, but they had saved an army.

Gourko sent an envoy to ask for Baker's surrender the next morning. The envoy was dumbfounded when he stumbled upon the dummy sentries and the unoccupied ridge. Baker's column had vanished in the night. The Russian sentries, so exhausted from the previous days of marching and fighting, were oblivious of the Ottoman withdrawal.

'Little Papa' could only watch as his chance to cut off Shakir's army vanished. Forbes captured the disappointment of Gourko:

It was the only occasion on which I saw Gourko's composure greatly disturbed. He threw himself on his horse, and galloped up to the crest behind the *han*, where he drew rein and looked down upon the empty plain where he had expected to find the Turkish army.

The frustrated Russian general turned with the majority of his force back towards Sofia, detaching segments of his army to pursue Shakir's retreat.

Looking back to the engagement at Tashkessen after the war, Baker shared these words to describe how he would remember the battle for the remainder of his life:

There are moments in the past of many a man's career that stand out clear and defined after the lapse of even many years: life pictures, the very memory of which brings back a glorious thrill of pride and pleasure. This is the feeling which vibrates through me still, when I recall that last and closing scene which crowned the hard-fought fight at Tashkessen.

Regardless of his faults or past misdeeds, the Battle of Tashkessen was Baker's most glorious hour.

Chapter 7

Redemption or Perpetual Exile?

Colonel Baker possessed no social standing a year ago, when he left an English prison, but his service on behalf of the unspeakable Turks seems to have purged him, in the estimation of the distinguished people of London, from all former disgrace.

Ashtabula Weekly Telegraph, 19 July 1878.

The stand at Tashkessen remains one of the last genuine victories in the Balkans for the Ottomans leading up to the end of the war. The war entered its second and final phase in the aftermath of the battle, as Ottoman resistance in the Balkans deteriorated at an alarming rate. Despite his inability to encircle and destroy Shakir's army, Gourko was satisfied with his accomplishments leading up to Shakir's retreat from the Kamarli line. In a matter of days, he overcame daunting obstacles to successfully scatter the only tangible opposition that could hinder his advance on Sofia.

On the evening of 1 January 1878, Gourko's columns initiated the second phase to eradicate Ottoman resistance in western Bulgaria. The main column under the command of Major General Rauch – with Gourko accompanying him – was composed of sixteen battalions and twenty-six guns, turned back to seize Sofia. Gourko ordered Lieutenant General Kataley to pursue Shakir's army to the ends of the earth with sixteen battalions and the same number of guns. Kataley was to unite with Major General Dandeville's column of nine battalions, fourteen guns, and six squadrons of cavalry at Bunova. Dandeville was caught in a fierce storm leading up to Tashkessen and had lost 800 men due to frostbite in his first attempt to pass the flank of the Kamarli line and cut off Shakir's retreat at Petric. The remaining detachments of Gourko's army were to bivouac in the Kamarli plain, and prepare to move in the direction of Adrianople.

The village of Acha Kamarli was occupied by Kataley's advancing column as Shakir's army retreated south-east towards the village of Otlukoi. Sten Wallin recorded an incident that demonstrated the brutal nature of the war that existed between the Ottomans and Russians. The hungry Finnish soldier entered the village of Acha Kamarli in search of something to eat, and came upon two Bulgarian Christian civilians who pointed out a sick or wounded Ottoman soldier lying in the snow. Thinking he would receive some food in exchange of ridding them of this burden, he recorded, 'I went over to him and rolled him down a slope. He gazed up at me with a glance that I have been unable to forget even [today].' He did not win the favour of the Bulgarian civilians for his act, or receive any food; instead, the despairing stare of the murdered Ottoman soldier was scorched into his memory for a lifetime.

Contact was made between skirmishes of the opposing forces on 2 January 1878, two days after the Battle of Tashkessen. General Kataley – accompanied by one of his brigade commanders, General Philosof, and their aides-de-camp – irrationally rode forwards to observe the progress of the skirmish line. A well-aimed volley from Ottoman soldiers hidden in the rocks tore into the imprudent party of officers. General Kataley was pierced and instantly killed, while Philosof died soon after from his wounds. A mistaken telegraph arrived to Constantinople rejoicing that Gourko had been killed instead of Kataley, eager that his death would lead to a delay in the Russian operations.

Beyond Kataley's persistent harassment, Shakir's army suffered from the unremitted cold that 'fell upon them like pitiless knives.' The more fortunate men of Baker's command were bundled up in Russian Imperial Guard greatcoats to protect themselves from the cold, taken from the dead bodies on the night of 31 December 1877. Each evening that Shakir's army halted, his men would collect as much firewood as possible, and cluster around these fires to avoid falling victim to hypothermia. The soldiers pulled the hoods of their coats tightly over their heads to provide protection from the piercing cold, and tried to get a few hours of sleep.

Starvation was also widespread among the men in Shakir's army as 'hunger gnawed at their entrails.' Meals usually consisted of a large dry biscuit short of any protein. 'It was generally so hard that the strongest teeth cannot masticate it,' Baker remembered of the unsatisfactory biscuit. To remedy the biscuit's rock-like toughness, soldiers would soak it in icy water for a short period of time and then toast it over hot coals. In the rare instances that Baker was able to procure meat, he would distribute it to his men to help them sustain their bodies against the extreme temperatures and physical exertions of the retreat.

Disorder reigned supreme as the Ottoman retreat caused morale to plummet and discipline to dissipate. Baker was disgusted by the poor discipline and selfishness of many Ottoman officers he encountered, which trickled down to the common soldier. He recalled:

> Generals of brigade would ride on, thinking only of their own personal arrangements; colonels would follow their example; the battalion commanders took no trouble to keep their battalions together; company officers lost their companies; and every man marched as he liked.

Fleeing Muslim villagers accompanied the army, further clogging the roads and narrow footpaths. 'They clung round it like an octopus, and strangled all its freedom of action,' Baker recollected with disgust.

Distance was measured from one village to the next as men travelled at a snail-like pace along the winding roads to the village of Petric. The demoralized army managed to traverse a number of frozen streams to reach the village as its first stopping point. Baker and his staff appropriated a fairly clean and decent sized home with several rooms in the village. Baker, Shakir, and their staffs bedded there for a single night. The next day, they began to move to the next destination, the village of Matchka.

Though Matchka was only several miles from Petric, it took hours for the dispirited army to travel over the slick roads layered in a sheet of ice. Baker described the homes of the villagers when he arrived as 'mere sheds with thatched roofs'. One female villager of Matchka, in her late sixties, fell madly in love with the fair-skinned Allix – to his reluctance – and devoted herself to his company. His handlebar moustache and the manner in which he wore his crooked fez must have enticed the Bulgarian woman. This gave Baker and his fellow staff members a moment for amusement during these despairing stretches of the retreat.

When the vanguard of the army finally reached Otlukoi, a telegraph awaited Shakir addressed from Adrianople. To Shakir's surprise, he discovered that Süleyman had fled Sofia in the wake of Gourko's descent on the Sofia plain to retrieve reinforcements from Adrianople. Süleyman left vague instructions for Shakir to hold his current position at all costs, until he could bring up his army of 20,000 from the vicinity of Adrianople. Süleyman was wise to flee from Sofia; it was under siege by the time Shakir's army began to gather at Otlukoi.

Ottoman officials boasted that the strategically situated city of Sofia had not been occupied by a Christian army since the fifteenth century. Gourko threatened to disrupt this 400-year-old legacy when he encircled the city with his column on 2 January 1878. The Governor of Sofia, Osman Pasha – not the same Osman of Plevna – commanded a garrison of 12,000 men and fifteen to twenty field guns positioned within five defensive redoubts and a network of entrenchments surrounding the city. Osman talked of rivaling his namesake and turning Sofia into a second Plevna days before Gourko's arrival, but would prove that he did not have an equal backbone.

Gourko anticipated that the defenders would put up a fierce fight and projected the loss of at least few thousand Russian soldiers in the grand assault. To his astonishment, the Ottoman defenders evacuated the city without resistance during the night, abandoning 1,500 of their own wounded in the hospitals. Osman fled with his garrison in the direction of Otlukoi, seeking to unite with the armies of Süleyman and Shakir. On 4 January 1878, the triumphant soldiers of Gourko's army entered Sofia greeted by hordes of liberated Christians. The father-like Gourko gave his men a stern warning that pillaging would be not be tolerated as they paraded past, and warned that perpetrators would be severely punished.

The fall of Sofia was the second most devastating blow for the Ottomans next to the fall of Plevna. Over 8 million rations of flour, rice, barely, salt, sugar, coffee, bread and salted beef were abandoned and fell into the hands of the Russians, enough to supply Gourko's whole army for a month. The fleeing Ottoman soldiers even left their tents and over 4 million rounds of stockpiled ammunition behind. Gourko's soldiers remained in the city for five days to allow 'those men of iron who for the last three weeks had been accomplishing the labours of giants' to have a brief period of respite by filling their bellies and getting some well-earned rest. Reinvigorated after the short stay in the city, Gourko divided his column into four separate detachments and began the final advance towards Adrianople and to crush Süleyman's army on 9 January 1878.

As Ottoman resistance in western Bulgaria was crumbling, Baker proposed a bold plan to Shakir to invigorate the army when they arrived at Otlukoi. He maintained that a lone Russian brigade of guardsmen headed the Russian vanguard since the Ottoman departure from Matchka. The remainder of Kataley's pursuing column, now under the command of Dandeville, was strung out for miles back to Petric. Baker suggested that Shakir should about-face with the three brigades at his disposal, and deliver a well-directed jab against the isolated Russian brigade. This deed would check the advance of the pursuit and provide some hope to the disheartened ranks.

Shakir rejected the offensive manoeuvre pitched by Baker, but allowed him to make a limited reconnaissance towards Matchka. He ordered Baker to capture and burn the village, *only* if it was unoccupied by Russian units. He particularly selected the 'shattered, but excellent remnant of the Tashkessen brigade' for this mission. On 6 January 1877, Baker led his men back to the outskirts of Matchka. He could observe Russian activity within the confines of the village, but could not determine how many Russians units occupied it.

With his usual bravado, Baker disregarded Shakir's timid orders and launched an assault. He sent out what remained of the Chasseur battalion – at half strength with less than 125 men – as skirmishers to divulge the Russian strength. They engaged four Russian companies strongly entrenched and positioned on a high hill. Baker ordered up the El Bassan, Touzla, and the Uskub battalions as support, holding the Prizrend battalion in reserve. He was able to outflank the Russian defenders despite the fierce resistance, and drove them to the opposite edge of the village.

'We must burn that village,' Baker uttered to Allix. Without hesitation, the mounted Allix and one orderly rushed through the avenues of the village and tossed a smoldering flame on a pile of dry straw, the whole time under fire at less than 300 yards distance from Russian infantrymen and angry Bulgarian civilians. Smoke and flames engulfed the village, fanned by a gentle breeze. Fred Burnaby afterwards praised Allix's deed, stating it 'would have won him the Victoria Cross' if they were fighting in a British war. With the village of Matchka submerged in flames, the Tashkessen veterans fell back to Otlukoi with their mission complete.

Baker's achievements at Tashkessen, and during the Ottoman retreat to Otlukoi, were transmitted to Constantinople by Shakir. In recognition of these services, he received a personal telegraph from Abdülhamid, thanking him and promoting him to ferik, the equivalent of lieutenant general in his prior army. The exploits of the 'Inglese Pasha' gave hope to those who surrounded him during these desolate weeks. The army would need every sliver of it.

Süleyman turned up at Otlukoi on 5 January 1878 with his army of 20,000, which was proceeded by Osman's 12,000 from the Sofia garrison. He made an inspection of a portion of the Ottoman army accompanied by Baker and Shakir. Baker observed that he did not seem to carry his usual air of self-confidence; instead, he showed signs of a 'most undecided and unsettled state of mind'. The war was taking a psychological toll on Süleyman. He was exceedingly suspicious towards his own division commanders to the point of paranoia, while also weighed down by immense pressure to turn the tide of the war. His poor psychological disposition altered his ability to make rational and thoughtful decisions during this critical period.

Süleyman nearly brought his subordinate commanders to munity over the indecisive and irrational manner in which he was directing the final operations of the war. Rumors circulated in the army that he may have betrayed his own countrymen and swindled a deal with the Russians, intending to sabotage the war effort or allow his army to disintegrate under the stress. What was needed most at this critical moment was a bold and inspiring general, one who had the ability to unite these scattered columns and revitalize Ottoman morale. Osman of Plevna fame would have been an ideal choice in this capacity, but he was serving his prisoner of war sentence in Russia. The Ottoman army was instead left under the leadership of an officer, who Baker felt remained in a 'state of wild confusion'.

On 10 January 1878, unfortunate news was received from the Eastern Theatre. Vessil Pasha's army of 36,000 stationed at Shipka Pass – the last opposition between General Radetzky's army of 56,000 men and Adrianople – had surrendered. Süleyman returned to Tatar-Bazardjik after receiving this news, and exposed symptoms of a nervous breakdown. He ordered a retreat to Adrianople, vacating the surrounding defensive positions in the mountains following the news of the surrender at Shipka Pass. False rumors of an armistice between the Russian and Ottoman governments put a halt on military operations for a couple of days, but they soon resumed after this was established to be untrue.

Despite the recent setbacks, Süleyman could have still feasibly salvaged the Ottoman war effort. A railway line directly connected Adrianople to Constantinople, where reinforcements could have easily been transported to support the city's defences. Greene had his own theory of how Süleyman could have turned defeat into victory for the Ottomans. He justified that Süleyman could have gathered what was left of his forces and 'strike against first one and then the other of the invading columns – which were widely separated – as Napoleon did in 1814, and then as a last resort have fallen back upon the strong fortifications of Adrianople and made a new Plevna of it.' Greene proclaimed that 'the war could at least have been prolonged till the next summer, and Turkey as a military power would not have collapsed in 1878.'

Greene alluded in his statement that Adrianople could have been turned into a second Plevna, which the Russians could ill afford to undertake. The public had grown weary of the war, and the swelling loss of life around Plevna demoralized many Russian families. A lengthy winter siege of Adrianople would have forced the war to drag on for an ambiguous amount of time, and would have strained the already fragile Russian supply lines stretching back to Romania. A protracted war could also permit the British to seriously consider military intervention. The Russians needed to bring the war to an end fast, and a fierce defence of Adrianople could have provided the obstacle to bring the war to a standstill.

Süleyman instead gave the order to halt the extended column near the city of Philippopolis, still 100 miles from Adrianople, and summoned his division commanders together for a council of war. The imprudent order to halt was met with bitterness by his subordinate commanders as Gourko's approaching columns closed in for the kill. His division commanders pleaded that they should continue on to Adrianople as rapidly as possible in order to make a stand within the city's defences and in close proximity to the provisions in Constantinople, instead of allowing Gourko's Russians to engage them. Baker remembered the events of the council of war:

It was in vain that we urged upon him the advantage of maintaining the start we had gained over Gourko. This determination on the part of Süleyman was so extraordinary and inexplicable that it gave us all the idea that he wished to lose the army.

This was the breaking point for the officers, and Baker recorded that 'this decision destroyed any remaining confidence that was felt by the generals of division in the commander-in-chief.'

Amid this debate, a distant but a fierce eruption of gunfire could be heard on a section of the Ottoman line, bringing the meeting to an abrupt end. Gourko had caught up to Süleyman with his four columns – each under the command of Wilhelminoff, Shouvaloff, Krüdener, and Schilder-Schuldner. Süleyman and his officers discovered soon afterwards their retreat to Adrianople had been blocked by Radetzky's army advancing from Shipka Pass. Adrianople was occupied without opposition despite the city being defended by 10,000 men under the command of the inept Ahmed Eyoub – the former commander of the Ottoman I Corps of Mehmed Ali's Lom army – on 22 January 1878.

Cut off from all angles, Süleyman had no choice but to order a retreat further south over the Rhodope Mountains in the direction of the Aegean Sea on 15 January 1878. He left a strong rearguard of 20,000 men at Tatar-Bazardjik under the command of Fuad Pasha to cover his disintegrating army's retreat. Süleyman intended to collect what remained of his army along the shores of the Aegean Sea, and transport it by an Ottoman fleet back to Constantinople. The heroic rearguard by Fuad fortunately held Gourko at bay for three days, but his units were eventually driven back and scattered in confusion by the overwhelming numbers.

After routing Süleyman's rearguard, Gourko turned the bulk of his army east in order to unite with Radetzky at Adrianople, while detaching a small column of his army to pursue Süleyman. On 27 January 1878, Gourko's men united with Radetzky, and began preparations to move on to Constantinople. Süleyman took his shattered army and continued southwards, essentially segregating itself from the main theatre of the war.

The remaining elements of Süleyman's army continued to diminish due to desertions or deaths as it crawled back to the port of Kara-Aghatch.

Physically and emotionally depleted men dragged their feet onwards, stepping over the bodies of comrades. Men simply collapsed or deserted due to fatigue, starvation, or resentment. Frozen bodies of horses and mules cluttered the roadside. One of these desolate scenes from the retreat remained fixed in Baker's memory after the war: 'One gipsy girl sat by the roadside, beating her breasts, and wailing over her dying husband, who, outstretched upon the snow, was giving his last gasp.'

Baker and his staff suffered equally in the hardships, but no one faced it with greater stamina than George Radford. Radford, having not slept in over forty hours, crashed to the ground from his horse on several occasions from sheer exhaustion. In one of these falls, he dislocated his thumb. Dr Gill rode up to the drowsy Radford with usual professional air, and grabbed hold of his hand while he was still mounted, and shoved his thumb back into the socket. Burnaby noted that when food was scarce, Radford would bring his biscuit ration and offer it to him, even though he failed to eat for days at a time.

One bitter cold evening along the journey south, an old Muslim man and his family accommodated Baker and Burnaby on their farmstead. The hospitable farmer provided them with 'some dilapidated *yorghans*' and lit a large fire in a little room for the weary travellers for the night. Baker and Burnaby rolled up these cotton bags stuffed with wool and used them as pillows. These makeshift pillows proved to be a godsend, and both men fell fast asleep under the warmth of the fire with thoughts of home in their dreams.

A faint dream of flames consuming his body made Baker toss and turn. To his dismay, he woke and found that his *yorghan* was half seared and on fire. No water was nearby to stop the flames from spreading and engulfing the all-wooden shelter. Burnaby woke from the commotion, and bolted outside of the shelter. He rushed back inside with an armful of snow, and dumped it on the fire, extinguishing the flames.

After a sigh of relief, the two occupants were again fast asleep. Baker made sure this time to scoot a safe distance away from the flames. Before falling back into a deep slumber, Baker again awoke to find his *yorghan* on fire. He panicked and grabbed hold of it, and tossed it out of the dwelling and into the snow. He resigned himself to make do without a pillow, attempting to salvage some rest for the remainder of the night.

Baker and the members of his staff experienced another unusual occurrence before reaching Kara-Aghatch. Upon their arrival at Gumurdjina, only 15 miles from Kara-Aghatch, a Greek archbishop of the district, in his glittering finery, met the party and made arrangements to allow these fellow Christians to rest for the night is his large estate. Invited to dine on some stewed meat and wine the next morning, the officers filled their stomachs and shared in some fine tobacco. They thanked their host, and headed on their way around 2.00 pm.

Less than half an hour later, Baker, Burnaby, and Shakir Bey became violently ill, complaining of 'constriction of the throat, burning pain down the course of the gullet [oesophagus] and at the pit of the stomach'. The three were overtaken by persistent vomiting, numbness of the limbs, and severe disorientation that carried into the following day. Dr Gill and other doctors accompanying the column came to the conclusion they had been poisoned with arsenic or copper, and administered large doses of water and salt to alleviate their suffering. It was never determined if this had been done intentionally by the cordial archbishop during the morning feast, or done by one of his many servants in a fit of revenge against Ottoman rule. All three fortunately recovered after the debilitating effects wore off.

The depleted remnants of Süleyman's army, roughly 35,000 stragglers, gathered at the port of Kara-Aghatch on 25 January 1878. When soldiers of the vanguard climbed over the summit and were able to view the choppy waves of the Aegean Sea, cries rang out of in the ranks of 'The Sea! The Sea!' To all of the survivors, the sea represented the end of their hardships. Awaiting them was the *Selimiye*, one of the largest fifty-gun frigates in the world, weighing over 4,000 tons, accompanied by another transport steamer. The sea was too shallow for the two transports to get close enough to the shore, so an army of wooden boats made countless journeys back and forth until the two vessels were loaded to maximum capacity.

Baker, his staff, and a total of 5,000 soldiers crammed on to the *Selimiye*. The deck was so congested with men that one could walk across them without touching the wooden walkway. 'I doubt whether so large a number of men had ever been previously conveyed for a sea voyage upon one vessel,' Baker later recalled. The soldiers suffered severely from thirst due to an inadequate supply of water. All 5,000 men disembarked at Gallipoli, ecstatic to escape the misery, and from there Baker travelled alone to Constantinople.

Baker found Constantinople in a state of complete pandemonium from the highest levels of society down to the lowliest Ottoman peasant. The Russian armies prepared to advance from Adrianople, only two hours from the capital. Abdülhamid was frantically seeking asylum for himself and his family from the British ambassador, Sir Austen Henry Layard, in preparation for the Russian assault on the capital. The defence of the capital was virtually overlooked in the state of terror, and most of its residents, including top officials, threw up their arms and fatalistically accepted defeat. Baker professed that 'this passive resignation and acceptance of defeat was perfectly heartbreaking.'

Abdülhamid found a scapegoat in Süleyman for the recent misfortunes, and placed him under arrest in order to face a court martial. The mock trial dragged on for eight months, ending with Süleyman sentenced to rot in a dungeon for fifteen years. In one heated instance during the trial, the president of the tribunal called for Süleyman's head, and in response, Süleyman lunged his breast towards a guard's bayonet and yelled 'Coward! That would be a soldier's death,' tempting the soldier to skewer him on the spot. Süleyman was eventually pardoned and exiled to Baghdad, but returned to the capital and died in 1892.

The political pressure of Great Britain spared the residents from a mass exodus and triumphant Russian occupation of the Ottoman capital. The potential capture of Constantinople by Russian soldiers posed an economic threat to British interests. It also possessed a major strategic threat; a strong Russian presence in the Balkans would allow them to set up future outposts to intimidate British spheres of influence in the Persian Gulf, the Bosporus, the Dardanelles, and most importantly, the breadbasket of Great Britain, India. Great Britain was prepared to take direct military action to protect these interests, just as they had done by propping up the Ottoman Empire during the Crimean War in the 1850s.

The British policy towards supporting the Ottomans had fluctuated over the preceding nine months of the war. Then everything changed overnight. Most Britons were horrified at the thought of Constantinople falling under Russian suzerainty, enough so as to overlook the censure the Ottoman administration received for the horrendous atrocities committed two years before in Bulgaria. The level-headed cabinet members sought diplomatic means to pressure the Russians to halt their advance instead of a formal declaration of war. Intoxicating patriotic fever swept the country, calling for war, and in the streets of London, war birds sang:

> *We don't want to fight,*
> *But by Jingo! if we do,*
> *We've got the ships,*
> *We've got the men,*
> *We've got the money too!*

Queen Victoria possessed a fervent animosity towards the Russians in line with the newfound public opinion. She sent a memorandum to her cabinet on 12 January 1878, stating that the occupation of Constantinople had to be acted upon at all costs to maintain British prestige. Great Britain needed to demonstrate that it was still the leading overseer of the balance of power among the European nations. A British fleet was ordered to pass through the Dardanelles as a demonstration of strength, while thousands of Indian troops were transferred to Malta to intimidate the Russians from occupying Constantinople. Fred Burnaby spelled out his frustration in a letter home dated 17 February 1878, angered with the shallow display of military strength instead of tangible military intervention: 'And so England does not mean to fight for Constantinople after all. What a wretched lot of shopkeepers we are! The country would seem to have lost all its backbone.'

On 3 March 1878, the signing of the Treaty of San Stefano between Ottoman and Russian politicians officially ended the war before British military intervention was required. However, none of the leading European nations were satisfied with its provisions imposed on the humiliated Ottomans. Austria-Hungary and Great Britain viewed the most provoking provision of the treaty as the creation of a Russian satellite nation of Bulgaria; the massive state would stretch from the Black Sea to the Aegean Sea. A conference was called together by the heads of the principal European nations to amend the Treaty of San Stefano, and administer the division of the Balkans on favourable terms to all influential parties.

The outcome of the conference led to the Treaty of Berlin on 13 July 1878. The revised treaty helped to diminish Ottoman losses in the Balkans imposed by the Russians in the first treaty. However, it still signified the dismemberment of the Ottoman Empire's foothold in Europe. Romania, Serbia, and Montenegro were declared independent and severed their Ottoman ties. An independent Bulgaria was created, but it was reduced by half the size compared to the massive state proposed by the Russians in the first treaty. The provinces in the southern part of the Balkans remained under Ottoman yoke, but a special provision was created that forced Abdülhamid to pledge to safeguard the remaining Christian subjects under his control.

Frederic Villiers of the *Graphic* recorded an unusual affair that occurred while diplomats hammered out the peace terms. General Skobelev of Plevna fame praised the exploits of Baker in the final months of the war to Villiers, uttering in one instance, 'Well, I should like to meet that man and shake him by the hand.' A dinner meeting was arranged at the Club Commercial et Maritime in Constantinople between the two folk heroes of the opposing armies. Villiers recorded the encounter:

> The two men, whose heroic exploits had for months attracted the attention of the whole civilized world, quietly linked their arms and walked up and down the room, chatting over their past experiences. As I looked at Baker in his smart general's uniform, his face sunburnt and bright with satisfaction of the moment, I could hardly recognize the disappointment, dejected applicant for the Turkish gendarmerie command I used to lunch opposite to in that very room a few months before.

Villiers proclaimed that 'I shall never forget that event.'

Baker decided to return to his homeland from exile before the ink dried on the first treaty, 'utterly disgusted' with the manner the Ottoman high command handled every aspect of the war. He held that the trained Ottoman foot soldier was not subject to any of the blame for defeat, specifying that:

> The trained Turkish soldier seemed to possess every military virtue. Patient and enduring, submissive to discipline, of strong physique and

a good marcher, cool and brave in moments of danger, and possessing to a high degree that military instinct which is so valuable in the loose formations demanded by modern warfare, the Turks form the beau-ideal of a soldier.

He felt defeat could have been diverted if there had been cooperation and altruism among senior leadership; not jealously, intrigue, and corruption. The war may have played out differently if an offensive approach had been adopted instead of a paralyzing defensive strategy early in the war.

His staff was made up of an eccentric combination of foreigners far from home, who formed a bond through their common heritage and religion. Baker was in gratitude to all of them. He even praised his servant Reilly, stating that, 'My faithful servant Reilly reached the coast with us, being this the only one of our party who had remained constantly with me from the commencement of the campaign on the Lom until we reached the sea.'

For most of the members of his staff, the war proved to be their finest hour; life after the conflict varied for them, some fading into ignominy. Allix left Baker's staff shortly before reaching the Aegean Sea with Süleyman's army, travelling to Constantinople 'on business of importance'. He was afterwards awarded the Order of Osmanieh for his actions at Matchka, and travelled to Cairo to serve as the aide-de-camp to the Khedive of Egypt. He died a poor man at the age of 79 in 1925. George Conrad Sartorius served in Egypt and lived a long life, but remained the odd man out among his other two brothers – never earning a Victoria Cross. He died in 1912 at the age of 79.

The altruistic Dr Gill was decorated with the Order of the Medjidie for his actions in the war. He afterwards acted as a civilian surgeon during the Anglo–Zulu War, and was wounded, which resulted in the lameness of one of his legs. He passed away at his sister's residence in Shrewsbury on 12 July 1898, after a 'long and painful illness'.

Charles George Baker, VC, who was supposed to be evacuated from Strigli under orders from Baker, was captured by the Russians. The doctors in Strigli objected to leaving the rest of the sick and wounded to evacuate him on Baker's orders, and chose to remain behind. Baker discovered the fate of his companion when he reached Petric, and composed in large letters with chalk a message on an abandoned wall of a home requesting for Russian officers to look after his friend. Baker, VC eventually recovered from his illness after being captured, and travelled to Egypt to serve in the gendarmerie, until his death at the age of 76 in 1906. His tombstone is inscribed with the modest, but powerful epitaph, 'There is no death.'

Fred Burnaby returned to Great Britain after the war. Baker wrote of his most trusted friend that he 'used to watch me like a child, and was always ready with some sustenance that might prevent my strength from failing.' The hardships of war brought the two closer together than ever before, and Burnaby initiated a public campaign for Baker's reinstatement into the British Army.

Burnaby's servant, George Radford, met an unfortunate fate after contracting typhoid fever during the retreat to the Aegean Sea. By the time Burnaby and Radford arrived home to Dover, his servant 'was almost unconscious.' Burnaby made sure 'everything that human skill could device was brought to bear, the best medical attendance was secured,' to no avail, noting, 'it was too late.' Despite Burnaby's efforts to save his friend, Radford died on 22 February 1878, and Burnaby inherited the responsibility of looking after the financial welfare of Radford's widow and children.

Burnaby had every intention to commemorate his faithful servant in perpetuity. Over his burial spot in the St James Cemetery in Dover, he had a tombstone erected bearing this heartfelt epitaph:

George Radford, Private in the Royal Horse Guards. Died at Dover, February 22nd, 1878, aged 42, of typhus fever, contracted during the retreat of Suleiman Pasha's Army across the Balkans in Turkey. George Radford was a brave solder, a faithful servant, and as true as steel. This stone is erected to his memory by the man whom he served so well.

Formerly shunned, Valentine Baker made a triumphant homecoming to Great Britain as 'Baker Pasha'. Author Anne Baker indicated he was 'spoken of as a romantic and mysterious figure, much as Lawrence of Arabia was described in the next century.' Baker provided Great Britain with a masculine hero that embodied all Britons when international politics failed to deliver a war to the public. A correspondent from *The New York Times* reported from

Adrianople that the exploits of Baker in the war sustained that, 'English pluck showed itself, as it always does.' All of the stereotypical qualities of what should define a British officer – gallantry, decisiveness, fortitude and zeal – were demonstrated by the outcast on the battlefields of Bulgaria.

Baker's leadership qualities at Tashkessen and afterwards received an abundance of praise in the press with such axioms as 'brilliant', 'wonderful', 'marvellous', 'magnificent', and 'heroic'. In March 1878, an anonymous contributor to *Vanity Fair* described Baker as a 'marvellous general' who was 'quite unassailable by fatigue'. The column further elaborated by claiming that 'those who have seen him in action hold that there never was a general at once so calculated to inspire confidence in the soldier and so able to wrest a victory for his standard from the very jaws of defeat.' The *Dundee Evening Telegraph* praised his 'skill and courage' while covering Shakir's retreat after Tashkessen. In the event of a war between Russia and Great Britain, the newspaper declared that the nation 'could ill afford to dispense with his services.'

Baker gained re-admittance into the aristocratic drawing rooms and social clubs he had been banned from since his exile. The *Ashtabula Weekly Telegraph* recorded an instance of Baker's treatment upon his jubilant return:

> The Duke of Sutherland gave a banquet to Valentine Baker, Pasha, on the latter's return to London, which was attended by many noblemen, generals and ambassadors. Colonel Baker possessed no social standing a year ago, when he left an English prison, but his service on behalf of the unspeakable Turks seems to have purged him, in the estimation of the distinguished people of London, from all former disgrace.

The outspoken Fred Burnaby made a public crusade in Baker's favour, petitioning for his friend to be re-elected into the Army and Navy Club, and the rousing accounts of his heroism were met with toasts from the members of the Savage Club, including Wolseley, who shook him 'heartily by the hand'.

Some overlooked the sexual assault charges in lieu of his exploits during the heightened frenzy, but others failed to forget what had brought him to Constantinople in the first place. The *Dundee Evening Telegraph* stated in reference to Baker's checkered past that 'a man's faults should be written in water, and his good deeds engraved in brass.' In one instance, a member of the Savage Club refused to acknowledge Baker when Burnaby called for his toast, and stormed out of the assembly in protest. *The Public Ledger* recorded the love-hate sentiment that some individuals still harboured:

> His return to England was quite a triumph. He had been re-admitted to all the clubs which expelled him after the trial, and has been received by the whole fashionable world, from the Duke of Sutherland downwards. It is, however, whispered that this change of public feeling in his favor has taken place, not because his railcar escapade is forgotten, but because he has once shown, during his service in Turkey, that he is one of the best cavalry officers England can boast of.

One person not consumed with this 'Baker Pasha fever' – the most important advocate for Baker's restoration into the army – was Queen Victoria. She had not forgotten the scandalous incident that brought international attention and dishonor to her army. Though all the glamour surrounding his return was pleasing, Baker hungered most for an opportunity to be reinstated back into the army. His most diehard advocates, including the Prince of Wales and the Duke of Cambridge, pleaded with Victoria on numerous occasions to overlook Baker's past and allow him to be restored for his valuable service in Great Britain's interests during the war. On 2 December 1879, Lord Ponsonby referred to one of these requests in a reply letter to the Duke of Cambridge:

> Sir, I have the honour of receiving his Royal Highness's letters, and communicating them to the Queen. The Prince of Wales was very anxious I should inform your Royal Highness that he had communicated to the Queen a request from Baker Pasha for restoration to the British Army. The Queen is by no means favourable to this proceeding, but if the Ministers insist on it as an absolute necessity will not oppose it. But Her Majesty will not receive him at court. I do not understand in what manner Baker Pasha desires to be restored.

Even with the glamorous attention he received from his role in the recent war, Queen Victoria refused to sanction his reinstatement. The ministers baulked at the idea of challenging her ruling and gaining her disfavour. So Baker's exile would endure. He was permitted to represent British interests in an unofficial capacity – gaining glory for his country and capturing the popular imagination – but he would never again be regarded as an officer of Her Majesty's Army or even have the dignity of being treated as a gentleman. He only remained in Great Britain for a few months, disillusioned and in a virtual state of ignominy, and instead returned to his exiled post in Constantinople to resume his duties with the Ottoman Army.

Baker submerged himself in reforming and reorganizing the Ottoman armed forces following the disastrous defeat in the late war. In August 1880, while investigating affairs in Armenia, one agitated officer reported back to his superior that Baker expressed to the Christian subjects the benefits of British suzerainty, and also began to encourage the discussion of an independent Armenia. The combination of boredom and the sultan's conceivable displeasure of his actions in Armenia left Baker discontent in Constantinople. *The Argus* reported that on 27 September 1882, 'Baker Pasha (Sir Valentine Baker) started today for Egypt. Much comment has been excited by the fact that he sailed without waiting for the Sultan to intimate his consent to his quitting the Turkish service.' Baker embarked on another 'special mission' in the name of Great Britain in an attempt to redeem his honor by the point of his sword. This time his adventures took him to Northern Africa.

Baker was offered command of the newly reformed army in Egypt, recommended by none other than Lieutenant General Wolseley, in command of the British forces in Egypt. A nationalistic and anti-foreign rebellion led by Colonel Ahmed Urabi against the pro-European regime of the Khedive Tewfik tore the country apart in 1879. British forces intervened and bombarded Alexandria in 1881, and squashed Urabi's army at the Battle of Tel-el-Kebir on 13 September 1882. Egypt became a quasi-protectorate of Great Britain, and their army needed to be rebuilt and restructured along British military standards. Baker's aptitude for organization made him a perfect fit to lead the overhaul and reorganization of this new British-officered army.

Baker, his faithful wife Fanny, and his two daughters, Hermione and Sybil, sailed from Constantinople to Cairo in the autumn of 1882. They arrived in October, and the Baker family found residence in the celebrated Shepheard's Hotel of Cairo. Fanny Wormald, a cousin of his wife, came to stay with the Bakers for a short time and would chronicle her experiences with the family. By 1882, the 16-year-old and golden-haired Hermione began to attract a number of suitors to the Baker household. However, some of these young men were deterred when they discovered that under Hermione's natural beauty lingered a young girl in fragile health.

The 30-year-old Captain Herbert Kitchener – to whom Baker had been introduced upon his visit to the Kamarli line during the Russo-Turkish War – became a frequent visitor to their residence. Kitchener became an exception to the timid suitors, unmoved by Hermione's poor health, and fell in love with her. They were rumored to have secretly agreed to an engagement. The couple did not plan to release the news until Hermione's health improved.

One afternoon, the spirited Wolseley assembled a group of ninety friends and colleagues for a 'picnic' outing to visit the ancient burial grounds of Saqqara. What Wolseley had in mind – intentionally or unintentionally – was far from a pleasurable afternoon outing to visit the pyramids and tombs; it would be more of a test of endurance. Baker must have missed the memo for the dress code and was completely unprepared for the brutal climate, as General William Butler observed, 'for some reason known only to himself, [he] had come to the picnic in a fashionable London frock coat, a tall black silk hat, and the rest of his costume in due keeping.' Butler reported that the combination of the 'heat of the sun' and the 'stifling atmosphere' caused the clothing of the explorers to become 'bedraggled and saturated', most especially 'our Piccadilly clad Pasha'. Baker looked more like a gypsy than a gentleman explorer by the end of the journey:

Words could not paint that picture: the silk hat was bent and broken by frequent contact with the roof of the rock cavern and tomb chamber; the frock coat looked as though several policemen had been tussling with its owner; the legs of the fashionably cut trousers had worked up under the exigencies of the donkey saddle until the ankles were where the knees ought to have been.

The exhausted members of the outing arrived back to a vessel waiting on the Nile, 'with a thirst for tea such as only the dust of 6,000 years of mummy powder could give us.'

Controversy developed before Valentine Baker even had a chance to get assimilated in the new duties of his command. British officers were to be loaned out to Khedive Tewfik on temporary assignment to be given a chance to distinguish themselves in the new army. Queen Victoria was irate when she heard Baker was being appointed to command the new army, fuming that this dishonoured officer would be allowed to command British officers. Some unhappy officers even hesitated to serve under him due to his unsavory notoriety. Baker was removed from command in late November, and Evelyn Wood – one of Queen Victoria's favorite generals – replaced him, leaving him unemployed.

Those closest advocates of Baker pleaded that his removal was backhanded and needed to be reconsidered. The Prince of Wales criticized cabinet members in a letter of 27 November 1882:

> It is not for me to comment on the decision of the Cabinet, but I must confess I think Baker Pasha has been very hardly and unfairly treated. To deprive him now of the important command, which the Khedive conferred upon him, is simply to ruin him.

Wolseley also attempted to intercede and 'risked his Sovereign's favour' in a vain attempt to secure Baker's restoration. General Henry Brackenbury later explained that he was disturbed by the 'blow which had been mercilessly inflicted on my old friend', and concluded that 'If ever a man had purged his offence, it was he. But the spirit of Puritanism prevailed over the quality of mercy, and the uncompromising fiat went forth bidding him abandon all hope.' Cabinet members simply responded that they had never invited Baker to go to Egypt in the first place, and that he went of his own accord without their official consent.

Baker had to instead settle for a lesser command – that of the Egyptian gendarmerie. It was similar to the position he held for a short while in Ottoman service. Baker was devastated; the shadow of disgrace still trailed close behind, and his dream to be reinstated in the British Army through his 'heroic' achievements kept fading further and further away from reality. He accepted the second-rate post with the hope that at some point, active military service would provide a chance for distinction on the battlefield. He did not have to wait long.

The British inherited Egypt's difficulties as soon as they crushed Urabi's army at the Battle of Tel-el-Kebir – most notably, the Sudan. The Sudan was made up of a 1 million-square-mile wild frontier region of desert that bordered Egypt to the south. Warlike and unconquerable tribes were scattered through the brutal landscape. A Sudanese religious man by the name of Muhammad Ahmad made a significant proclamation on 29 June 1881 to the fragmented tribes, proclaiming to be the new messiah, or the Mahdi. He declared a new holy war, and called to peasants from all of Sudan to rise up, unite, and overthrow the oppressive Egyptian rule.

The Mahdi's followers became known as the *Ansars*, or 'Helpers', and grew from a dozen to many thousands overnight. The *Ansars*, or Dervishes to the British, developed a reputation as tough and fanatical fighters, and would launch furious melee assaults from several directions in an attempt to entrap and cut off enemy armies. It was rumored that Muhammad Ahmad could turn enemy bullets into water – along with other mystic powers that gave his followers a sense of invincibility. It was not long before he was in almost complete control of the Sudan.

Colonel William Hicks, a career British officer now in Egyptian service, was tasked with crushing the Mahdi's uprising. Hicks had been recommended for command of the Egyptian expedition by Baker. Hicks Pasha led 10,000 ill-trained Egyptian soldiers into the desert of the Sudan against a portion of the Mahdi's army under his efficient subordinate, Osman Digna. Near the village of Kashgil, Hicks's army was ambushed and the 10,000-man force was nearly annihilated to a man in early November 1883. The decapitated head of Bill Hicks was proudly presented to the Mahdi in Omdurman.

On 23 December 1883, a second expedition composed of the Egyptian gendarmerie and other units landed in Suakin, a Red Sea port located in Eastern Sudan. Baker had been ordered by Khedive Tewfik to prevent the port city from falling into the hands of the Mahdi, and to relieve the besieged Egyptian garrisons in Tokar and Sinkat. He transported his column to Trinkitat, only 18 miles away from Tokar. He had orders from Tewfik to act with prudence and not directly engage the Mahdi's armies. His inadequate force was to only safeguard these Egyptian interests.

In November 1883, Fanny Wormald detected the strain of the task assigned to her cousin's husband before he departed for Suakin. 'Val is overwhelmed with work, in consequence of this terrible disaster to Hicks in the Sudan. He looks thin and ill, and is very anxious about Hermione,' she observed. Baker was most depressed at the thought of having to leave his oldest daughter while in her failing health. This depression was reinforced by the fact that Fanny pleaded for him not to join the expedition, with a pre-eminent feeling that disaster would befall the column. Baker did not falter from doing his duty despite his reluctance to depart from Cairo.

On 3 December 1883, Fred Burnaby received an emotional plea from Fanny that 'Val' needed the support of his old companion more than ever on the eve of the campaign. She excused her husband for not writing personally to Burnaby, weighed down by the burden of preparing for the logistical nightmare of conducting the expedition. A telegraph arrived to Burnaby from Fanny that indicated her concern:

> I am really terrified about Val's chances. Of course whenever there is a chance of fighting I am always very much frightened, but hitherto I have always been able to think of him as surrounded by brave soldiers who would follow him anywhere.

The words 'We are longing for you' at the end of the letter must have struck deep at Burnaby's sentiments. Bored with the current affairs in Great Britain and always looking for a new adventure, the maverick army officer did not hesitate to come to the aid of an old friend.

The men of the Egyptian gendarmerie fell short of the fine material found in the Bosnian and Albanian battalions seven years before at Tashkessen. The gendarmerie was trained to patrol the streets of Cairo as a quasi-police unit, not to fight battles. Many of the Egyptian officers in the ranks were retired army officers too old for active service. This ill-prepared force was all the Egyptian government could spare to send at the time, as they were deprived of 10,000 soldiers due to the most recent disaster. Many of the men openly wept on their departure from Cairo, certain their assignment would be their last.

Baker nonetheless led his ill-fated column over the sandy summits with his usual gusto towards the besieged garrison at Tokar. He was accompanied by Burnaby, who arrived just in time to join the column. The old associates reunited for the first time on an active military campaign since Süleyman's retreat in 1878. Burnaby once again dressed like a man ready to attend a parlour game rather than one about to be entering a battle; he rode beside Baker carrying only a huge umbrella to protect his fair skin from the sun, and carried a pistol holstered to his waist. Another familiar companion complemented the Russo-Turkish War reunion: George Conrad Sartorius, commanding a portion of Baker's column.

Despite the poor quality of Baker's soldiers, they still held some advantages when faced with a Dervish onslaught. The Egyptian policemen were armed with modern breech-loading rifles, accompanied by four Krupp guns, and two Gatling guns, against a foe armed with spears, shields, and a blend of dated and modern firearms. Baker managed to acquire a small detachment of brave and well-disciplined Sudanese soldiers on which he could rely. With their superior armaments, and the hope he could instill a little discipline into his column, Baker set out to liberate the defenders at Tokar. On 31 January 1884, the seven-year anniversary of the Battle of Tashkessen, Baker cabled back to Cairo that he had 'every chance of success'.

Before reaching Tokar, Osman Digna and 1,000 of the Mahdi's men launched an ambush on Baker's column near the village of El Teb on 4 February 1884. The frenzied attack sliced through Baker's densely packed square formation, causing many of Baker's men to panic and flee. The disorder caused by the disintegrating lines led to a wild confusion as camels, mules, horses and men became intermixed. Some Egyptians of the gendarmerie tried to hide behind each other, and others begged for mercy on both knees, only to be unsympathetically speared in the back and or have their throats slit. In one instance, a fanatical Dervish warrior picked up an Egyptian rifle, but not knowing how to operate it, used it as a club to beat in the owner's skull.

Baker rode forwards with the cavalry from the sanctuary of the square to curtail the assault. The Dervish hordes managed to get between the cavalry and the crumbling Egyptian square. To avoid being cut off, Baker and the survivors had to cut their way back through the Mahdist tide to escape. Baker nearly met the same fate as Bill Hicks, when two Dervish warriors heaved their spears directly at him, both nearly skewering him. Baker departed the field of battle when all hope of rallying his shattered ranks was futile.

The 'battle' lasted less than ten minutes. Out of the 3,500 men of the Egyptian column, 2,225 men and ninety-six officers were dead. Only about 1,100 shattered men remained alive to make the protracted retreat back to Trinkitat. If Osman Digna's force had been larger, it is likely the column would have been slaughtered to a man. All of the Egyptian Gatling and Krupp guns fell into the hands of the Dervishes. Burnaby expressed that Baker made sure he 'was the last man into Trinkitat'.

Baker was ashamed of the performance of the Egyptian gendarmerie. He sent a telegraph back to Cairo dated 6 February 1884 that attributed the disaster to the disheartening performance of his men. A section of his telegram to Cairo indicated this displeasure: 'On the square being only threatened by a small force of enemy, certainly less than 1,000 strong, the Egyptian troops threw down their arms and ran, allowing themselves to be killed without the slightest resistance.' The defeat at El Teb was the second shattering blow to Anglo–Egyptian prestige in the Sudan.

The defeats at both battles proved to be too overwhelming for British pride to tolerate. Many shortsighted individuals asked how two armies led by British officers, viewed as the finest officers in the world, could be defeated by two poorly armed mob armies. The same individuals demanded that British regulars must be sent to relieve Tokar and recapture the lost British prestige in the Sudan. Major General Gerald Graham was dispatched with a force composed of roughly 3,000 men made up of the cream of the British Army to salvage this lost prestige: the Black Watch, the Gordon Highlanders, 60th Rifles, and the 10th and 11th Hussars.

Baker was 'terribly down under bad luck' following the disaster. He may have wished that he had perished in the battle to evade the shameful rebuke he received from the press for the second time in his life. A letter addressed from Major General Charles George 'Chinese' Gordon to Sam Baker on 26 February 1884, in reference to his brother's defeat, had these words of encouragement for Val: 'By your letter, 26th January, you are at Cairo. Hope all well. Sorry Suakin business. Tell your brother, heads or tails up here! but will trust.' After the disaster, Baker acted as an intelligence officer in

Graham's expedition, in a sense on probation for his poor performance at El Teb. Graham and Baker had known each other from their Crimean War days, and had a good working relationship, which may have been the only reason Baker was allowed to accompany the expedition in any capacity. This was a demotion from his former role, but it at least provided him with a chance to get back into the action.

Tokar fell on 21 February 1884, before Graham was able come to the rescue of its Egyptian garrison. Nevertheless, his column marched in the direction of a 6,000-man Dervish army with the intention of defeating them in battle. The two forces collided on 29 February 1884, with the British soldiers formed in their usual square formations to meet the onrush of the Dervish tide. Wave after wave of Dervish warriors armed with daggers, knives, spears, swords, and firearms fanatically charged forwards but were cut down by well-directed British gunfire. This time discipline prevailed as Graham inflicted nearly 2,000 casualties on the Dervish force at the loss of 189 British soldiers.

Baker recklessly exposed himself in the action in an attempt to provide a source of inspiration to the men and to redeem his lost honor. A 2-ounce iron ball suddenly smashed into his face and lodged into his cheekbone, barley missing his eye – thought to be from one of the Egyptian guns captured at Tokar. Maintaining his balance in the saddle, he rode over to the field hospital and had the wound temporarily bandaged up. He disregarded the shooting pains that came from his cheek, and rode in view of his old regiment, the 10th Hussars, with a bloody tourniquet wrapped around his head and jaw. Only visible were his piercing grey eyes and the sound of his resonating voice identifying him as the ex-colonel of the 10th Hussars. Burnaby was also wounded in the action, hit by flying shrapnel in the arm, and also had a horse shot out from under him.

Baker rode up to his old associate Frederic Villiers in the heat of action, attached to the column as a war correspondent. 'I hope you are not badly hurt,' Villiers inquired as he grasped Baker's hand during their greeting, noticing the cloth wrapped around his head and jaw. Baker replied in his usual casual manner, 'No, my dear Villiers, not seriously hurt,' but Villiers felt the tremble of his hand, saw tears swell up in his eyes, and observed droplets of blood dripping from the wound upon his dusty tunic. He was in excruciating pain, but refused to leave the field until the Mahdi's warriors were routed.

Melton Prior, of *The Illustrated London News*, reported that Baker was escorted back to HMS *Sphinx* by a few officers upon the conclusion of the battle, steadied in his saddle as he struggled to remain conscious. Baker returned to Cairo for treatment of this serious wound, where it was discovered that he had numerous splinters of bone impacted into his face, and that the large bullet had shredded his cheekbone. He sat in an armchair for nearly an hour, without chloroform, as a surgeon poked and twisted to extract these bone fragments and iron ball from his disfigured face. He was said to have sat motionless except for one instance when he fainted from the agony. The bullet was saved and mounted on an ebony stand in Baker's study to be displayed to all visitors.

The Prince of Wales again implored for Baker to be nominally restored as a retired officer upon hearing of his exploits in Graham's battle. Khedive Tewfik of Egypt even requested 'as a personal favour to himself' that Queen Victoria reconsider his reinstatement. This was corroborated with Graham's commendable battle report from Camp Tokar on 2 March 1884:

> My thanks are due to Lieut General Baker Pasha for the valuable information and assistance rendered by him throughout the operations. General Baker was, I regret to say, severely wounded in the early part of the action on the 29th February. His wound was in the face, and must have been very painful; notwithstanding which, after getting it dressed, he returned to the field, and only at the end of the action could I persuade him to retire to the base.

Queen Victoria once more snubbed the request. The hope for redemption withered away for the aging warrior.

In May 1884, Baker returned to Great Britain after it was decided that his wound needed to be examined by a more specialized surgeon. A crowd gathered to greet him at Charing Cross Station in London. He was revered by the public for his exploits in the recent battle, but memory of his disgrace and recent defeat at the Battle of El Teb still lingered with some. He did not return to Egypt for another four months, until September 1884. The next year was the hardest of Baker's life.

Death took away those closest to Baker in the early months of 1885. On another grand adventure, Fred Burnaby joined the relief column tasked with rescuing 'Chinese' Gordon bottled up in Khartoum. On 17 January 1885, the 'latter-day Paladin' was killed at the Battle of Abu Klea. There a Dervish warrior speared the gallant Burnaby in the throat while he met an onrush of Dervishes outside of the British square with his four-barrelled Lancaster pistol. As he lay down on the field of battle gasping his last breath, another Dervish warrior came up and split his skull nearly in two with a two-handed sword. He was remarkably still clinging to life when his body was found 30 yards from the square after the battle.

In a matter of moments, Burnaby bled out. One observer noted that his face 'wore the composed and placid smile of one who had been suddenly called away in the midst of a congenial and favourite occupation; as undoubtedly was the case.' His body was draped with the Union Jack, and he was buried alongside the other fallen officers on the field of battle, only identified by a collection of stones gathered from the barren landscape. In his will, Burnaby left Baker as the guardian of his 4-year-old son in the event of his widow's death.

His beloved Hermione was the next to leave his side. His 18-year-old daughter had been in fragile health since coming to Egypt from Constantinople. She passed away on 21 January 1885, 'after long weary watching', at the end of the same month as Burnaby, succumbing to an outbreak of typhoid fever in Cairo. Baker had a Worcester stone mason fashion a piece of Sicilian marble into a monument to be sent and placed at her gravesite. The *Worcester Chronicle* revealed that 'the cross on the top is formed by three carved lilies with the stem as the shaft of the cross, from which hangs a bud partly broken,' which sat on a black marble plinth, with the religious epitaph quoting 2 Kings 4:26 engraved into it: 'It is well with the child. And she answered, It is well.' Her coffin was covered in white flowers and the Union Jack, trailed by more than 100 carriages on its journey for burial in the cemetery.

It was rumored that Hermione's heartbroken fiancé, Captain Kitchener, wore a gold locket of her image around his neck for the remainder of his life.

Kitchener went on to become a household name in Great Britain, drowning in 1916 during the First World War while serving as the Secretary of State for War. He never married.

The final and most devastating blow came when Fanny died at the end of February, six weeks after the death of Hermione. Just as his daughter, his loyal and faithful wife died of typhoid fever, most likely contracted from tending to Hermione. She had been his anchor through all of his mishaps, and stood by him in his darkest moments. The *York Herald* reported that, 'Mrs Baker had been to him a most devoted companion, and nobly stood by her husband in his time of greatest distress and obloquy.' In a rare show of compassion, Wolseley professed:

> I am so grieved for poor Val Baker: he had just lost his eldest daughter, and he now telegraphs to say his wife is dead. She was the best of wives to him, and heaven knows she had many trials to put up with on his account.

'Quite overcome by his affliction' due to these devastating losses in such a short period, Baker fanatically dedicated his time to reforming the gendarmerie. Since its defeat at the Battle of El Teb, Baker moulded the organization into a well-trained and well-disciplined force to be proud of. He was 'almost worshipped' by Egyptians and Britons alike in Cairo for his accomplishments, and many spoke of him 'with tears in their eyes'. It is thought-provoking to wonder what if the gendarmerie was at this level of proficiency when he met the Mahdi's warriors at El Teb.

In April 1887, Baker and his remaining daughter, Sybil, travelled to Great Britain for a much needed six-month leave to escape the sorrows of Egypt. He still received no special mention for his service and sacrifice thus far for his country. Other members in Egyptian service had received their due praise. Upon Gerald Graham's own return to Great Britain, he was made a lieutenant general for his distinguished service, and four other soldiers were awarded the Victoria Cross in the same battle where Baker received his disfiguring facial wound.

The correspondent Edward Vizetelly noted that he could distinguish the physical and psychological wear on Baker over the years since his dismissal in 1875. 'Baker Pasha was no longer the Colonel Valentine Baker of former years,' he recalled. He continued that:

A long absence from the English army, a long residence in Turkey, made him quite a different man from the former dashing cavalry officer. He had never been able to forget the past. You could see that written on his face plain enough. Although still as brave as a lion, he had grown stout and flabby, he had degenerated into a Turkish Pasha, and had lost half of his former energy. He was kindness itself, and it required quite an effort on his part to say nay to anyone.

Villiers corroborated Vizetelly's concern when he ran into Baker while in Paris. 'He looked far from well, and was much changed in appearance; the energetic soul of the man seemed to have already left him.'

Queen Victoria seemed to have been feeling sympathetic on 15 June 1887, five days before her Jubilee. She sent a reluctant note to her son, the Prince of Wales: 'As regards General Baker, after consulting some important people in whose judgment I can rely, I now propose that his re-instatement in the Army might take place by and by,' but made sure to mention it was 'not on the account of my Jubilee'. The decision for reinstatement was delayed because it had to go through the proper channels before a formal ruling could be finalized. It was not until later that year that it was deemed official.

Baker began his return journey to Cairo in July 1887, still without receiving the verdict of his reinstatement. He was accompanied by his daughter Sybil, and his brother Sam's two daughters, Ethel and Agatha. Sam's daughters planned to stay for a short time with their Uncle Val before they continued on to Ceylon. The group's journey ended up being delayed, and they did not arrive at Port Said until November 1887.

Baker was both mentally and physically in decline by the time he reached Cairo. He had a high fever that he could not shake off, and was in a melancholy mood. His recent losses, coupled with the reminder that he was still an exile among his own people, weighed heavily upon his heart. On 17 November 1887, after consuming a bowl of curry for supper, he complained to his daughter of sharp pains in his shoulders and chest, uttering, 'I hope it is not another attack of dengue fever coming on.' One of his nieces gave him a helping of laudanum to calm his restlessness. While under the spell of this opiate, Baker passed away in his sleep around 11.00 am the next day at the age of 60.

His death cast a dark curtain over all of Cairo. His niece Ethel wrote that, 'All dear Uncle Val's friends seemed as if they had lost a father or brother in him.' His funeral was attended by nearly all foreigners and members of the military living within Cairo, and the funeral procession twisted through the streets for over three quarters of a mile. His casket was transported on a gun carriage draped with the Union Jack and covered in garlands, escorted by nine pallbearers – one from his Russo-Turkish War days, Baker, VC. He was buried next to his daughter Hermione, in the English cemetery of Cairo.

Tragically, the order for Baker's reinstatement travelled at a slothful pace, reaching its recipient posthumously. *The Times* recorded soberly:

There is something extremely pathetic in the obscure and gloomy close to what at one time promised to be a career of singular lustre. The favourite of society, the dashing cavalry officer, the lion of so many a gay coterie, has died far away from friends and home, and it is in a foreign land that his old comrades pay the last honours to his name.

One of Baker's surviving sisters captured the tragic irony of her brother's life and the psychological strain he suffered:

Dear Val was laid very near his darling Hermione, just on the other side of the path, with all possible military honours of a British general, which he would have been, had he lived a few *days* longer! It is all heartbreaking – but he rests at last – no one can hurt him anymore. Dr Sandwich says that a year ago there were obscure symptoms of heart disease – or rather, I fancy, a worn-out heart – one may also say literally a broken heart, broken by many sorrows, he told me himself.

Heartbroken and shunned, he died without any knowledge of being absolved of the humiliation he suffered twelve years before, having sacrificed so much for his country and having gained so little in return.

The current condition of Baker's tombstone in the English cemetery of Cairo is unknown, and a tablet constructed in the original All Saints' Cathedral of Cairo – erected through funds raised to perpetuate his memory – has vanished today, obliterating any evidence of Baker Pasha's saga. His own surviving daughter, at the time a minor, inherited £3,728 and all of his property upon his death. Sybil Baker married the wealthy Sir John Craven Carden, 5th Baronet (1854–1931) on 10 February 1891. She gave birth to one son, named Sir John Valentine Carden, 6th Baronet (1892–1935) in honor of her father. Sybil Martha (Baker) Carden died on 1 July 1911.

Chapter 8

A Most Brilliant Action?

I think it is a shame to us that this, the finest story of a rearguard action in history – an action successfully carried out by an Englishman in command of Turkish troops in the most recent continental war, should be forgotten.
The words of Colonel Sir John Frederick Maurice
in his presentation to the Military Society of
Ireland on 16 November 1892.

T he stand at Tashkessen was applauded by Baker's colleagues as a prototype of effective leadership, an aggressive defence, and the successful display of the 'spirit of tactics' that should be studied by all students of war. Edmund Ollier, author of *Cassell's Illustrated History of the Russo-Turkish War*, composed these visionary words when he described Baker's battle: 'The action at Tashkessen in particular will always remain as a model of a rearguard engagement scientifically, stubbornly, and successfully fought.' On 16 November 1892, fifteen years after the battle, Colonel Sir John Frederick Maurice was invited to give a lecture on the Battle of Tashkessen to British officers of the Military Society of Ireland. A professor of military history at the Staff College, Maurice was regarded as an expert on all military matters, having taken part in the Ashanti campaign of 1873–74, the Anglo-Zulu War, and the Egyptian expedition of 1882.

Baker's old ally, Garnet Wolseley, inaugurated the forum by claiming that the Battle of Tashkessen was 'one of the most important events in the war between the Turks and the Russians in 1877'. Maurice followed up with a play-by-play presentation of the events surrounding the battle. At one point in his lecture, he remarked that it was 'the most wonderful rearguard action of our times, if not of all times'. He ended his presentation with this declaration:

I think it is a shame to us that this, the finest story of a rearguard action in history – an action successfully carried out by an Englishman in command of Turkish troops in the most recent continental war, should be forgotten. It is a brilliant example and less as to what may be accomplished under such circumstances by a man in the direst difficulty. A careful study of the exact steps Baker took at each phase of battle is the very best instruction that anyone can have. In my judgment, a knowledge of the facts of this little incident is in itself much more valuable to an officer than any theories we can lay down about.

The forum was opened up to questions by Wolseley after Maurice concluded his presentation. Captain Bewicke Copley rose and expanded on how 'people on the other side' – the Russians – viewed the engagement. He stated several of the Russian battalion commanders at the battle commended afterwards on 'how exceedingly successfully General Baker moved his troops on that occasion' and also noted 'that he handled them with such skill that the Russians completely failed to realize what was going on [on] his side of the fight.'

Wolseley concluded the lecture by giving his own appraisal of the action. He proclaimed to all of the young officers present that it was surely 'a most brilliant action in all its various phases' and to urge upon all of them 'the study of it in its very fullest detail'. He hinted to the officers that if Baker's offensive vigour would have been adopted earlier in the war by the Ottoman high command, 'the result would have been a very different one, indeed.'

Most accounts corroborate Maurice's claim that the battle was all but forgotten within a decade. In *A Military Geography of the Balkan Peninsula*, Lionel W. Lyde deviated from describing the geography of the region to mention that Baker's action at Tashkessen was 'little remembered' by the time he published his book in 1905. In his 1912 article, 'A Subaltern in the Balkans', William G. Knox explained that, 'History relates but little of Valentine Baker's career with the army which he threw in his lot.'

If the engagement was as marvellous as stipulated by Maurice and Wolseley, then why was the battle and Baker's role in the war relegated to obscurity a decade or so later? Tribute to the battle and Baker's role in the war may have been clouded by his own the murky legacy. Francis of *The Times* provided an alternative reasoning for the slide into obscurity, explaining that 'Owing to the rapid march of succeeding events, it did not attract the notice it deserved.' The individual occurrences of the war drifted into ignominy as other events took a greater precedence in the years before the turn of the century. In consequence, of any number of these factors, the memory of the part Baker played in the conflict suffered.

Is there any foundation in the claim made by Maurice that the battle was the 'most wonderful rearguard action' of its time? Or was the acclaim all hype to boost the vanity of Baker's fellow officers? To further determine if this action is worthy of the applause that it received, an unprejudiced survey of other 'successful' rearguard actions of the nineteenth century must be conducted and compared to Baker's rearguard action. The mutual elements that led to success in the five rearguard actions selected will be uncovered and semblance drawn to Baker's fight in 1877.

What defines a rearguard? A rearguard action is a military operation in which a detachment is tasked with protecting the retreat or strategic withdrawal of a parent formation. Once the retreat or strategic withdrawal of the parent formation has been successfully executed, the detachment would then begin its own extraction. The rearguard detachments were typically outmatched by at least a 2:1 ratio in the engagements studied – with the exception of Young's Bridge. The expectation is that the detachment is sent to stall the enemy for a limited amount of time, not to win a decisive victory.

The five rearguard actions chosen for this study are listed in chronological order: Schöngrabern (1805), Peacock Hill (1814), Young's Bridge (1862), Monocacy (1864), and Sankelmark (1864). These successful rearguard actions took place in a period ranging from the early to middle of the nineteenth century. Each took place either during the War of the Third Coalition, the Anglo-Nepalese War, the American Civil War, or the Second Schleswig War. All four shared mutual elements leading to their success:

• Sound tactical arrangements to maximize the defensive position.
• Appreciation of the significance of time management and the prevention of overcommitment.
• Resourceful leadership qualities of the rearguard commander.
• Combination of the loyalty and the discipline of the men making up the defending detachments.

A brief investigation of each engagement will further divulge the shared mutual elements that led to success.

Schöngrabern [Hollabrunn], 1805

General Mikhail Kutuzov's Austro-Russian army was in a precarious situation following the bloody repulse at Dürenstein in November 1805. His army rapidly retired towards Moravia to evade encirclement from the French and to unite with reinforcements marching from mainland Russia. A 37,000-man detachment of Napoleon's Grand Armée, under the command of Joachim Murat, was rapidly gaining on the defeated Austro-Russian force. Kutuzov's weary and battered columns could trudge no further despite this threat, forcing him to call for a halt to save his army from disintegrating under the stressful retreat. He ordered a detachment to make a defensive stand in order to stall Murat to save his army from being overrun.

Kutuzov called for one of his most trusted generals – the Georgian-born Peter Bagration – to conduct what he saw as a forlorn task. In his twenty-three years of service, Bagration had gained a reputation for his composure in a crisis, boundless bravery, decisiveness in action, and his aptitude for striking the enemy at the right moment. He headed towards Schöngrabern with 7,000 cold and hungry Russian and Austrian soldiers leased to him by Kutuzov. What the soldiers lacked in strength, they made up for in their loyalty to Bagration. As they departed for their desperate mission, Kutuzov broke down and wept, convinced that he was sending these men to their inevitable deaths.

On 15 November 1805, Bagration established his force near the village of Schöngrabern. The terrain selected provided an excellent defensive position for his men to make a stand. The landscape was broken by vineyards and bogs, restricting the employment of cavalry, which made up a significant portion of Murat's command. Bagration positioned his men in a line running behind the village of Schöngrabern, and ordered those closest to the village to occupy its buildings. He placed his artillery across the road leading from Schöngrabern, and positioned six battalions of infantry and cavalry on either side of the guns, holding two battalions in reserve.

When Murat arrived with his command, he miscalculated the strength of the enemy command to his front. He was reluctant to engage what appeared to be a superior sized force. He further delayed the assault when a factious armistice arrived from Kutuzov. Both delays infuriated Napoleon, not yet on the scene, who ordered Murat to stop loitering and to attack at once. Murat launched the assault with a total of four divisions against Bagration's small command.

Bagration managed to fend off the overpowering assault of five times his number for some time. When his line began to disintegrate from the mounting pressure, he gave the order to commence a fighting withdrawal back towards the village of Grund. Fighting continued until Napoleon arrived on the scene at midnight, ordering Murat to conclude the bloody contest after seven hours of non-stop combat. When Bagration received the news that Kutuzov passed out of danger into Moravia with the main army, he slipped away with what remained of his command under the cover of darkness. The action cost Bagration half of his command, but their sacrifice allowed Kutuzov to outpace Murat's exhausted men, thus saving his army from a foreseeable disaster.

Peacock Hill, 1814

From October–December 1814, the East India Company's invasion of Nepal was plagued by setbacks and embarrassments. On 27 December 1814, Major William Richards' 600 men were rooted on Peacock Hill after a failed attempt to capture the Nepalese stronghold of Jaithak. Richards felt reassured that fresh ammunition and reinforcements would arrive soon – until he received a disheartening message from his commander, Major General Gabriel Martindell. The timid general ordered Richards and his command to return immediately to Nahan, vacating their strong forward position.

Martindell's order put Richards and his men in a perilous predicament. They would be forced to stumble back to Nahan in the dark of the night through the hills down a zigzagging pathway, while at the same time under pursuit by a Nepalese force three times their number. Richards had no choice but to delegate a portion of his men to sacrifice their lives for the salvation of the rest of the column. Richards chose Lieutenant Thomas

Thackeray – known for his 'extraordinary valour' – and his company for the forlorn mission.

In all, 200 Indian sepoys and English officers assembled to form the rearguard. Nearly 1,300 Nepalese soldiers, eager to shed blood, appeared from the jungle as the remainder of Richards' column shuffled through the hills single-file back towards the village of Nahan. Thackeray formed his men in two squares on the wooden heights to meet the Nepalese horde. The sepoys were ordered to fix bayonets, and to hold until the last man of Richards' column escaped.

Thackeray's men fought ferociously to keep the Nepalese combatants at bay. They succeeded in checking the pursuit for over an hour. Owing to the mounting casualties, the two squares began to disintegrate. More than half of the original 200 were either killed or wounded. When Richards' column was out of harm's way, Thackeray ordered his men to disperse into the jungle in order to escape complete annihilation.

He led the survivors in a concentrated effort to penetrate the swarms of Nepalese combatants in the direction of Nahan. Fighting was vicious, and men became engaged in small clusters of melee combat. Thackeray suddenly collapsed from a shot in the chest, falling to the ground mortally wounded, and soon after expired. Those soldiers not killed outright were captured. The remnants of the rearguard fled through the jungle.

Major Richards and his column made it safely back to Nahan. Though half of Thackeray's detachment perished in his rearguard action, some stragglers managed to make it back to Nahan and report the fate of the command. Francis Rawdon-Hastings, the Commander-in-Chief of India, issued a special order honouring Thackeray, 'whose heroic spirit and personal example animated his little band', and to the Bengal Native Infantry, whose 'zeal and courage' had yet to be surpassed. A marble obelisk was erected in Nahan by the surviving officers of Richards' column in memory of Thackeray and his men.

Young's Bridge, 1862

Following the Confederate repulse at the Battle of Corinth in October 1862, Major General Earl Van Dorn's 20,000 men of the Army of West Tennessee crawled towards the Mississippi Valley in search of sanctuary. Van Dorn's 500 slow-moving wagons and thousands of dispirited soldiers extended several miles in an accordion-like column as they made the protracted retreat south. Union Major General William S. Rosecrans, with 20,000 of his Army of the Mississippi, began his pursuit from the east. Another Union detachment, made up of 5,000 men under the command of Major General Edward O.C. Ord, moved from the west to cut off Van Dorn's line of retreat. Not only did the Confederate army face being enclosed by the Union pincer movement, it also had to contend with fording the flooded and swift-moving Hatchie and the Tuscumbia rivers in order to reach the Mississippi Valley.

On 5 October 1862, Van Dorn tasked Brigadier General John S. Bowen with his lone brigade of 2,000 to stall Rosecrans' attempt to cross over the Tuscumbia at Young's Bridge. The 32-year-old Bowen was eulogized by author Phillip Thomas Tucker as the 'Stonewall of the West', reinforced by his exceptional military record until his tragic death from dysentery in 1863. But in 1862, the intrepid Bowen was celebrated for his expertise in conducting rearguard actions. Although he was recognized as a strict disciplinarian, he maintained the undying loyalty of his men, and would never ask them to do anything he was not willing to undertake himself.

Bowen's defensive arrangements at Young's Bridge were carefully set up to maximize his musketry and artillery firepower. He positioned his veteran brigade along the elevated bank and heavily timbered landscape north of the wooden bridge. He ordered his men to utilize every hill, tree, and fence for protection, and camouflaged his guns in the underbrush and timber to enfilade the Union pursuers as they approached. His goal was to inflict as much damage on the enemy with minimal loss to his own command.

As the sun began to set, Union Colonel John D. Stevenson's brigade of Brigadier General James B. McPherson's Provisional Division emerged from the woods leading Rosecrans' vanguard. The second brigade of the division, under the command of Colonel Michael Kelly Lawler, followed close behind. McPherson ordered his two brigade commanders to drive the Confederates back across the river and capture Young's Bridge intact before nightfall. He planned to split Bowen's line down the centre and into two isolated pockets, destroying each in detail with their backs against the river.

Bowen's skirmishers were easily driven back when the Union soldiers advanced in a dense column, fading into the forest towards the elevated ground of Bowen's main position. The core of his command remained concealed and ready to spring their well-planned ambush. McPherson's confident soldiers followed the skirmishers in pursuit, unaware of the trap. When McPherson's soldiers were within a few yards of the Confederate line, he gave the order to unleash hell. The punishing fire from the camouflaged defenders caught the advancing Union line off-guard, and stunned McPherson's brigades.

Bowen led his men from their concealed positions in an audacious counter-attack. The effect of the close-range gunfire coupled with the bold counter-attack brought McPherson's division to a grinding halt. When darkness fell over the battlefield and the fighting came to an end, Bowen safely retired his brigade across Young's Bridge. Once all of his men successfully crossed to the other side, he ordered the wooden bridge to be burned, hampering any Union advance in pursuit of Van Dorn's army. Bowen suffered less than twenty casualties during the battle, while aiding in preventing a catastrophe and allowing Van Dorn's army to fight another day.

Monocacy, 1864

In the autumn of 1864, Confederate Major General Jubal Early and 20,000 men were detached from the Army of North Virginia for an offensive planned to penetrate the Shenandoah Valley. This army would move into Maryland, and threaten Washington, DC, the Union capital and permanent residence of President Abraham Lincoln. No significant amount of Union soldiers remained in the Shenandoah Valley to counter Early's invasion. The majority of those Union units safeguarding the capital had previously been sent to reinforce the Army of the Potomac in Virginia. General Robert E. Lee, of the Army of North Virginia, hoped that this movement would cause Lieutenant General Ulysses S. Grant to detach a significant portion of his army around Petersburg and Richmond to counter this threat.

Early scattered the negligible Union units in the Shenandoah Valley, leaving him within two days' march of the capital. The only force adequate to counter General Early's threat was the Baltimore garrison under the command of Major General Lew Wallace. Wallace's men were made up of inexperienced militia that had never before seen combat. Even worse, some of them were bounty men paid $950 a head for their service, far from the quality soldiers with Grant in Virginia.

The 37-year-old Indiana native had an unspectacular career leading up to 1864. Lew Wallace had fallen out of favour with the most powerful man in the army two years before, due to his lackluster performance at the Battle of Shiloh. Grant's criticism cast a shadow over his name, and he was shunned from taking an active part in the war. He was instead given backwater administrative assignments. Wallace was looking for an opportunity to redeem himself, and Early's threat to Washington was his chance.

President Abraham Lincoln's administration ordered Wallace to first and foremost protect the city of Baltimore. He disobeyed these specific orders and risked everything by moving his garrison directly in the path of Early's advancing army. He believed that if he could stall Early's army for a day or so, it would at least allow for reinforcements to arrive from Grant by vessel to bolster Washington's defence. Fortunatly for Wallace, reinforcements from Grant were already on their way, composed of a veteran division detached from the VI Corps under the command of Brigadier General James B. Ricketts. Between the Baltimore garrison and Ricketts' division, Wallace would muster 7,000 men to face Early's 20,000 hardened veterans.

Wallace moved his command south of the city of Frederick and positioned it at Monocacy Junction. He arranged his men on the elevated ground overlooking the Monocacy River, forcing Early to either cross a single bridge or ford the river at a shallow point to drive him back. On 9 July 1864, with an air of self-confidence, Early ordered his men to drive what he presumed was militia from Monocacy Junction. He couldn't have been more wrong. The green soldiers of the Baltimore garrison and Ricketts' veterans provided stiff resistance, inflicting heavy casualties on Early's army that they could ill afford to lose.

By 4.00 pm, Wallace had no choice but to order a retreat after six hours of continuous combat. Wallace may have lost the battle, but it cost Early vital time and manpower. Due to his stand at Monocacy, Grant was able to rush the remainder of the VI Corps to Washington and funnel troops into its defences. The sharp engagement at Monocacy triggered Early to act cautiously for the remainder of the campaign in the Shenandoah Valley.

He was ultimately defeated by a Union army under Major General Phil Sheridan at the Battle of Cedar Creek in October 1864, and driven from the Valley, thanks to the role Wallace and his men played at Monocacy.

Sankelmark [Oeversee], 1864

On 6 February 1864, the 1st and 11th Danish Regiments of the 7th Brigade took position under frigid temperatures to cover the retreat of the main Danish army to Dybbøl. The 56-year-old Colonel C.F. 'Max' Müller had orders to bring the 2,752 men of the 7th Brigade forwards to stall the Austrian pursuit. In pursuit of the Danish army were Major General Nostitz and his 5,079 men of the 3rd Brigade, under the overall command of General Ludwig von Gablenz of the II Corps. Müller and his command were detached to protect the thousands of fleeing Danish soldiers until they at least had passed the village of Flensburg.

Müller had a notorious reputation as being a tough Danish officer with a short temper. He was quick to challenge fellow officers to duels if he felt unjustly censured. Despite this irrational behaviour, he was respected and admired by his men. He stated to a fellow general on the eve of his deployment to Sankelmark that 'halting the enemy is not enough, I must attack him.' He was the ideal officer to stand toe-to-toe against the confident and numerically superior Austrian brigade.

Müller sandwiched his men between the Sankelmark Woods and the Sankelmark Lake. His right flank was pushed up against the Sankelmark Lake, and his left flank rested against the Sankelmark Woods, with the main road cutting down his centre towards Flensburg. The lake itself was frozen, but not solid enough to allow enemy soldiers to cross over it and outflank his position. Close to the main road, a dike provided a manmade barrier, while the 11th Regiment was positioned in a hollow, 200 feet to the rear of the 1st Regiment. Two guns were placed on top of a small hill behind the main line, which gave Müller the ability to fire over his men's heads into the advancing Austrian soldiers.

Austrian hussars initiated the battle when they crashed into the bayonet-spiked defensive square of the 1st Regiment. Soon after, Austrian infantry support arrived, and the two sides engaged in a close-range firefight and in fierce hand-to-hand combat. Müller ordered the 11th Regiment to pull back into the Sankelmark Woods in order to cover the withdrawal of the hard-pressed 1st Regiment. The withdrawal of the 1st Regiment dissolved into chaos despite Müller's fervent attempts to rally them. The 11th Regiment began its own slow fighting withdrawal, as pockets of reformed soldiers from the 1st Regiment attached themselves to the regiment's flanks to continue the fight.

The Austrian attack lost its momentum as their soldiers grew tired of the fierce resistance put up by the Danish defenders. Müller saw the opportunity and struck. He led a bold counter-attack that crashed into the tired and exhausted Austrians, sending them reeling back in retreat. Losses were high for both sides when the battle came to an end, as the Austrians suffered 600–700 casualties compared to the 900–1,000 Danish casualties. Müller successfully delayed the Austrian pursuers long enough to allow the Danish army to withdraw safely back to the fortified position at Dybbøl, and reluctantly initiated his own withdrawal that night.

Analysis

The commanding officers of each rearguard action made sound tactical arrangements on their respective fields of battle to maximize the strength of their defensive positions. Every hill, ridge, fence, boulder, lake, or building was employed to the defender's advantage. At Schöngrabern, Bagration shielded his men from Murat's cavalry by placing them among the vineyards and bogs, and commandeered buildings of the village. Müller situated his right flank against the impassible Sankelmark Lake and his left against the Sankelmark Woods, and positioned his men inside a hollow and a dike to provide shelter. Thackeray, Bowen, and Wallace carefully arranged their men on elevated ground and utilized the natural landscape to further hinder and delay their attackers.

Valentine Baker masterfully selected and exploited the landscape surrounding Tashkessen for his defence. He designated the region as a resourceful place to conduct a defensive action weeks before the actual engagement. He first positioned his men on the three commanding knolls behind the village of Tashkessen, exploiting the elevated ground. Fragmented boulders and a line of excavated entrenchments provided shelter to his men. He afterwards withdrew his battalions to an even stronger position on the ridge anchored by the *han*, where he was able to beat back additional assaults.

It was critical for each rearguard commander to appreciate the time required to accomplish their missions, and to avoid over commitment at all hazards. Once a commander completed the task assigned of his rearguard, it was vital for him to extradite his detachment or face the threat of being cut off or annihilated. An 1887 article published in *The Illustrated Naval and Military Magazine* specified that the main goal of a rearguard is to 'retard rather than to repel an enemy, to gain time rather than to inflict loss'.

All of the commanders studied were mindful of every second, minute, hour, or day essential to delaying the enemy and saving their parent formation. Wallace's goal was to intercept Early's army and delay it until no longer feasible; he ordered a retreat after six hours when it became apparent he could no longer hold back the enemy's pursuit. Thackeray held back the Nepalese horde long enough for his parent formation to escape, but unfortunately, his command was overwhelmed before it could conduct an orderly withdrawal. Bagration and Bowen were fortunate enough to be able to slip away using the cover of darkness after their missions had been accomplished. The overly aggressive Müller was reluctant to recall his men even with his mission accomplished, but better judgment prevailed, and he removed his men when nightfall provided a chance to escape.

Baker's silver pocket watch proved to be his most vital article at Tashkessen. He monitored each passing hour he gained to allow Shakir to escape with his army. The words used by Fred Burnaby when describing the delay at Tashkessen must have echoed in Baker's own mind during the course of the battle: 'Every moment gained was so much time lost to the enemy.' Baker indulged the Russians to approach his line with restraint on 28 December 1877, inducing them to squander three more days on his front. He was able to hold the overconfident Russians for ten hours on the actual day of the battle, until nightfall allowed him to vacate his position under the cover of darkness to join Shakir's army already evacuated to Acha Kamarli.

A rearguard commander must be resourceful and possess excellent leadership qualities. Tranquility in action and a rational mind is essential, as rearguard commanders are placed under a tremendous amount of pressure from both the enemy and the burden of their assignments. He must demonstrate decisiveness in action and must be bold enough to exploit his enemy's weaknesses – even if this means adopting an aggressive defence. Courage in the heat of battle is crucial to sustain the morale of the men and inspire them to preserve, despite the daunting odds. Under a weak, uninspiring, and unimaginative leader, a rearguard is destined to fail.

All five rearguard commanders exhibited resourceful and excellent leadership qualities in some capacity. Bowen and Müller both led decisive counter-attacks on their imprudent and over optimistic enemies. Wallace demonstrated his boldness by intercepting the enemy with his inexperienced command, while also demonstrating his composure by enduring the repeated blows from a veteran army. All five officers demonstrated instances of fearlessness under fire in order to steady the morale of their men in a time of crisis. Thackeray paid with his life for this bravery, and Bagration would die of wounds received in another battle in 1812.

Baker certainly demonstrated exceptional leadership qualities at Tashkessen. Francis celebrated him for his 'endless resource', 'unflinching determination', and 'unconquerable energy', while Knox praised his 'stout heart' and 'well-taught mind'. Ollier extolled him for exercising independent command 'in a manner showing the highest genius for war'. In his study titled 'Cover, Screen, and Illusion', Major M. Martin of the Royal Engineers commended Baker for 'a good illustration of the advantages of screen', stating that at Tashkessen he 'employed cover, screen, and illusion, and gave a further instance of the last before his retirement during the night.' He conducted an aggressive defence in a similar fashion to Bowen, ordering bold counter-attacks despite being desperately outnumbered, driving Russian assaults back in both instances.

His courage and pluck were unparalleled. He exposed himself with a selfless disregard to steady the morale of his men and officers during the battle. His deeds inspired the equally daring Burnaby to comment that at Tashkessen, 'Baker was in the foremost and most exposed place, standing in a hail of rifle bullets and shellfire, encouraging his men.' His coolness in action prevailed when Allix sent back the alarming dispatch of Shakir's supposed betrayal and premature evacuation of the Kamarli line. Baker displayed his ability to face hardship with a positive and aggressive attitude.

The loyalty and the discipline of the men engaged in each rearguard action weighed heavily upon their success. Each commander held an aura of respect and loyalty over their men – enough so that each soldier was willing to die for his commander. The commands of Bagration, Bowen, and Wallace persevered due to their discipline when panic could have easily led to their destruction. Even though assailed on all sides, the discipline of Thackeray's men kept the lines steady long enough to allow Richards' command to escape to safety. When the 1st Danish Regiment broke, Müller was able to stabilize the situation with the well-disciplined 11th Danish Regiment.

Despite his own white Anglo-Christian background, Baker possessed the loyalty of the men under his command – even though his soldiers were devout Muslims and he was unable to speak more than a word or two of Turkish. Baker's men overlooked the religious and cultural barriers because he took special care to look out for their welfare and shared in their hardships. He treated his men and officers as equals rather than inferiors, as Francis put it, he had a 'peculiar insight into the feeling of the men he commands, and wonderful tact in managing them'. The account of Kitchener while visiting the Kamarli line provides further insight into this unspoken dedication that existed between the two:

> Baker Pasha is the only general who has looked after the interior economy and sanitary arrangements of his men, and his division's camps are in striking contrast to those of the rest of the army. The men are very fond of the Inglese Pasha, as they call him, and have thorough confidence in him.

For these reasons, he was idolized in the ranks.

His mere presence on the battlefield or in camp inspired a sense of *esprit de corps* that intoxicated those who surrounded him. Ollier proclaimed that he had 'an extraordinary power of inspiring his troops with confidence under trying circumstances'. Skobelev heard his name whispered among Ottoman prisoners in the wake of Süleyman's retreat, prompting his desire to arrange an audience with the famed Englishman. Macpherson admitted that soldiers at Tashkessen were 'not in the best position, physically or morally, for gaining victory', but under Baker's leadership their discipline prevailed and 'the few Englishmen who witnessed the battle were filled with admiration at the determined and enthusiastic manner [with] which they fought.'

After evaluating the other five rearguard actions and comparing them to Tashkessen, does the battle rise above them as the 'most wonderful rear guard action' of the nineteenth century? The evidence suggests that Tashkessen is worthy of the contemporary acclaim it received, not an amplification from Anglophiles wishing to glorify the battle or seeking to enhance Baker's legacy. Baker perfected the four elements essential for conducting a successful rearguard action, aiding to divert a major catastrophe. To declare the Battle of Tashkessen as the 'most wonderful' rearguard action of the nineteenth century would lead to undervaluing the other rearguard actions. If not a superlative model, Tashkessen certainly ranks in the top echelons of nineteenth-century rearguard actions.

Contemporary military experts were adamant that the memory of this battle should be preserved as a future instrument in the tactical study of war. Their advice should be heeded. The battle can certainly serve in this role to students at military colleges and academies even 140 years later. Its study not only provides interesting reading material for military history enthusiasts, but also value to army officers of how sound tactical arrangements, time management, resourceful leadership, and the loyalty and the discipline of the regular soldier are vital to conducting a rearguard action. For this reason, the memory of Baker and the Battle of Tashkessen should be revived.

Bibliography

Newspapers
Aberdeen Express
Ashtabula Weekly Telegraph
Australian Town and Country Journal
Border Watch
Cromwell Argus
Dundee Evening Telegraph
Evening Post
Evening Star
Man of Ross, and General Advertiser
New York Tribune
Northern Argus
North Otago Times
St James Gazette
York Herald
Warwick Argus and Tenterfield Chronicle
Western Daily Express
Worcester Chronicle
Worcester Journal
Vanity Fair
The Argus
The Bee-Hive
The Bible Echo
The Brisbane Courier
The Daily Bulletin
The Illustrated London News
The New York Times
The Maitland Mercury & Hunter River General Advertiser
The Mineral Argus
The Pall Mall Budget
The Public Ledger
The Morning Post
The Spectator
The Sydney Morning Herald
The Times

Manuscripts
Mirliva Süleyman to an unknown Ottoman official, 30 August, 1880. Baker Paşa ve seyyar konsolosların çalışmalarının Anadolu halkı arasında İngiltere nüfuzunun ve Ermenistan'ın bağımsızlığını düşünenlerin sayısının artmasına sebep olduğu. Republic of Turkey General Directorate of State Archives. http://www.devletarsivleri.gov.tr/icerik/2399/baker-pasa-ve-seyyar-konsoloslarin-calismalarinin-anadolu-halki-arasinda-ingiltere-nufuzunun-ve-erme/.

Ulysses S. Grant to General Alfred T.A. Torbert, Consul Gen., of the US in Paris, France. Athens, Greece, 9 March 1878. Ulysses S. Grant Comments on the Refugees – Many, Bulgarian Jews – Who Have Fled to Constantinople Before Russian Invaders 9 March 1878. The Shapell Manuscript Collection. http://www.shapell.org/manuscript/ulysses-s-grant-tours-ottoman-empire-1878.

Both Anne Baker and Dorothy Anderson attest that any significant trace of correspondence from the introvert Valentine Baker is virtually non-existent – Bonhams auctioned off a small lot of Baker's papers to a private seller in 2009. The scant amount of manuscript material cited in this book can be attributed to this, relying heavily instead on additional primary sources material to establish the true character of Valentine Baker.

Published Works

Primary
Baker, Samuel White, *Wild Beasts and their Ways: Reminiscences of Europe, Asia, Africa and America*, Macmillan, London, 1890.
Baker, Valentine, *Clouds in the East: Travels and Adventures on the Perso-Turkoman Frontier*, Chatto & Windus, London, 1876.
Baker, Valentine, *War in Bulgaria: A Narrative of Personal Experiences*, 2 vols., Sampson Low, Marston, Searle & Rivington, London, 1879.
Boyle, Frederick, *The Narrative of an Expelled Correspondent*, Richard Bentley & Son, London, 1877.
Brackenbury, Sir Henry, 'Some Memoirs of My Spare Time, 1856–1885, VI', *Blackwood's Edinburgh Magazine* 185, no. 1122 (April 1909), pp. 483–505.
Bulwer-Lytton, Edward Robert, *Personal and Literary Letters of Robert, First Earl of Lytton*, vol. 2, edited by Lady Betty Balfour, Longmans, Green & Co, London, 1906.
Burnaby, Frederick Gustavus, *On Horseback through Asia Minor*, rev. ed., Cosimo, Inc., London, 2007.
Butler, Sir William, *Sir William Butler: An Autobiography*, Charles Scribner's Sons, New York, 1911.

Coope, Colonel William Jesser, *A Prisoner of War in Russia: My Experiences Amongst the Refugees with the Red Crescent*, Sampson Low, Marston, Searle & Rivington, London, 1878.

Cunynghame, General Sir Arthur Thurlow, *My Command in South Africa, 1874–1878, Comprising Experiences of Travel in the Colonies of Africa and in the Independent States*. 2nd ed., Macmillan & Co, London, 1880.

Denison, Colonel George T., *Soldiering in Canada: Recollections and Experiences*, George N. Morang and Company, Toronto, 1900.

Edwards, Jennie, *John N. Edwards: Biography, Memoirs, Reminiscences and Recollections*, MO, Jennie Edwards, Publisher, Kansas City, 1889.

Fife-Cookson, John, *With the Armies of the Balkans and at Gallipoli in 1877–1878*, Cassell, Petter, Galpin & Co, London, 1879.

Forbes, Archibald, *Czar and Sultan: The Adventures of a British Lad in the Russo-Turkish War of 1877–78*, Charles Scribner's Sons, New York, 1894.

Forbes, Archibald & Januarius A. MacGahan, *The War Correspondence of the 'Daily News', 1877–78, continued from the Fall of Kars to the signature of the preliminaries of peace with a connecting narrative forming a continuous history of the war between Russian and Turkey*, Macmillan and Co, London, 1878.

Francis, Francis, *War, Waves, and Wanderings: A Cruise in the 'Lancashire Witch'*, 2 vols., Sampson Low, Marston, Searle & Rivington, London, 1881.

Fulford, Roger, ed, *Darling Child: Private Correspondence of Queen Victoria and the Crown Princess of Prussia 1871–1878*, Evans Brothers, London, 1976.

Graham, Gerald, *Life, Letters, and Diaries of Lieut General Sir Gerald Graham*, ed. by R.H. Vetch, Blackwood, London, 1901.

Hawkins, Sir Henry, *The Reminiscences of Sir Henry Hawkins*, ed. by Richard Harris, Edward Arnold, London, 1905.

Herbert, Frederick William von, *The defence of Plevna, 1877, Written by one who took part in it*, Longmans, Green & Co, London, 1895.

Huysche, Wentworth, *The Liberation of Bulgaria: War Notes in 1877*, Bliss, Sands & Foster, London, 1894.

King, Edward, *Descriptive Portraiture of Europe in Storm and Calm: Twenty Years' Experiences and Reminiscences of an American Journalist*, C.A. Nichols & Co, Springfield, MA, 1888.

Kitchener, Horatio Herbert, 'A Visit to Sophia and the Heights of Kamerleh – Christmas 1877', *Blackwood's Edinburgh Magazine* 123, no. 748 (February 1878), pp. 194–200.

Knox, Major General William G., 'A Subaltern in the Balkans in the Winter Campaign of 1877', *The Nineteenth Century and After* 72, no. 329 (November 1912), pp. 889–912.

Macpherson, Richard B., *Under the Red Crescent: Or, Ambulance Adventures in the Russo-Turkish War of 1877–78*, Hamilton & Co, London, 1885.

Moltke, Helmuth Graf von, *Field-Marshal Count Helmuth von Moltke as a Correspondent*, translated by Mary Herms, Harper & Brothers, New York, 1893.

Murray, David Christie, *Recollections*, John Long, London, 1908.

Oliphant, Lawrence, 'Moss from a Rolling Rock: IX – Crimean and Circassian Experiences during the War, 1854–55', *Blackwood's Edinburgh Magazine* 140, no. 849 (July 1886), pp. 52–66.

Ryan, Charles Snodgrass, and John Sandes, *Under the Red Crescent: Adventures of an English Surgeon with the Turkish Army at Plevna and Erzeroum, 1877–78*, Charles Scribner's Sons, New York, 1897.

Sartorius, Ernestine, *Three Months in the Soudan*, Kegan Paul, Trench, & Co, London, 1885.

Stephenson, Frederick Charles Arthur, *At Home and on the Battlefield: Letters from the Crimea, China and Egypt, 1854–1888*, ed. by Mrs Frank Pownall, John Murray, London, 1915.

Vereshchagin, Vasil, *The War Correspondent: A Story of the Russo-Turkish War*, J.R. Osgood, McIvaine & Co, London, 1894.

Villiers, Frederic, *His Five Decades of Adventure*, vol. 1, Hutchinson & Co., London, 1921.

Villiers, Frederic, *Peaceful Personalities and Warriors Bold*, Harper & Brothers, London, 1907.

Villiers, Frederic, 'The Story of a War Correspondent's Life', *The Cosmopolitan* 10, no. 6 (April 1891), pp. 702–21.

Vizetelly, Edward, *From Cyprus to Zanzibar by the Egyptian Delta*, C. Arthur Pearson, Ltd., London, 1901.

Wellesley, Colonel Frederick A., *With the Russians in Peace and War*, Eveleigh Nash, 1905.

Secondary

Achtermeier, William O., 'The Turkish Connection: The Saga of the Peabody-Martini Rifle', *Man At Arms Magazine* 1, no. 2 (March/April 1979), pp. 12–21, 55–7, http://www.militaryrifles.com/Turkey/PeabStory/PeabodyStory.htm.

Adams, Michael, *Napoleon and Russia*, Hambledon Continuum, 2006.

Aksan, Virginia H., 'The Ottoman Military and State Transformation in a Globalizing World', *Comparative Studies of South Asia, Africa and the Middle East 27*, no. 2 (2007), pp. 259–72.

Alexander, Michael, *The True Blue: The Life and Adventures of Col Fred Burnaby, 1842–1885*, Rupert Hart-Davis, London, 1957.

Anderson, Dorothy, *Baker Pasha: Misconduct and Mischance*, Michael Russell Publishing Ltd., London, 1999.

Anderson, Dorothy, *The Balkan Volunteers*, Hutchinson, London, 1968.

Anderson, John P., *Conrad's Lord Jim: Psychology of the Self*, Universal Publishers, Boca Raton, FL, 2005.

Anglesey, Marquess of Paget, George Charles Henry Victor, *A History of the British Cavalry 1816–1919*, vol. 3, 1872–1898, Leo Cooper, Secker & Warburg, London, 1982.

Badem, Candan, *The Ottoman Crimean War (1853–1856)*, E.J. Brill, Leiden, 2010.

Baker, Anne, *Question of Honour: The Life of Lieutenant General Valentine Baker Pasha*, Leo Cooper, London, 1996.

Baker, Anne, 'The Making of Baker Pasha: The High and the Low', *Soldiers of the Queen* 146 (September 2011), pp. 18–21.

Baker, James, *Turkey in Europe*, Cassell, Petter, & Galpin, London, 1877.

Baker, Valentine, *The British Cavalry*, Longman, Brown, Green, Longmans, & Roberts, London, 1858.

Barber, Noel, *The Sultans*, Simon & Schuster, New York, 1973.

Barry, Quintin, *War in the East: A Military History of the Russo-Turkish War 1877–78*, Helion & Company Ltd., Solihull, 2012.

Beckett, Ian F.W., 'Retrospective Icon: The Martini-Henry', in *A Cultural History of Firearms in the Age of Empire*, ed. by Karen R. Jones, Giacomo Macola, & David Welch, pp. 233–50, Ashgate Publishing Co., Surrey, 2013.

Beckett, Ian F.W., *The Victorians at War*, Hambledon, London, 2003.

Benson, Captain G.E., 'The Tactical Operations of the Future (Including Questions of Supply and Transport of Ammunition) As Affected by the Introduction of Magazine Rifles, Machine and Quick-firing Guns, and Smokeless Powder', *Journal of the Royal United Services Institute for Defence Studies* 25 (1891), pp. 395–454.

Best, Brian, *The Victoria Crosses that Saved an Empire: The Story of the VCs of the Indian Mutiny*, Frontline Books, London, 2016.

Bilmes, Murray, 'Macho and Shame', *International Forum of Psychoanalysis* 1 (December 1992), pp. 163–8.

Bilmes, Murray, 'Shame and Delinquency', *Journal of Contemporary Psychoanalysis* 3 (1967), pp. 113–33.

Bodinson, Holt, 'Britain's Big .577 Snider', *Guns Magazine* (March 2006), pp. 18–22.

Brockett, Linus Pierpont and Porter Cornelius Bliss, *The Conquest of Turkey: Or, The Decline and Fall of the Ottoman Empire, 1877–1878*, Hubbard Bros., Philadelphia, 1878.

Castle, Ian, *Austerlitz and the Eagles of Europe*, Leo Cooper, London, 2005.

Chesney, Colonel Francis Rawdon, *The Russo-Turkish Campaign of 1828 and 1829, with a View of the Present State of Affairs in the East*, Redfield, 1854.

Conrad, Joseph, *Lord Jim*, J.M. Dent and Sons Ltd., London, 1946.

Cooling, Benjamin Franklin, *Monocacy: The Battle That Saved Washington*, White Mane Publishing, 1997.

Cowles, Virginia, *Edward VII and His Circle*, Hamish Hamilton, London, 1956.

Cowles, Virginia, *The Russian Dagger: Cold War in the Days of the Czars*, Harper & Row Publishers, New York, 1969.

Curtiss, John Shelton, 'The Army of Nicholas I: Its Role and Character', *American Historical Review* 63, no. 4 (July 1958), pp. 884–6.

Curtiss, John Shelton, *The Russian Army Under Nicholas I, 1825–1855*, Duke University Press, Durham, NC, 1965.

Danilevskii, Nikolai Iakovlevich, *Woe to the Victors! The Russo-Turkish War, the Congress of Berlin, and the Future of Slavdom*, translated by Stephen M. Woodburn, Slavica, Bloomington, IN, 2015.

Davison, Roderick H., *Reform in the Ottoman Empire, 1856–1876*, Princeton University Press, NJ,1963.

Dixon, William Hepworth, *The London Prisons*, Murray, London, 1850.

Dolby, I.E.A., ed., *The Journal of the Household Brigade for the Year*, 1862–1880, W. Clowes, & Sons, London, 1877.

Dr John Gill, *Salopian Shreds and Patches* 3, (17 April 1878) pp. 33.

Drury, Ian, & Raffaele Ruggeri, *The Russo-Turkish War 1877: Men-at-Arms*, Osprey Publishing, Oxford, 1994.

Dunn, John P., *Khedive Ismail's Army*, Routledge, London, 2013.

Dwight, Henry O., *Turkish Life in Wartime*, Charles Scribner's Sons, New York, 1881.

Eklof, Ben, John Bushnell & Larissa Zakharova, eds., *Russia's Great Reforms, 1855–1881*, Indiana University Press, Bloomington, 1994.

Embree, Michael, *Bismarck's First War: The Campaign of Schleswig and Jutland 1864*, Helion & Company Limited, Solihull, 2006.

Epanchin, Nikolai A., *Operations of General Gurko's Advance Guard in 1877*, translated by Henry Havelock, Kegan Paul, Trench, Trübner & Co, London, 1900.

Erickson, Edward J., *Defeat in Detail: The Ottoman Army in the Balkans, 1912–1913*, Praeger, Westport, CT, 2003.

Fahmy, Khaled, *All the Pasha's Men: Mehmed Ali, His Army, and the Making of Modern Egypt*, American University in Cairo Press, 2002.

Farwell, Byron, *Queen Victoria's Little Wars*, Norton, New York, 1972.

Featherstone, Donald, *Omdurman 1898: Kitchener's Victory in the Sudan*, Osprey Publishing, Oxford, 1994.

Furneaux, Rupert, *The Breakfast War*, Crowell, New York, 1960.

Gall, Captain H.R., 'Modern Tactics', *Illustrated Naval and Military Magazine* 7, no. 37 (July 1887), pp. 115–24.

Goldie, Lieutenant Colonel M.H.G., 'Tactical Application of Field Defenses in Battles of Recent Campaigns', *Journal of the Military Service Institution of the United States* 21, no. 88 (July 1897), pp. 102–25.

Grant, Jonathan, 'The Sword of the Sultan: Ottoman Arms Imports, 1854–1914', *The Journal of Military History* 66, no. 1 (January 2002), pp. 9–36.

Greene, Francis Vinton, *Report on the Russian Army and Its Campaigns in Turkey in 1877–1878*, D. Appleton & Company, New York, 1879.

Greene, Francis Vinton, *The Campaign in Bulgaria, 1877–1878*, Hugh Rees Ltd., London, 1903.

Griffiths, Merwin Albert, 'The Reorganization of the Ottoman Army under Abdülhamid II, 1880–1897', PhD diss., University of California, 1966.

Grovenor, Bendor, 'Britain's "most isolationist Foreign Secretary": The Fifteenth Earl and the Eastern Crisis 1876–1878', In *Conservatism and British Foreign Policy, 1820–1920: the Derbys and their World*, ed. by Geoffrey Hicks, pp. 129–68, Ashgate Publishing Company, Farnham, 2011.

Harrison, Michael, 'Colonel Baker Goes too Far', In *Painful Details: Twelve Victorian Scandals*, edited by Michael Harrison, pp. 148–56, Max Parrish, London, 1962.

Hesseltine, William Best & Hazel Catherine Wolf, *The Blue and the Gray on the Nile*, University of Chicago Press, 1961.

Hill, Richard Leslie & Hogg, Peter C., *A Black Corps d'Elite: An Egyptian Sudanese Conscript Battalion with the French Army in Mexico, 1863–1867, and its Survivors in Subsequent African History*, Michigan State University Press, East Lansing, 1995.

Hozier, Sir Henry Montague, *The Russo-Turkish War: Including an Account of the Rise and Decline of the Ottoman Power and the History of the Eastern Question*, 2 vols., London, 1877–1879.

James, Major W.C., 'The Development of Modern Cavalry Action in the Field', *Journal of the Military Service Institution of the United States* 12, no. 52 (July 1891), pp. 807–29.

Jastrzembski, Frank, 'Baker's Spartan Stand: Buying Time at Tashkessen 1878', *Soldiers of the Queen* 159 (March 2015), pp. 3–9.

Jastrzembski, Frank, 'The Battle of Peacock Hill – How a Desperate Rearguard Action Saved a British Army', *Military History Now*, http://militaryhistorynow.com/2015/08/03/the-battle-of-peacock-hill-how-a-desperate-rearguard-action-saved-a-british-army-in-1814/.

Jessup, John E., *Balkan Military History: A Bibliography*, Garland Publishing, Inc., New York, 1986.

Kamenir, Victor, 'Plevna under Siege', *Military Heritage* (October 2004), pp. 32–9.

Karpat, Kemal H., 'The Social and Political Foundations of Nationalism in South East Europe After 1878: A Reinterpretation', In *Studies on Ottoman Social and Political History: Selected Articles and Essays*, ed. by Kemal H. Karpat, pp. 352–84, Brill, Leiden, 2002.

Katcher, Philip, *Great Gambles of the Civil War*, Cassell & Co., London, 1996.

Kaufman, Gershen, *The Psychology of Shame: Theory and Treatment of Shame-Based Syndromes*, 2nd ed., Springer Publish Company, New York, 1996.

Kostova, Emilia, 'The Russo-Turkish War in Bulgarian Historiography', *South-Eastern Europe* 2 (1979), pp. 246–56.

Laitila, Teuvo Tapana, 'Soldier, Structure and the Other: Social Relations and Cultural Categorization in the Memoirs of Finnish Guardsmen Taking Part in the Russo-Turkish War, 1877–1878', PhD diss., University of Helsinki, Finland, 2001.

Lehmann, Joseph, *All Sir Garnet: A Life of Field Marshal Lord Wolseley*, Jonathan Cape, London, 1964.

Levy, Avigdor, 'The Officer Corps in Sultan Mahmud II's New Ottoman Army, 1826–39', *International Journal of Middle Eastern Studies* 2, no. 1 (January 1971), pp. 21–39.

Liddell, Robert Spencer, *The Memoirs of the Tenth Royal Hussars (Prince of Wales's Own) Historical and Social*, Longmans, Green & Co, London, 1891.

Lieberman, Benjamin, *Terrible Fate: Ethnic Cleansing in the Making of Modern Europe*, Ivan R. Dee, Chicago, IL, 2006.

Lucas, Ray, *Armies of the Russo-Turkish War 1877–1878*, The Battery Press, London, 1994.

Lyde, Lionel W. & Mockler-Ferryman, A.F., *A Military Geography of the Balkan Peninsula*, Adam & Charles Black, London, 1905.

McClellan, George B., 'Capture of Kars and Fall of Plevna', *The North American Review* 126 (January–February 1878), pp. 132–55.

McGregor, Andrew James, *A Military History of Modern Egypt: From the Ottoman Conquest to the Ramadan War*, Praeger, Westport, CT, 2006.

'Marriages', *The Gentleman's Magazine and Historical Review* 1 (January 1866), pp. 116–20.

Martin, Major M., 'Military Notes: Cover and Screen', *Journal of the Military Service Institution of the United States* 20, no. 85 (January 1897), pp. 206–209.

Mason, Alfred Edward Woodley, *The Four Feathers*, The Macmillan Co., New York, 1902.

Maurice, Sir John Frederick, 'The Battle of Tashkessen', in *Military Society of Ireland: Mobilization for Home Defence*, ed. by Colonel W.R. Lascelles, pp. 79–96, Sibley & Co, Dublin, 1892.

Maurice, Sir John Frederick, *The Russo-Turkish War, 1877: A Strategical Sketch*, Swan Sonnenschein, London, 1905.

Maurois, Andre, *Disraeli: A Picture of the Victorian Age*, translated by Hamish Miles, D. Appleton, New York, 1928.

Menning, Bruce W., *Bayonets before Bullets: The Imperial Russian Army, 1861–1914*, Indiana University Press, Bloomington & Indianapolis, IN, 1992.

Menning, Bruce W., 'Train Hard, Fight Easy: The Legacy of A.V. Suvorov and his "Art of Victory"', *Air University Review* 38 (November–December 1986), pp. 79–88, http://www.au.af.mil/au/afri/aspj/airchronicles/aureview/1986/nov-dec/menning.html.

Mikaberidze, Alexander Peter, 'Peter Bagration: The Best Georgian General of the Napoleonic Wars', *The Napoleon Series*, http://www.napoleon-series.org/research/biographies/bagration/c_bagration1.html.

Miles, Nelson Appleton, *Military Europe: A Narrative of Personal Observation and Personal Experience*, Doubleday & McClure Co., New York, 1898.

Mösslang, Markus, Torsten Riotte & Hagen Schulze, eds., *British Envoys to Germany 1816–1866*, vol. 3: *1848–1850*, Cambridge University Press, 2006.

Murray, Douglas T. & White, Arthur S., *Sir Samuel Baker: A Memoir*, Macmillan, London, 1895.

Murray, Nicholas, *The Rocky Road to the Great War: The Evolution of Trench Warfare to 1914*, Potomac Books, Washington, DC, 2013.

O'Connor, Maureen P., 'The Vision of Soldiers: Britain, France, Germany and the United States Observe the Russo-Turkish War', *War in History* 4, no. 3 (1997), pp. 264–95.

Ollier, Edmund, *Cassell's Illustrated History of the Russo-Turkish War*, 2 vols., Cassell, Petter & Galpin, London, 1879.

Playfair, Giles, *Six Studies in Hypocrisy*, Martin Secker & Warburg, London, 1969.

Ralston, David B., *Importing the European Army: The Introduction of European Military Techniques and Institutions into the Extra-European World, 1600–1914*, University of Chicago Press, IL, 1996.

Raugh, Harold E., *The Victorians at War, 1815–1914: An Encyclopedia of British Military History*, ABC-CLIO, Santa Barbara & Oxford, 2004.

Reid, James J., *Crisis of the Ottoman Empire: Prelude to Collapse, 1839–1878*, F. Steiner Verlag, Stuttgart, 2000.

Royle, Charles, *The Egyptian Campaigns, 1882 to 1885: And the Events which Led to Them*, vol. 2, Hurst & Blackett, London, 1886.

Royle, Trevor, *The Kitchener Enigma*, Michael Joseph, London, 1985.

Royston-Pigott, G.E. & West Royston, George, *Savage and Civilized Russia*, Longmans, Green & Co., London, 1877.

Saks, D.Y., 'Botched orders or insubordination – The battle of Berea revisited', *Journal of the South African Military History Society* 9, no. 6 (December 1994), pp. 211–14, http://samilitaryhistory.org/vol096ds.html.

Sanders, Lloyd Charles, ed., *Celebrities of the Century: Being a Dictionary of Men and Women of the Nineteenth Century*, vol. 1, Cassell & Co, London, 1887.

Scott, Leslie, '"It Never, Ever Ends": The Psychological Impact of Wrongful Conviction', *American University Criminal Law Brief* 5, no. 2 (2010), pp. 10–22.

Shipman, Pat, *To the Heart of the Nile: Lady Florence Baker and the Exploration of Central Africa*, Perennial, New York, 2004.

Smith-Christmas, Kenneth L., 'Icon of an Empire: The Martini-Henry', *American Rifleman* 162 (November 2014), pp. 86–91, 108 & 109.

Stone, David R., *A Military History of Russia: From Ivan the Terrible to the War in Chechnya*, Praeger, Westport, CT, 2006.

Taylor, Antony, 'Aristocratic Debauchery and Working-Class Virtue: The Case of Colonel Valentine Baker', In *Lords of Misrule: Hostility to Aristocracy in Late Nineteenth and Early Twentieth-Century Britain*, ed. by Anthony Taylor, pp. 17–44, Palgrave Macmillan, Basingstoke, 2004.

'The Advance into Thessaly', *The United States Army and Navy Journal and Gazette of the Regular and Volunteer Forces* 34, no. 37 (May 1897), pp. 678–9.

The Armed Strength of Russia: Compiled in the Intelligence Brach of the Quarter-Master-General's Department, Horse Guards, War Office, printed under the Superintendence of Her Majesty's Stationery Office, London, 1882.

'The Late Dr Gill of Welshpool', *Bye-Gones: Relating to the Wales and the Border Counties, 1897–1898*, 5 (July 1898), pp. 426–7.

Thompson, Brian, *Imperial Vanities: The Adventures of the Baker Brothers and Gordon of Khartoum*, HarperCollins, London, 2001.

Torres, Walter J. & Bergner, Raymond M., 'Humiliation: Its Nature and Consequences', *J Am Acad Psychiatry Law* 38, no. 2 (June 2010), pp. 195–204.

Trenk, Richard, 'The Plevna Delay: Winchesters and Peabody-Martinis in the Russo-Turkish War', *Man at Arms Magazine* 19, no. 4 (August 1997), pp. 29–36, http://www.militaryrifles.com/Turkey/Plevna/ThePlevnaDelay.html.

Trotha, Captain Thilo Lebrecht Ernst Michael von, *Tactical Studies on the Battles Around Plevna*, translated by Lieutenant Carl Reichmann, Hudson-Kimberly Publishing Co, Kansas City, MO, 1896.

Trow, M.J., *The Adventures of Sir Samuel White Baker, Victorian Hero*, Pen & Sword, Barnsley, 2010.

Tucker, Phillip Thomas, *The Forgotten 'Stonewall of the West': Major General John Stevens Bowen*, Mercer University Press, Macon, GA, 1997.

Turan, Omer, ed., *The Ottoman-Russian War of 1877–78*, Middle East Technical University; Meiji University Institute of Humanities, Ankara, 2007.

Tyrrell, Henry & Haukeil, Henry A., *The History of Russia From the Foundation of the Empire to the War With Turkey in 1877–1878*, vol. 3, The London Printing & Publishing Company, London, 1879.

Uyar, Mesut & Erickson, Edward J., *A Military History of the Ottomans from Osman to Atatürk*, Praeger, Westport, CT, 2009.

Ware, J. Redding & Mann, R.K., *The Life and Times of Colonel Fred Burnaby*, Field & Tuer, The Leadenhall Press, E.C., London, 1885.

Wawro, Geoffrey, *The Austro-Prussian War: Austria's War with Prussia and Italy in 1866*, Cambridge University Press, 1997.

Wawro, Geoffrey, *Warfare and Society in Europe, 1792–1914*, Routledge, London, 2000.

Wilbraham, Lieutenant General Sir Richard, 'On the Causes which have led to the Pre-eminence of Nations in War', *Journal of the Royal United Service Institution* 21, no. 89 (February 1877), pp. 455–91.

Worthington, Glenn H., *Fighting For Time or the Battle That Saved Washington and Mayhap the Union*, Frederick County Historical Society, Frederick, 1932, and PA: Beidel Printing House, Shippensburg, 1985.

Wright, Thomas, *The Life of Colonel Fred Burnaby*, Everett & Co, London, 1908.

Ziegler, Philip, *Omdurman*, Collins, London, 1973.

Zurcher, E.J., 'The Ottoman Conscription System in Theory and Practice, 1844–1918', *International Review of Social History* 43, no. 3 (1993), pp. 437–49.

Index